"Anyone working in a Catholic ministry today '
identity is a hot-button issue. Multiple comple
the ministry contribute to the current challeng
eighties, in several acclaimed books, Father Ger
believers to ground their ministries in the narra
addresses contemporary ministry in a just-in-tir
a multifaceted descriptive account as well as pra
for the reader's consideration. This book is a mu. ... ...ose serving as
sponsors, senior leaders, mission leaders, or formators of tomorrow's leaders
in Catholic ministry. Eschewing a didactic methodology, social anthropologist
Arbuckle utilizes a more inductive, narrative approach to draw forth a deep
and lasting commitment to Church ministry."

> —Patricia Talone, RSM, PhD
> Catholic Health Association of the United States

"This book brings together the accumulated wisdom and experience of
Gerald Arbuckle's pioneering work on 'refounding' and applies it to an
urgent question of our time: preserving and furthering the Catholic identity
of educational and healthcare institutions. It is a must-read for anyone
concerned about the public face of the Catholic Church in an increasingly
secularized, postmodern world."

> —Robert Schreiter
> Author of *The New Catholicity*

"'Chaos' and 'Refounding' are the hallmark tropes of Gerald Arbuckle's
now huge literary corpus. With a magisterial command of contemporary
theological literature, Arbuckle applies his anthropological insights to the
'refounding' (not 'renewal'!) of Christian ministries, especially in education
and health care, for our 'chaotic' times. If his proposals on Catholic identities
(not 'identity'!) are implemented, there will be a rebirth of Christian
ministries appropriate for our postmodern age. Once again, the church owes
Arbuckle a huge debt."

> —Dr. Peter C. Phan
> The Ignacio Ellacuría Chair of Catholic Social Thought
> Georgetown University

"With characteristic clarity, depth, and wisdom, Gerald Arbuckle offers reflections on refounding and Catholic identity, two important elements in today's call to engage in a 'new evangelization.' For Arbuckle, the only real way to evangelize is to refound—to express who we are as Christians by a creative retelling of the Christian story. Readers who have been inspired and challenged by Arbuckle's earlier books will not be disappointed when they read this one."

—Stephen B. Bevans, SVD
Louis J. Luzbetak, SVD, Professor of Mission and Culture
Catholic Theological Union
Chicago, Illinois

Catholic Identity or Identities?

Refounding Ministries in Chaotic Times

Gerald A. Arbuckle, SM

LITURGICAL PRESS
Collegeville, Minnesota

www.litpress.org

1	2	3	4	5	6	7	8	9

Library of Congress Cataloging-in-Publication Data

Arbuckle, Gerald A.
    Catholic identity or identities? : refounding ministries in chaotic times / Gerald A. Arbuckle.
        pages   cm
    Includes index.
    ISBN 978-0-8146-3567-4 — ISBN 978-0-8146-3592-6 (ebook)
    1. Catholics—Religious identity.   2. Identification (Religion)   3. Catholic Church.   4. Church work—Catholic Church.   I. Title.

BX1795.P79A73   2013
282—dc23   2013019745

To Maria Cunningham, RSC, and Therese Vassarotti:
faith-filled and courageous refounders

By the same author

The Chatham Islands in Perspective: A Socio-Economic Review
(Wellington: Hicks Smith, 1971)

Strategies for Growth in Religious Life
(Alba House/St. Pauls Publications, 1987)

Out of Chaos: Refounding Religious Congregations
(Paulist Press/Geoffrey Chapman, 1988) (Catholic Press Award)

Earthing the Gospel: An Inculturation Handbook for Pastoral Workers
(Geoffrey Chapman/Orbis/St. Pauls Publications, 1990) (Catholic Press Award)

Grieving for Change: A Spirituality for Refounding Gospel Communities
(Geoffrey Chapman/St. Pauls Publications, 1991)

Refounding the Church: Dissent for Leadership
(Geoffrey Chapman/Orbis Books/St Pauls Publications, 1993) (Catholic Press Award)

From Chaos to Mission: Refounding Religious Life Formation
(Geoffrey Chapman/Liturgical Press, 1996)

Healthcare Ministry: Refounding the Mission in Tumultuous Times
(Liturgical Press, 2000) (Catholic Press Award)

Dealing with Bullies: A Gospel Response to the Social Disease of Adult Bullying
(St Pauls Publications, 2003)

Confronting the Demon: A Gospel Response to Adult Bullying
(Liturgical Press, 2003)

Violence, Society, and the Church: A Cultural Approach
(Liturgical Press, 2004)

Crafting Catholic Identity in Postmodern Australia
(Catholic Health Australia, 2007)

A 'Preferential Option for the Poor': Application to Catholic Health and Aged Care Ministries in Australia
(Catholic Health Australia, 2008)

Laughing with God: Humor, Culture, and Transformation
(Liturgical Press, 2008)

Culture, Inculturation, and Theologians: A Postmodern Critique
(Liturgical Press, 2010)

Humanizing Healthcare Reforms
(Jessica Kingsley, 2013)

Contents

Acknowledgments

It has been said that "a good book is the best of friends, the same today and for ever" (Martin Tupper 1810–1889). My hope is that this book becomes "the best of friends" for many readers, but a "good book" depends not just on the author but on the collaboration of many people: Hans Christoffersen, editorial director at Liturgical Press, who kindly accepted the book for publication; the community at Campion Hall, Oxford University, where most of the research and writing of the book took place; my Marist superiors who so generously support my ministry of writing; Martin Laverty, CEO Catholic Health Australia, for permission to use material in chapters 7 and 8 that I had previously published; and the wonderful Margaret Zucker, who again patiently read and corrected my grammar, as well as at times offered wise comments on the text. To these people and many others with whom I discussed the insights of this book—my sincere thanks. These people, however, are in no way responsible for the book's inadequacies.

Introduction

*By your favor, O Lord, you had established me as a strong
mountain;
you hid your face; I was dismayed.
To you, O Lord, I cried . . . "What profit is there in my
death, if I go down to the Pit?" . . .
You have turned my mourning into dancing;
you have taken off my sackcloth
and clothed me with joy. (Ps 30:6-9, 11)*

Chaos can be a blessing! Surprised? Not if we read the Scriptures
and find that chaos in its many synonyms is a dominant theme in both
the Old and the New Testaments. The Israelite prophets and the psalm-
ists often use the imagery of chaos in order to highlight the opposite,
namely, the ongoing inventive and redemptive action of God.[1] God's
face is suddenly hidden, throwing the Israelites into a state of despair
(Ps 30:7). Then through God's compassionate action they discover new
life in their experience of the chaos:

> You have turned my mourning into dancing; you have taken off my
> sackcloth and clothed me with joy (v. 11).

---

1. See Bernhard Anderson, *Creation Versus Chaos: The Reinterpretation of Mythical Symbolism in the Bible* (New York: Association Press, 1967), 132. Biblically,
"chaos" and its many synonyms such as "the Pit," "grave," "wilderness" mean a
state of utter confusion and fear, totally lacking in organization or predictability;
it is the antithesis of cosmos. Walter Brueggemann writes that "the Bible is much
more preoccupied with the threat of chaos than it is with sin and guilt. . . . The
storm produces a more elemental, inchoate anxiety, a sense of helplessness. . . . It
is bottomless in size and beyond measure in force" (*Inscribing the Text* [Minneapolis:
Fortress Press, 2004], 51).

We certainly need a better knowledge of this truth today. The late Cardinal Carlo Martini is right. In "affluent Europe and in America" we are a tired church.[2] The church is no longer perceived as "a strong mountain" (v. 6). We wrestle with scandals; trust in episcopal authority is disintegrating; people are leaving the church; priestly and religious vocations are in rapid decline; restorationist reactions to the chaos add daily to our sadness. Especially in the Western world the church had been a mighty self-contained fortress, "established . . . as a strong mountain" (Ps 30:7) of power and prestige, secure in a never-ending supply of vocations, schools, colleges, universities, hospitals. Suddenly God's face is hidden. We are dismayed. We have lost our way in the darkness!

The Scriptures invite us to relearn, though painfully, two fundamentally constructive lessons about our experience of this darkness.

- The first biblical lesson we need to learn is that in the chaos we can rediscover that we are humanly powerless without God's abiding help. Consider the theme of chaos in the book of Job, a remarkable text about the human struggle for meaning within an often messed up, wretched world (see Job 40:19). When Job suffers afflictions he returns to ponder the powerlessness of humankind. As God so beautifully explains to Job, when God's face turns away from us and we encounter the fear-evoking force of darkness and uncertainty, then as creatures of God we come into contact with the chaos out of which we were made and the lessons it symbolizes. That is, we encounter afresh, if we freely choose to do so, the roots of our being, our own helplessness, and at the same time the saving, the re-creative and energizing power of God in Christ. We relearn to detach ourselves from an overconfidence in our abilities to act without God: "I am poor and needy; hasten to me, O God! You are my deliverer; O Lord, do not delay!" (Ps 70:5).

- The second, specific lesson from the Scriptures is that chaos calls us to reexamine how we live and teach our faith. In view of the chaos in the church and the postmodern world, rediscovering the roots of our Catholic identities requires us to relearn the art of storytelling that Jesus Christ modeled so effectively in his ministry. We require a creative quantum leap in our thinking and action, not modifications of the traditional methods of adult formation.

2. Carlo Cardinal Martini, reported by *The Tablet* (8 September 2012), 8.

That is, there is need for refounding, not renewal, of how we train and form members of our institutions in Gospel values that are the ultimate foundations of Catholic identities. Renewal confines itself to polishing up formation methods of the past. That is not enough today.

Refounding focuses on the radical rethinking of our pastoral approach in the light of our contemporary postmodern age. We need to let cherished structures and processes die when they no longer serve the mission of our institutions. This demands courageous and creative leadership born of inner detachment from the reassuring, but now irrelevant, pastoral status quo and a skilled understanding of the Scriptures (see chapters 4, 5, 7, and 8).

This book argues that refounding pastoral instruction requires a return to the practice of storytelling, as modeled by Jesus in his use of parables. He knew that storytelling encouraged people to bridge the gap between the head and the heart, thus opening the way for the necessary creative, imaginative, and bold action. This is no time for complacency. Rather, it is a time that impels us to invest in boldly new pastoral initiatives.[3] Then we will discover that our mourning can be turned "into dancing" and we can again become "clothed . . . with joy" (Ps 30:11). This second lesson is surely at the heart of Cardinal Martini's testimony. He asks: how can the flame of love grow strong again in a church that has become tired? Focusing on the transformative power of the Scriptures for answers, he responds by asking further questions:

> Where are the individuals with the generosity of the Good Samaritan? Who have the faith of the Roman centurion? Or the daring of Paul? Who are the faithful like Mary Magdalene? . . . [We need] unconventional people to take on leadership roles. Those who are close to the poor, who can galvanise young people by being willing to try new approaches. We need to be challenged by people who are fired by the spirit so that it can be spread far and wide.[4]

Both lessons, but especially the second, are the themes of this book. Jesus knew that people take pleasure in storytelling and frequently attain

---

3. See John Paul II, *At the Beginning of the New Millennium* (Sydney: St Pauls Publications, 2001), 22.

4. Martini, loc. cit.

insight, energy, and support through doing so. In the politically and religiously chaotic world of his time he realized that as people listened to and retold his parables they would learn to create connections between their own life stories and the truths embedded in the parables. This would lead to the transformation of their lives. I was once present at a gathering of people belonging to a L'Arche community and witnessed members with significant learning disabilities miming the parable of the Good Samaritan. It was a deeply inspiring experience. Participants did precisely what Jesus had intended when he first recounted this parable. In the mime they were able to connect the experience of their own lives with that of the injured traveler and the Samaritan himself. For them the comforting and challenging message of Jesus Christ came alive in their actions.

The primary aim of this book, therefore, is to search for pastorally practical ways in which we can apply to our contemporary postmodern situation biblical insights that help us to move forward in faith, in particular by using the teaching method of storytelling that Jesus used so effectively.

Challenge: How to Be Catholic Today?

Pastors and religion educators in schools painfully know that old methods of evangelizing now rarely succeed. Equally, we recognize that previous systems of educating the staffs of our hospitals, universities, schools, and other institutions, who are the primary focus of this book, fail to affect their lives in any significant way. In this pluralistic age we employ in these institutions an increasing number of people with little or no faith background. We cannot expect to impose on them the beliefs of the Catholic Church such as the Trinity, the divinity of Jesus Christ, the sacraments, papal infallibility. However, our Catholic institutions, if they are to maintain their Catholic identities, have the right to require their staffs to behave in accordance with Gospel values and with the ethical and social principles of the Catholic Church.[5] When staff members live by values such as compassion, respect for the dignity of the person, and

---

5. For example, Pope Benedict XVI issued an apostolic letter, dated 11 November 2012, on "The Services of Charity." The document set out new rules to strengthen the religious identity of Catholic charities and ensure that their activities conform to church teaching.

justice they are in fact giving concrete expression in their workplace to the teachings of Christ, which are the foundation of Catholic identities.

The challenge is: How are these Gospel values to be instilled in a way that people's lives are transformed? How are individuals and institutions to craft stories that weave together the narratives of Jesus Christ and their own stories into a single, vibrant fabric? How are people in our institutions, whether they are professedly Catholic or not, to become so inspired by the story of Jesus Christ that they are moved to act individually and communally with compassion and justice?[6] What qualities do we need today in those called to teach our faith?

Traditional Pastoral Instruction: Weakness

Persons in authority such as teachers, politicians, and ecclesiastics are always tempted to tell people who they are and how they should behave. This didactic, top-down approach has been described with some truth by educator Paulo Freire as the "banking theory of education."[7] The psychologist Carl Rogers calls it the "jug to mug" theory of learning[8] because it stresses the transfer of knowledge through a one-way communication. The recipient is likened to an empty mug expecting to be filled with information from the jug, who is the teacher. If learning does occur, it usually does so at the cognitive level only. People are not expected to examine their emotional responses to the material imparted to them. Nor are they expected to express any dissent, as it is taken for granted that the information is objectively true because those in authority confirm this. In fact, it is assumed that the more passive the recipients the more effective will be the learning.

The didactic method was widely popular in the church in the centuries following the Reformation. People were instructed from above, often in minute detail, about what should identify Catholics from other Christians (see chap. 6). The norms defining our Catholic identities were viewed as rigidly static (see chaps. 1 and 2). Rome fostered a form of scholastic philosophy, "neoscholasticism," that provided the church with

6. See comments by Herbert Anderson and Edward Foley, *Mighty Stories, Dangerous Rituals: Weaving Together the Human and the Divine* (San Francisco: Jossey-Bass, 1998), 53.

7. Paulo Freire, *Pedagogy of the Oppressed* (Harmondsworth: Penguin, 1972), 46.

8. See n. 13 below.

a very coherent and rigid intellectual framework affecting all aspects of its ministries. Theology became highly rational. It was so self-contained that its supporters saw no need to listen to, much less learn from, the experiences of people being taught, or from other philosophies, biblical studies, and the social sciences. The task of teachers and preachers was to pass on dogmatic statements to members of the church whose task was to assent without question. Theology was reduced to manuals, with scriptural texts uncritically used in support of preexisting theological conclusions. Vatican II rightly called us back to the inductive teaching methods of Jesus Christ (see chap. 5), but we were ill-prepared for this and now chaos is the result (see chaps. 2 and 3).

Although didactic teaching and discursive or analytic learning definitely have their importance, they should never be the primary method of forming identities. For example, there are times when people need to be told that certain behaviors are acceptable or unacceptable in our institutions. However, behavioral conformity through fear does not in the long run build a culture of trust, good morale, creativity, and work satisfaction. Likewise, Catholic identities today need to be implanted by persuasion and sustained, ultimately, by love.[9] This inductive method of teaching and learning I call the process of "dynamic identification," and it will be explained in chapter 1.

Identities through Inductive Learning

Dynamic inductive identification processes that intimately involve people in their learning begin with their experience, just as Jesus, the expert in adult teaching, demonstrated. He knew that abstract principles are easier to grasp when viewed through the lens of a well-chosen story. Inductive teaching aims to involve as many different dimensions of the learner as possible. Its purpose is to foster integrated learning at the spiritual, cognitive, imaginative, affective, and behavioral levels, so that people are inspired to make real attitudinal and behavioral changes in their lives because they recognize and accept for themselves the relevance and importance of these changes. One of the positive gifts of our postmodern age is the appreciation that imagination holds a critical role in learning and in storytelling. Imagination has a fundamental mediat-

9. See Peter Steinfels, "Catholic Identity: Emerging Consensus," *Origins* 25, no. 11 (1995): 173–77, at 176.

ing role in human experience and in inductive learning,[10] and for this reason Jesus so vividly fostered the imagination of his listeners. Since imagination is the ability to picture intuitively "the world out beyond what we take as established given,"[11] it is a quality that surely threatens the power of authoritarian instructors.

Inductive learning encourages critical thinkers, people who are willing to critique the world around them according to Gospel values. It is a collaborative process involving "all participants, teachers and learners alike, in a process of mutual vulnerability and risk taking, of personal challenge and learning."[12] Teachers need, of course, to be competent in their subject at the levels of theory and experience, but they should be prepared to use a flexible approach that is adaptive to the learner's current knowledge and experience. As Thomas Groome writes: "Instead of a 'jug to mug' pedagogy, people in every generation need to come to their own cognition and recognition . . . of the truths and values discovered by those before us. . . . So . . . religious education must lead people to reflect on their own lives, as both a departure and a point of arrival in coming to 'know' their faith."[13]

Blessed John Henry Newman (1801–1890) found the neoscholastic method of teaching of his day arid, "rigorously abstract, ahistorical and deductivist."[14] For Newman, pastoral teaching and theological formation needed to be conducted in an inductive manner:

> [D]eductions have no power of persuasion. The heart is commonly reached, not through the reason, but through the imagination, by means of direct impressions, by the testimony of facts and events, by history, by description. Persons influence us, voices melt us, looks subdue us, deeds inflame us. . . . Logic makes a sorry rhetoric with the multitude; first shoot round corners, and you may not despair of converting by a

---

10. See Richard Tarnas, *The Passion of the Western Mind: Understanding Ideas That Have Shaped Our World View* (New York: Ballantine, 1991), 405.

11. Walter Brueggemann, *Disruptive Grace* (Minneapolis: Fortress Press, 2011), 296.

12. Tony Hobbs, in idem, ed., *Experiential Learning: Practical Guidelines* (London: Routledge, 1992), xiv.

13. Thomas H. Groome, *Will There Be Faith? A New Vision for Educating and Growing Disciples* (New York: HarperOne, 2011), 284.

14. Nicholas Lash, "Waiting for Dr. Newman," *America* (1–8 February 2010): 13.

syllogism. . . . After all, man is *not* a reasoning animal; he is a seeing, feeling, contemplating, acting animal.[15]

Theologian Nicholas Lash commented on Newman's support of the inductive method: "The interrogative, tentative, inductive temper of his arguments and his lack of specialization are more likely today than they were in the 19th century to be appreciated as virtues in a theologian." Lash is hopeful that contemporary Catholic theology "[has] by and large escaped from the aridities of neoscholasticism and has reestablished contact with the biblical and literary richness of patristic and medieval Christianity."[16] This inductive method so favored by Newman finds solid support in the ecclesiology of Vatican II, that is, an ecclesiology that calls the church to evangelize through dialogue by meeting people first at their points of need—their joys, hopes, and anguishes.[17] This is called a "narrative ecclesiology" or an "ecclesiology from below."[18]

Blessed John Paul II also showed passionate concern for an inductive approach to theology and pastoral teaching: the "secret of [the church's] educative power [is] not so much in doctrinal statements and pastoral approaches to vigilance, as in constantly looking to the Lord Jesus Christ. Each day the church looks to Christ with unfailing love, fully aware that the true and final answer to the problem [of identities] lies in him alone."[19] Encouraged by these words, we are to hold firm in returning to the inductive pedagogical method adopted by Jesus Christ to explain and build his kingdom of love, justice, and compassion.

The gospel stories and parables are well adapted to people's postmodern yearning to discover identities and the meaning of life through imaginative storytelling (see chaps. 2 and 4). Parables and biblical stories, for example, can become the refounding stories for people and institutions in search of Catholic identities today. With skilled educators,

---

15. John Henry Newman, cited by Ian Ker, *John Henry Newman: A Biography* (Oxford: Oxford University Press, 1988), 211.

16. Ibid.

17. See Pastoral Constitution of the Church in the Modern World (*Gaudium et Spes*) 1, in *Vatican Council II: Volume 1, The Conciliar and Post Conciliar Documents*, ed. Austin Flannery (Northport, NY: Costello Publishing Company, Inc., 1996).

18. See Gerard Mannion, *Ecclesiology and Postmodernity: Questions for the Church in Our Time* (Collegeville, MN: Liturgical Press, 2007), 43–74.

19. John Paul II, *Veritatis Splendor* (Vatican City: Libreria Editrice Vaticana, 1993), 130.

people can rediscover for themselves the roots of their Catholic identities and be inspired to relate their values to contemporary postmodern issues. Just as Christ did not presume his listeners had prior knowledge of his teachings, so also today we are being called to evangelize people and institutions with little or no knowledge of Christ's teachings. The wisdom writers of the Old Testament faced a world in many ways like our own because people wanted hope in the midst of meaninglessness and uncertainty. The sages did not respond with abstract and discursive language, but in colorful storytelling. Christ through his parables followed the example of these wise writers and so must we.[20]

It is this inductive, non-discursive approach to learning that should be the primary response to the call of Benedict XVI for a New Evangelization (see chap. 3). Otherwise, no matter how inspiringly worded the deliberations of the Synod on New Evangelization may be, nothing pastorally innovative will eventuate. Sustained pastoral change ultimately is a "bottom-up" process because it engages people at each stage of their transformation. Pope Francis is today a master of inductive evangelization—an engaging Gospel storyteller.

Identity or Identities?

I have used the words "Catholic Identities" in the title of this book and throughout the text to reinforce the point that there are many ways of identifying what "Catholic" means. As the human person has many identities, so also do the church and its members (see chaps. 1 and 2). Thus Peter Steinfels has wisely reminded us that we should "stop thinking about Catholic identity as though this were something univocal. . . . There may be some overarching principles . . . but there is no single way of embodying them, and it might be wiser to speak of Catholic identities in the plural."[21] Contemporary restorationist forces in the church are actively seeking to reverse this positive trend toward the inductive method of teaching and formation (see chap. 6). Restorationists would like to reduce Catholic identities to "something univocal," that is, to one single theme, namely, orthodoxy, meaning unquestioning conformity to Roman ways.

20. See Jill Y. Crainshaw, *Wise and Discerning Hearts: An Introduction to Wisdom Liturgical Theology* (Collegeville, MN: Liturgical Press, 2000), 161–91.

21. Peter Steinfels, *A People Adrift: The Crisis of the Roman Catholic Church in America* (New York: Simon & Schuster, 2003), 147–48.

However, if we isolate one expression of identity to the detriment of other identifying qualities we end up in fundamentalism with its oppressive and arrogant rigidity. No discussion or loyal dissent allowed! Then a culture of fear results. Fear gives way to distrust and internecine theological warfare. People fear to be pastorally creative lest they be reported to the local bishop or to Rome itself. Then the church fails "to be a symbol of God's reign, God's kingdom, where the love of God flows freely so that divisions can be healed and peace prevails."[22] It is a fact of life that the more there is trust and transparency in an institution, including the church, the healthier it is and the more it can blossom. People feel authorized to be creative. Conversely, the less trust exists, the sicker an institution becomes. If the level of trust becomes too low, the institution wilts and dies. Sadly, the levels of trust within the church today are dangerously low, so low that people are not encouraged "to show boldness"[23] in creating innovative ways to preach the Gospel.

In this book, therefore, the term "Catholic identities" means the church-engaging-with-the-contemporary-world (chap. 3), that is, the mythology of the life, death, and resurrection of Jesus Christ, engaging-with-the-world as mediating through such realities as the Scriptures, the church, magisterium, authentic tradition, theology, sacraments, liturgies, moral and social teachings, "culture champions" such as institutional founders, refounders, and all values-committed people (chap. 4). The process of engaging and mediating is expressed in an ever-changing variety of Catholic identities. In summary, "Catholic identities" refers to the engagement of the church with the contemporary world, and this will manifest itself in a constantly changing diversity of ways. The more people are trusted to live and preach the Gospel, the more vibrant and relevant will be these identities.

Structure of the Book

This work is written to assist a wide range of people in their various ministries, such as bishops, theologians, pastoral workers, and staff members in schools, healthcare, business organizations, and tertiary

---

22. R. Kevin Seasoltz, *A Virtuous Church: Catholic Theology, Ethics, and Liturgy for the 21st Century* (Collegeville, MN: Liturgical Press, 2012), 199.

23. *Lineamenta* (Preparatory Document for Synod 2012), "The New Evangelization" (Nairobi: Paulines, 2011), § 6.

institutions. The book draws on several disciplines: for example, theology, Scripture, and history, but particularly cultural anthropology. Anthropology is about how people feel and communicate with one another and across cultures. It is often about revealing the cultural forces that motivate people and their institutions, though they are so often unaware of the existence of these forces and their ability to control behavior.[24] This discipline has been called by anthropologist Raymond Firth "an inquisitive, challenging, uncomfortable discipline, questioning established positions . . . peering into underlying interests, if not destroying fictions and empty phrases . . . at least exposing them."[25]

- Chapter 1, *Catholic "Identity" or "Identities"?* explains that individuals and institutions have multiple sociological identities. The identity that is operative at a particular time will depend very much on the context. Storytelling is the preferred way of discovering and negotiating identities.

- Chapter 2, *The Catholic Story: Identities' Crisis*, describes from a cultural-anthropological perspective how the theological and cultural changes over the last fifty years have led to very different understandings of Catholic identities. Before 1965 the markers of Catholic identities in the centuries following the Reformation remained stable and universal; this is no longer the situation because of the combined impact of such factors as Vatican II, the rising social and economic status of Catholics, and postmodernity.[26]

- Chapter 3, *Ministries: Crisis of Identities*, looks closely at the breakdown of traditional Catholic identities in the particular ministries of healthcare and education. There is an urgent need to find ways to refound Catholic identities in these ministries. Traditional or didactic methods of teaching and learning are no longer effective.

- Chapter 4, *Founding and Refounding Identities*, emphasizes the important distinction between "renewal" and "refounding": the

---

24. See Gerald A. Arbuckle, *Culture, Inculturation, and Theologians: A Postmodern Critique* (Collegeville, MN: Liturgical Press, 2010), 19–48.

25. Raymond Firth, "Engagement and Detachment: Reflections on Applying Social Anthropology to Social Affairs," *Human Organization* 40 (1981): 192–201, at 200.

26. This chapter updates material published in my book *Refounding the Church: Dissent for Leadership* (Maryknoll, NY: Orbis Books, 1993), 36–97.

first deals with the symptoms of a problem; the second goes to the roots of a challenging issue. The qualities of refounders are described and illustrated with examples.

- Chapter 5, *Founding and Refounding Identities: Scriptural Experiences*, demonstrates why the Old Testament prophets are refounders of the Israelites' identities as a nation. Also, the preferred method of Jesus Christ for founding and refounding faith-based identities among his followers is the inductive or narrative method, for example, in his use of parables or storytelling. This biblical narrative style is particularly adapted to inspire leaders with refounding qualities who can creatively respond to pastoral needs of people in our contemporary postmodern times.

- Chapter 6, *Catholic Normative Identities: A Critique*, highlights various normative theological models that traditionally shape Catholic identities. It has commonly been assumed that these definitions of identities can be imposed from above. Since this didactic or "top-down" pedagogy is ineffective in our postmodern age, the process of crafting identities needs to be based first on the inductive style of biblical storytelling. Pastors, religious educators, and people entrusted with the task of maintaining Catholic identities in our institutions urgently need to model this inductive approach.

- Chapter 7, *Healthcare and Welfare: Refounding Catholic Identities*, is a practical explanation of how the Good Samaritan parable, the foundational story of healthcare, socioeconomic development, and welfare ministries, can be used as the catalyst for people to craft their value-based Catholic identities.

- Chapter 8, *Crafting Catholic Identities in the Business World*, illustrates in practical ways why many of the parables of Jesus Christ offer opportunities for people to reflect on their moral obligations to act with justice and compassion.

- Chapter 9, *Adult Rural Education: Refounding Catholic Identities*, describes why a rural education project in a developing country is uniquely successful. The case study illustrates that devotion, a critical factor behind the project's success, can be "taught" and "caught" when educators skillfully draw on lessons inherent in the popular religiosity of their trainees through a process of storytelling.

Personal Experience

When I first began to conduct workshops on the constituent elements of Catholic identities in Catholic healthcare facilities in North America and Australia I followed a normative or didactic approach: lectures, then discussion and questions. The approach was a failure. People were bored, uninterested, and very suspicious that I was "forcing religion on them." Then in desperation I turned to an inductive approach, beginning always by inviting participants to identify issues of concern in their experience as staff members. In the light of what emerged I would choose and briefly explain a parable or a biblical story, then invite participants to identify values relevant to their experience in their healthcare ministry. In other words, participants in workshops in a sense set the agenda, based on their personal experiences of working in Catholic healthcare facilities. After reflecting on the values inherent in the parables, people discovered for themselves, for example, the need to understand and adhere to the ethical principles that should characterize Catholic healthcare institutions. The atmosphere in the workshops radically changed. True, I certainly covered far less material in this method, but the energy and learning of the participants increased immensely. No longer did participants complain that religion was being imposed on them (see chaps. 7 and 8).

I have previously written on the theme of refounding: *Out of Chaos: Refounding Religious Congregations* (1988); *Earthing the Gospel: An Inculturation Handbook for Pastoral Workers* (1990); *Healthcare Ministry: Refounding the Mission in Tumultuous Times* (2000); and *Humanizing Healthcare Reforms* (2012). This book updates and applies material originally contained in my *Refounding the Church: Dissent for Leadership* (1993) and *Culture, Inculturation, and Theologians: A Postmodern Critique* (2010). But unlike them, this book specifically focuses on the importance of refounding adult formation for Catholic ministries and the practical ways to achieve this by first returning to the Scriptures and the methods of teaching that Jesus Christ himself used with such authority and effectiveness.

Chapter One

Catholic "Identity" or "Identities"?

All the world's a stage. And all the men and women
merely players: They have their exits and their entrances;
And one man in his time plays many parts. (William
Shakespeare, As You Like It*)*[1]

Late have I loved you, beauty so ancient and so new: late
have I loved you. (Augustine, Confessions*)*[2]

This chapter explains that:

• in the postmodern world there is a proliferation of potential identities

• for individuals and institutions identification is a process
  of "engaging-with-contexts"

• this process is one of storytelling or the creation of
  narratives

• in narratives of identity people draw on individual and
  collective "myths"

• narratives can restrict, or even contradict, the original
  myths, as is the case with Catholic fundamentalism in
  the church

• in times of institutional chaos people of refounding
  qualities are needed to create relevant identities

---

1. William Shakespeare, *As You Like It*, II.vii.139.
2. St Augustine, *Confessions*, trans. Henry Chadwick (Oxford: Oxford University Press, 1991), 201.

Shakespeare is perceptively right again. Every person on the daily stage of life plays a multitude of roles, of "identities."[3] This introductory chapter explains theoretically why Shakespeare's insights into the meaning of identity will always be relevant. We all know more or less what the word "identity" means, but settling on a precise definition is not so easy. We know that identity connotes two paradoxical realities: sameness and uniqueness. We share similar qualities with other human beings, but at the same time we know that each of us has unique characteristics that mark us as different.[4] But what makes each one of us distinctively different? There is no simple answer.

Until recent times the popular modern view, a remnant of Enlightenment thinking, was that the self is an autonomous, stable, structural entity composed of factors and traits that "add up" to a total person without that person's active involvement, and transcending her or his particular place in culture, language, and history.[5] According to this view identity is something static, unchanging. That is not the case. Rather, identity is a process of "self-engaging-with-context."[6] As the context changes, so there is potentially a new identity, a new identifying role to play, that a person must acknowledge in some way or other. So it is more accurate to say that a person has many identities, not just one, because the context in which he or she lives is changing. For example, we behave differently with our peers and with children, in informal and formal situations, in our work environment and in our homely settings. Our identity is far from unitary; rather, we all have a multiplicity of identities, and often there are tensions, even conflicts, between our different identities. Madan Sarup is right: "identities, our

3. In this foundational chapter I summarize, but further develop, material I have previously published. See Gerald A. Arbuckle, *Culture, Inculturation, and Theologians: A Postmodern Critique* (Collegeville, MN: Liturgical Press, 2010), 1–18.

4. See Steph Lawler, *Identity: Sociological Perspectives* (Cambridge: Polity, 2008), 1–5.

5. See Frank Johnson, "The Western Concept of Self," in *Culture and Self: Asian and Western Perspectives*, ed. Anthony J. Marsella, George Devos, and Francis L. Hsu (New York: Tavistock, 1985), 91–138.

6. Thomas K. Fitzgerald, *Metaphors of Identity: A Culture-Communication Dialogue* (New York: SUNY Press, 1993), ix.

own and those of others, are fragmented, full of contradictions and ambiguities."[7]

It will be helpful to explain these points further. In traditional societies where change is very slow, people interact with the *same* people in their neighborhoods, workplaces, and at leisure. Identities are for the most part unchanging because the context remains generally stable. But it is very different for the average person in the Western postmodern world. No longer can we view a culture as a unifying, unchanging, and homogenizing force. The relationship between an individual and his or her culture is a dynamic and ambivalent one; individuals possess multiple, often contradictory and constantly changing, identities. That is, individuals have a multiplicity of potential identities because the context in which they are living, working, and recreating is continually changing. Identities become more compartmentalized and fragmented; within the space of one day most individuals must interact with a great variety of *different* people, depending on the context. In summary, who we are is primarily to be found in the way we live day by day within a particular cultural context or environment, not just in what we think or say about ourselves. Identity is always a process of "being" or "becoming," never a final and settled issue.

Identification Processes: Clarification

Identification is the process whereby we understand "who we are and who other people are, and, reciprocally, other people's understanding of themselves and of others (which includes us)."[8] This process whereby we become aware that we are distinctly different from, or similar to, other people is achieved in either *normative* or *dynamic* ways (see fig. 1.1). Through the *normative* identification process we discover that we must conform to preset identities; society or institutions tell us how we must behave with little or no involvement on our part. The *dynamic* identification process, however, places the emphasis on individual decision making in choosing identities. Of course, if we opt to emphasize

---

7. Madan Sarup, *Identity, Culture and the Postmodern World* (Edinburgh: Edinburgh University Press, 1996), 14.

8. Richard Jenkins, *Social Identity* (London: Routledge, 2008), 18. See also Victor J. Seidler, *Embodying Identities: Culture, Differences and Social Theory* (Bristol: Policy Press, 2010), 1–52.

dynamic identification we have to decide to accept or reject identities that have been normatively set by others.

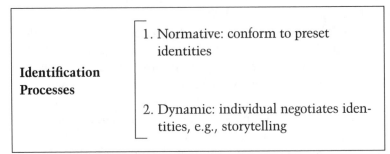

Figure 1.1 Identification Processes

In our postmodern world individual identity is less and less a question of conforming to definite, set roles and more and more an issue of trying to make sense of who I am through monitoring my own actions, depending on the ever-changing social environment in which I find myself. It frequently involves a complicated process of decision making in the face of numerous social situations. It is as though I must constantly tell stories to myself to remind me of my identity in a particular context. Sociologist Anthony Giddens refers to this process as the "reflexive self," that is, a process whereby "self-identity is constituted by the reflexive ordering of self-narratives."[9] Through self-narratives or storytelling individuals write and rewrite the story of their selves and the many worlds in which they live.[10] Giddens further comments that "the narrative of self has in fact to be continually reworked, and lifestyle practices brought into line with it," and in consequence, "life-style choices are constitutive of the reflexive narrative of self."[11] Through storytelling, individuals are constantly reflecting

9. Anthony Giddens, *Modernity and Self-Identity: Self and Society in the Late Modern Age* (Cambridge: Polity, 1991), 244.

10. Psychoanalyst Roy Schaefer writes that "more generally the so-called self may be considered to be a set of narrative strategies or storylines each person follows in trying to develop an emotionally coherent account of his or her life among people. We organize our past and present experiences narratively." *Retelling a Life: Narration and Dialogue in Psychoanalysis* (New York: Basic Books, 1992), 34.

11. Anthony Giddens, *The Transformation of Intimacy: Sexuality, Love and Eroticism in Modern Societies* (Cambridge: Polity, 1992), 75.

on their experiences in order to define their changing identities and create a sense of personal stability.

Stories and Storytelling

When someone asks me who I am, I tell a story, that is, I describe my present circumstances in light of my memories of the past and what I think is relevant to the questioner. Storytelling is a process of narrating "that enriches our understanding of the world and of the people who affect our lives."[12] Storytelling puts people's minds and hearts in contact with the knowledge and feeling of being alive. Stories give people a foundation "for making strategic choices about actions and communication with others."[13]

Richard Jenkins describes the process of self-identification through storytelling as one of negotiation. Individuals create "an image of themselves—of self—for acceptance by others"[14] and implicitly or explicitly negotiate with them to determine what is an acceptable identity in particular contexts. Sometimes identities are in constant tension: for example, the fact that a woman may be both a parent *and* a professional business person will create stress at times. She must negotiate with herself ways to control this stress. Self-identification is thus an increasingly complicated and contentious process because, owing to the ever-increasing speed of change both locally and globally, relationships and power must be forever negotiated.[15] There is also a complex relationship between narrative, time, and memory, for we can amend and edit the remembered past to fit with our identities and the context at the present moment. For example, I may be an aging person but at times I will deny this and claim the physical identity of someone much younger.

12. Michael Kaye, *Myth-Makers and Story-Tellers* (Sydney: Business & Professional Publishing, 1996), xix.

13. Ibid., 17. A British moral philosopher, Alasdair MacIntyre, provides a philosophical foundation for organizational storytelling in his book *After Virtue: A Study in Moral Theory* (Notre Dame, IN: University of Notre Dame Press, 1984).

14. Jenkins, *Social Identity*, 93.

15. See Anthony D. Buckley and Mary C. Kenney, *Negotiating Identity: Rhetoric, Metaphor, and Social Drama in Northern Ireland* (Washington, DC: Smithsonian Institution Press, 1995).

In brief, identities are not fixed, immutable, or primordial. They are sociocultural in their origins and are thus at least potentially flexible, situational, and negotiable.[16] We effectively negotiate our way through daily life by storytelling that explains who we are and what we are doing, and by having these stories grafted onto the stories that others recount.

Institutional Identities

Statements of identity—mission statements, for example—are ideal expressions of institutional identity. They set normative standards to measure behavior. This means they establish values and behavioral patterns that theoretically classify their uniqueness. Members are expected to act according to these standards, in ways that differentiate them from non-members; there will be clear boundaries that separate members from non-members. People become aware of their uniqueness when they stand at the boundaries of these institutions and discover that the values and behaviors of others are different from their own.[17]

More accurately, however, an institutional identity, like personal identity, is an ongoing process of "engaging-with-context." How an institution acts, not what it says about itself, realistically defines its identity. As the economic, social, and cultural contexts change, so an institution must constantly adjust its identity to this reality, demanding constant rethinking and renegotiating on the part of those in charge of institutions. The mere statement of institutional identity will achieve nothing by itself unless there is this constant process of actually engaging-with-context.

When the context is complex there will be many identities, some more important than others, depending on the context. For example, the primary role of hospitals until the 1960s was for the most part to *care* for people. Many diseases and injuries could not be cured. But with the arrival of miracle drugs the task of hospitals changed dramatically. Now hospitals became institutions primarily to *cure* people. Hospitals today symbolize this change in all kinds of ways, for example, through developing more and more specialized departments with their own particular identities and rituals, accompanied by new and expensive machinery with the precise purpose of curing patients in the shortest possible time. A hospital will

16. See Jenkins, *Social Identity*, 19, and Ken Roberts, *Key Concepts in Sociology* (Houndmills: Palgrave Macmillan, 2009), 128.

17. See Anthony P. Cohen, *The Symbolic Construction of Community* (Chichester: Ellis Horwood, 1985).

go out of business if it fails to adjust its services, and therefore its set of identities, to the changing technologies of healthcare and the needs of patients. The same is true for schools or universities. Unless they are constantly adapting their curricula and teaching methods, their identities, to the changing times, they will have no future. They will slip into history. The truth is simply this: if institutions are not continually engaging and responding to new needs, they die. An institution cannot be expected to survive if it thinks it can hold on to exactly the same set of identities it had twenty years ago. The particular identity to be emphasized will depend on the specific situation in which the institution finds itself.

Maintaining Institutional Identities: Key Insights

We are now in a position to make four key points that will influence the remainder of this book:

1. Institutional identities, like individual identities, are socially constructed. They are shaped in particular cultural and historical contexts. Since these contexts are constantly changing, institutions themselves must be in continuous change and reconfiguration if they are to survive. Identities belong to the present and the future as much as to the profound influences of the past. Far from being eternally fixed in some unchanging realities of the past, identities are subject to the continuous play of history, culture, and power. To know an institution's identity, therefore, and of course to be able to shape it, we must know the *context* in which it is operating, interacting, or engaging now.

2. Institutions that refuse to allow their identities to change in view of changing contexts cease to exist. This means that there can be no constructive change at all, even in the church, *unless* there is some form of dissent. A reasonable degree of diversity and dissent is essential for any organization if it is to have a future. People who invented automobiles were dissenters. Cars were at first considered to be dangerous and troublesome disturbers of the peace. Imagine what would have happened if they had been effectively marginalized from society. We would today still be riding horses! By "dissent" I mean simply the *proposing of alternatives*—and a system that is not continuously examining alternatives, that is, new expressions of identity, is not likely to evolve creatively.

Open organizations encourage people who propose alternative ways of doing things because they know that institutions age and produce deadwood. New ideas and ways of doing things may guarantee that life and vitality will continue. They are the seedlings out of which the future is born. However, as seedlings are very frail, so also new proposals for acting are fragile and can be quickly smothered long before they have had a chance to develop. Anthropologists frequently observe that once cultural patterns are established, they tend to endure. This is not only because people are more comfortable with the familiar. The power of vested interests is as often responsible for maintaining the cultural status quo as are ingrained habits or mere complacency. In contrast, creative or dissenting people are designed to give birth to what has never been in existence before. The alternatives they propose, along with their different identities, frighten people who take comfort in the predictable and/or sense that their vested interests are threatened.

Authentic dissenters respect the past but carefully distinguish between values that must never change and how these values are to be expressed because the context has altered. A good example is the confusion among many Catholics about the meaning of *Tradition* and how it differs from *traditions*. Tradition with a capital "T" connotes the unalterable living out of the Gospel message given by Jesus Christ to the apostles and their successors, but traditions with a small "t" are "those changeable customs, laws, and practices which the Church had adopted over the centuries in order to facilitate and further [its] mission."[18] For example, Tradition tells us that Mary is the Mother of God and we venerate her for this reason. Over the centuries people have developed different ways to express this veneration, such as the rosary, processions, and pilgrimages, but these are not integral to Tradition. Times have radically changed. Most people today no longer have the leisure time for long devotions. Authentic dissenters call us to find new ways, that is, new identities, for expressing veneration of Mary. In brief, Tradition is not synonymous with traditions.

In summary, every institution, the church included, faces a joint task: it must engender a degree of conformity to the existing order of

---

18. Lawrence S. Cunningham, *An Introduction to Catholicism* (Cambridge: Cambridge University Press, 2009), 12.

boundaries, but at the same time it must allow for those "heretics" of each age, the people with apparently outlandish ideas and customs, who have often become the pastoral innovative heroes of the next.

3. For an institution to maintain its identity, it requires four qualities. First, it must have a founding story that defines how it is to engage or negotiate through narratives with its surrounding contexts; thus, a healthcare institution will interact with its surrounding social, political, and economic context in a way that is significantly different from that of an engineering firm. Second, the institution will have clearly defined symbolic and ritual markers that identify its unique story and its cultural boundaries. People become aware of their culture when they stand at its boundaries; if the boundaries are not clear, people become confused about their identities. Third, it will foster responsible dissenters who are prepared to propose new narratives of thinking and acting in view of changing circumstances and needs. Fourth, the institution will have formal and informal educational programs that ensure its members remain in touch with the founding story.

4. As contemporary societies encourage people to decide for themselves whether or not they wish to have a religious identity, faith-based institutions must be increasingly concerned to construct and maintain their religious identity.[19]

Identities: Myths and Narratives

The process of acquiring identities will now be more deeply examined. Given that contemporary identities are increasingly fragmented, blurred, and unstable, the key question is: how are people at the personal, group, institutional, and cultural levels to attain reassuring identities?

Identities are clarified in one of two ways, didactically or inductively. As explained in the Introduction, when the didactic approach is used, people are told who they are; this is the "mug" and "jug" approach in which learning occurs, if at all, almost entirely at the intellectual level. The recipient of a preset identity is like an empty mug waiting to receive information poured into them from the source of knowledge, the

19. See Arthur L. Greil and Lynn Davidman, "Religion and Identity," 549–65, in James A. Beckford and N. J. Demerath, eds., *Sage Handbook of the Sociology of Religion* (London: Sage, 2007), 560.

jug. That is, only people at the top of the hierarchy of power determine identities, which are then imposed on others. This is a passive method of learning in which people are not required to examine their own emotional and intellectual responses to identities handed down from above. Those who object to this imposition of identities feel smothered by an avalanche of information and decrees from above and may angrily struggle to dissent, but often without success.

On the other hand, in the experiential or inductive approach people negotiate for themselves and others who they are and who they are not. Through storytelling, individuals write and rewrite the story of their selves and the many worlds in which they live. As individuals construct stories from experience, so also groups of all kinds, such as business organizations, communities, governments, and nations, assemble preferred narratives that feelingly tell them who they are at this moment in time, where they have come from, what is good or bad, and how they are to organize themselves and maintain their sense of unique identity in a changing world.

In reflexive storytelling or narratives people and groups draw on myths. Myths are stories handed down from the past that explain to people the *origins* of natural and social realities and interrelationships; they are stories that claim to reveal in an imaginative and symbolic way fundamental truths about the world and human life;[20] they are efforts to explain what usually is beyond empirical observation and to some degree outside human experience. They speak of reality and experience *other* than in the physical world. Myths help us to articulate the deepest issues of our lives. Myth and history do not contradict each other because each relates to facts from its own standpoint; history observes facts from the "outer physical side, myth from the inner spiritual side."[21]

Myths can evoke deep emotional responses and a sense of mystery in those who accept them, simply because they develop out of the very depths of human experience. No matter how seriously we seek to deepen our grasp of the meaning of myths, they will remain somewhat ambiguous and mysterious because they attempt to articulate what cannot be fully articulated. Myths remain the revelations of mysteries rather than clever illustrations or didactic entertainments on the part of mere human persons.

---

20. See Gerald A. Arbuckle, *Earthing the Gospel: An Inculturation Handbook for Pastoral Workers* (Maryknoll, NY: Orbis Books, 1990), 26–43, and *Culture, Inculturation, and Theologians*, 19–42.

21. Morton Kelsey, *Myth, History and Faith: The Demythologizing of Christianity* (New York: Paulist Press, 1974), 4.

The use of symbols and mythical language is crucial for the evoking of mystery. Avery Dulles, SJ, has written: "Unlike historical or abstract truth mystery cannot be described or positively defined. It can only be evoked."[22]

Example

The Lincoln Memorial is located at the end of the National Mall in Washington, DC. At the heart of this strikingly beautiful memorial is a massive statue of Lincoln, who led the nation through its greatest constitutional, military, and moral crisis—the Civil War. The monument is deliberately designed to inspire mythological mystery or awe in the hearts of visitors. Words alone can never adequately describe the qualities of this man and the debt the nation owes him. Visitors leave the monument with the feeling that there is something wonderfully mysterious about Abraham Lincoln and the values of liberty and justice he stood for.

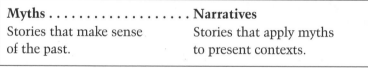

Myths . . . . **Narratives**
Stories that make sense   Stories that apply myths
of the past.   to present contexts.

Figure 1.2 Myths and narratives

Myth and narrative are two sides of the one coin (see fig. 1.2). Although myths and narratives are stories, there is a significant difference. Myths make our lives intelligible in the *past*, but the retelling of these stories in light of *present* needs is what we call narrative. Narrative is the actual recounting of the myth, but within changing times. In the process of retelling, the myth itself is altered or modified according to the circumstances of time and place. That is, in narratives myths from the past are applied to what concerns people today and in the process the myths are enlarged, altered, or even discarded.[23] The founding myth of

---

22. Avery Dulles, "Symbol, Myth and the Biblical Revelation," *Theological Studies* 27 (1966): 1–26, at 1.

23. See Arbuckle, *Culture, Inculturation, and Theologians,* 72.

modernity, for example, asserts that the individual is perfectible through his or her own efforts; governments must not interfere. This myth, the foundation of capitalism, was challenged in the period of the Great Depression and again with the recent global economic downturn. Thus the myth of capitalism has had to be significantly modified by a new narrative in the United States. Now we have a narrative that tells Americans that the federal government has a right to intervene directly at times in national monetary policies to protect the employment and health of people, even if this means reducing the freedom of the wealthiest. Politically, however, Republicans (more so than Democrats) would severely restrict any narrative that encourages federal government intervention in monetary matters (and even in health issues).

Every narrative has a plot or purpose that shapes its structure. That is, not only must a narrative be more than one event following another, but some form of meaningful connection between them is necessary. The connection is provided by the plot of the narrative; the raconteur chooses how to do this, depending on the audience.[24] The plot is the vehicle whereby the overall purpose of the narrative is achieved. As Paul Ricoeur writes: "By plot I mean the intelligible whole that governs a succession of events in any story. . . . A story is *made out of* events to the extent that plot *makes* events *into* a story."[25]

Narratives are therefore:

- about creating identity in the here and now, all the while drawing on myths of the past;

- stories that recount in a variety of ways, such as images, music, and gestures, but particularly language, a series of temporal events so that a meaningful succession is depicted, which is the plot;

- everywhere, to be found in all forms of human communication, so much so that human beings can be called "narrating animals."

24. See Anthony Kerby, *Narrative and Self* (Bloomington, IN: Indiana University Press, 1991), 39.

25. Paul Ricoeur, "Narrative Time," *Critical Inquiry* 7 (January 1980): 169–90, at 171.

The following are examples of the ways in which narratives create identities. Though each narrative is described as a separate entity in practice, there is often an overlap so that each may contain elements of other narratives.

Narratives of Deception

In the aftermath of the Japanese bombing of Pearl Harbor in 1941 over 120,000 Japanese Americans, the large majority of whom were United States citizens and included second and third generations, were relocated and interned. A false racist narrative was constructed to legitimize this.[26] A similar deceiving narrative was developed by the Bush Administration to justify the invasion of Iraq in 2003.

Narratives of Cultural Romanticism and Amnesia

Narratives of cultural romanticism idealize a cultural past. Historical imperfections and injustices are ignored or deliberately denied. Cultural romanticism is alive and well in the Catholic Church, especially when people accept and encourage creeping centralized infallibility. The church has never made mistakes, it is said, and the pope's pronouncements have been, and must be, always right. Romanticists ignore the enormous mistakes of the past (and present). For example, until the nineteenth century church documents often justified slavery. As recent as 1866 the Holy Office declared that "slavery itself . . . is not at all contrary to the natural and divine law."[27] Rome finally, in 1890, accepted the fact that there can be no such thing as just slavery, though the British government had outlawed slavery in all its colonies in 1838.

Also, it is sometimes said that the church by its founding mythology is not a democracy—it has never been and will never be one, and so Rome can justifiably ignore the values of participative or consultative leadership. Here, there has been a myth drift. Not only is this contrary to the spirit of Vatican II, but it ignores the original practice of the church for a significant period of history. Historian Leonard Swidler concludes that the choice of bishops by clergy and people remained effective until the twelfth century. John Carroll, the first bishop of the United States,

26. See Catherine K. Riessman, *Narrative Methods for the Human Sciences* (Los Angeles: Sage, 2008), 46.

27. See Maureen Fiedler and Linda Rabben, *Rome Has Spoken: A Guide to Forgotten Papal Statements and How They Have Changed through the Centuries* (New York: Crossroad, 1998), 81.

was chosen with Rome's approval by the priests of the country. As late as the beginning of the twentieth century fewer than half of the world's bishops were directly chosen by the pope.[28]

Narratives of Fundamentalism

Political and/or religious fundamentalism is apt to occur in almost every society or organization in reaction to a breakdown of order following rapid change. People yearn for simplistic, clear-cut identities in the midst of this confusion. There are no gray areas of uncertainty, only absolute answers. Fundamentalism is organized anger that groups of people feel because they sense that history has gone awry and their task is to restore it to "normality" as defined by themselves.[29] For example, the Know Nothing political movement in the United States in the early 1850s was characterized by political xenophobia, anti-Catholic sentiment, and occasional violence against groups. It was a reaction to anti-slavery agitation and the increasing presence of Catholic immigrants from Ireland and Germany. Supporters felt that the founding mythology of the Constitution was being violated and they were going to restore it to its original purpose. Abraham Lincoln condemned them: "When Know-Nothings get control, [the founding document] will read 'all men are created equal, except Negroes, and foreigners, and Catholics.'"[30] The contemporary Tea Party movement is a further example of an American narrative fundamentalism. It emerged from the Tea Party protests that occurred in 2009 against the government's bank bailouts and healthcare reform proposals. It campaigns against government spending, is opposed to tax increases, and presses for the reduction of the national debt. Adherents loudly and angrily assert that the country must return to an authentic interpretation of the Constitution, which means for them that the rights of the individual must have precedence over the common good.

Within the Catholic Church fundamentalism is present in different forms in reaction to the changes introduced by Vatican II. Thomas

28. See Leonard Swidler, "Democracy, Dissent, and Dialogue: A Catholic Vocation," 306–24, in *The Church in Anguish*, ed. Hans Küng and Leonard Swidler (San Francisco: Harper & Row, 1986), 310.

29. See Gerald A. Arbuckle, *Violence, Society, and the Church: A Cultural Approach* (Collegeville, MN: Liturgical Press, 2004), 195–214.

30. Abraham Lincoln, quoted by Orville V. Burton, *The Age of Lincoln* (New York: Hill and Wang, 2007), 65.

O'Meara, OP, defines Christian fundamentalism as "an interpretation of Christianity in which a charismatic leader locates with easy certitude in chosen words, doctrines and practices, the miraculous actions of a strict God saving an elite from an evil world."[31] This is an apt description of Catholic fundamentalism. Sects like Catholics United for the Faith (CUF) were formed to defend the church against "the evils of secular humanism," "the loss of orthodoxy," or "the liberalizing excesses that Vatican II inspired." The Latin Mass movement gave some Catholics the nostalgic support they craved, and some moved into schism within the Lefebvre sect. Catholic fundamentalists are highly selective in what they see as pertaining to the church's identity, insisting on accidentals, not the substance of issues, and they readily ignore papal teaching on social justice. They are especially insistent on "restoring" the hierarchical model of the church centered on Rome; they downplay collegiality and the emphasis given by Vatican II to the church as servant, people of God, mission, sacrament, and pilgrim. Catholic identity means for Catholic fundamentalists "adherence to orthodoxy," that is, unquestioning obedience to the hierarchy.[32] "Catholic identities" are to be interpreted in the singular as "Catholic identity"; other Catholic identities do not and cannot exist.

Narratives of Boundary Setting and Scapegoating

Every group, including the church, has the right to define its boundaries or what it considers to be its authentic symbols of identity and orthodoxy. But in boundary setting two principles must be kept always at the forefront: that what is stated to be orthodox must in fact be authentically orthodox; that the process of discerning what is or is not orthodox must follow the religious and secular norms of truth, transparency, and objectivity. Anthropologists, however, point out that in times of cultural disintegration, when cultural boundaries are seriously threatened or break down, scapegoating crazes commonly occur. Scapegoating (or witch-hunting) is the process of passionately searching for and eliminating agents believed to be causing harm to the cultural identity of individuals and groups, demanding that they adhere to traditional orthodox principles. By passing the blame for their afflictions on to others, people

31. Thomas F. O'Meara, *Fundamentalism: A Catholic Perspective* (New York: Paulist Press, 1990), 18.
32. See Tom Roberts, *The Emerging Catholic Church: A Community's Search for Itself* (Maryknoll, NY: Orbis Books, 2011), 154.

are able conveniently to distract themselves from the real causes of chaos and the efforts they must make to remove them.[33]

Vatican II articulated a mythology of church that must guide the formulation of narratives of Catholic identities. However, there are two levels in the contemporary church at which the above two principles of boundary setting are not always being observed by people in practice, namely, at the grassroots and the hierarchical levels, especially in Rome. The mythology they adopt as the foundation of their narratives of identity is that of the pre-conciliar church. Both levels represent fearful groups in the church that seek the simplistic and instant order of a bygone ethnic Catholic culture (see chap. 3) and pursue a witch-hunt against those who do not agree with them. The more witch-hunters at the grassroots know that Rome favors restorationism, the more avidly they go about their work of scapegoating those assumed to be unorthodox members of the church. They undertake their task in a variety of ways, including direct communication to their bishops or Rome itself. Witch-hunting is far more serious at the church's hierarchical level because it is deliberately planned and sanctioned from the top. Theologians are particularly the targets of this witch-hunting.[34] What James Provost, then-professor of canon law at the Catholic University of America, wrote in 1989 is still very much true today: "The rejection of any type of 'dissent' from non-infallible positions has been severe, despite the exception made for many years in the case of Archbishop Lefebvre. There has been an on-going harassment of theologians . . . which often appears as an attempt to appease influential minorities." While acknowledging issues of orthodoxy as a legitimate concern of papal authority, Provost commented that the way this authority is being used on occasion "has the appearance of a defensive effort to exercise centralized control—defensive against the 'evil' world in contrast to the Second Vatican Council's views . . . defensive of a very limited school of theology."[35]

---

33. See Arbuckle, *Violence, Society, and the Church*, 136–51.

34. See Daniel S. Thompson, *The Language of Dissent: Edward Schillebeeckx on the Crisis of Authority in the Catholic Church* (Notre Dame, IN: University of Notre Dame Press, 2003), 1–9; Bradford E. Hinze, "A Decade of Disciplining Theologians," 3–39, in Richard R. Gaillardetz, ed., *When the Magisterium Intervenes: The Magisterium and Theologians in Today's Church* (Collegeville, MN: Liturgical Press, 2012).

35. James Provost, "The Papacy: Power, Authority, Leadership," 189–215, in Bernard Cooke, ed., *The Papacy and the Church in the United States* (New York: Paulist Press, 1989), 205.

The victims of the theologians' "witchcraft" are thought by Rome to be the church itself and the integrity of papal authority. As in all orthodoxy crazes, respect for truth and human rights can suffer sadly, as the following description of the judicial process established by the Congregation for the Doctrine of the Faith (CDF) indicates. It remains substantially unchanged since it was inaugurated in 1971:[36] the CDF is prosecutor, judge and jury; the person being investigated is not told of the inquiry until stage thirteen (of eighteen stages) and may never know the identity of his or her accusers; the defendant is unable to choose a defender or even know the latter's identity, nor is there access to material relating to the allegations against the accused; no publicity is permitted concerning the proceedings and there is no right of appeal.[37] Serious injustices can occur. There is constant recourse to secrecy by the CDF in the judicial process. Secrecy is a powerful instrument of control in narratives of witch-hunting and it is particularly characteristic of cultures that are strongly hierarchical. It is used by elites to hold on to their positions of power through the possession of special knowledge, and by non-elites to defend themselves against the intruding power of the elite. Egalitarian cultures, however, stress values of openness and publicity.[38] It is not surprising, therefore, that the more Rome tries to

36. In 1997 the Holy See promulgated new procedural rules called "Regulations for the Examination of Doctrines" that modified previous norms governing the investigation of theologians. However, they do not substantially change the previous rules. As canonist Ladislas Örsy writes: "for anyone educated in the sensitivities of jurisprudence, [they] do not respond, as they were intended, to the demands of the present day. . . . They have their roots in past ages; they were not born from the vision of human dignity and the respect for honest conscience that is demanded the world over today. . . . They are not rooted in any divine precept." Örsy, *Receiving the Council: Theological and Canonical Insights and Debates* (Collegeville, MN: Liturgical Press, 2009), 102–3. Theologian Elizabeth Johnson had not heard that the Committee on Doctrine of the United States Bishops Conference had investigated and severely criticized her book, *Quest for the Living God*, until the day before the publication of their document. She had never been invited to enter into a conversation with the committee. See Richard R. Gaillardetz, "The Elizabeth Johnson Dossier," 177–275, in *When the Magisterium Intervenes*, 178.

37. This description comes from Bernard Quelquejeu and is quoted by Richard A. McCormick and Richard P. McBrien, "L'Affaire Curran II," *America* 16, no. 6 (8-15 September 1990): 127–32, 142–45, at 128.

38. See Donald N. Levine, *The Flight from Ambiguity: Essays in Social and Cultural Theory* (Chicago: University of Chicago Press, 1985), 33; Gerald A. Arbuckle,

restore the pre–Vatican II vertical hierarchical structures, the more it opts for greater secrecy.

There are times when secrecy is essential, for example, to protect the welfare of a person or group, but it must not be habitually used as a cloak for anything any organization does or wants to keep from public gaze. And the habit of secrecy often leads to a very unpleasant quality: the justification of infringing laws and human rights "for the sake of the common good." Secrets give power of control over others, even more so when those who cultivate them are accountable to no public group; secrecy was used to intimidate victims of the Inquisition, and this can still occur. There is no Gospel reason to justify the present form of judicial process for investigating theologians, since the CDF is not publicly accountable to anyone. The church is not above the Gospel and it is imperative that we respect human rights everywhere, first and foremost within the church itself, otherwise the church contradicts what it is trying to preach.[39]

In 1991 theologians Richard McCormick and Richard McBrien, when analyzing the 1990 Vatican "Instruction on the Ecclesial Vocation of the Theologian," wrote that the document provided a further disturbing insight into how Rome is using secrecy to control and orientate the church back to its pre–Vatican II mythology and structures. Theological reflection, according to the "Instruction," is to be the preserve of a select, safe few. This, concluded McCormick and McBrien, is contrary to Vatican II.[40] The council recognized that all believers can contribute to theological reflection and progress when it expressed the hope that laypeople, not just clerics, be well informed in the sacred sciences. It stated: "But for the proper exercise of this role, the faithful, both clerical and lay, should be accorded a lawful freedom of inquiry, of thought, and of expression, tempered by humility and courage in whatever branch of study they have specialized."[41]

Confronting the Demon: A Gospel Response to Adult Bullying (Collegeville, MN: Liturgical Press, 2003), 65–94.

39. See Paul VI, Apostolic Letter *Evangelii Nuntiandi* (Sydney: St Pauls Publications, 1982), 42.

40. See McCormick and McBrien, "Theology as a Public Responsibility," *America* 165, no. 8 (28 September 1991): 184–89.

41. *Gaudium et Spes* 62, in *Vatican Council II: Volume 1, The Conciliar and Post Conciliar Documents*, ed. Austin Flannery (Northport, NY: Costello Publishing Company, Inc., 1996), 968.

This encouragement to all within the church to ponder theologically is a consequence of the council's respect for the church as the people of God; all by baptism journey with Christ, enjoy the presence of the Holy Spirit, and have the right to share that experience for the support and growth of the church. In the "Instruction," however, this model of church is downplayed and replaced by the hierarchical or pyramidal pre–Vatican II theology. The consequence of this model reversal in the "Instruction" is to make theology a privatized discipline, that is, it is reduced to a Gnostic-like science or a secret to be shared by the hierarchical magisterium and a docile group of theologians. They must confine their writings to professional journals and avoid speaking to the media. But this is an impossible restriction in an age that specializes in mass-media communication because, as canonist Ladislas Örsy, SJ, wrote in 1990, professional theological gatherings are open to journalists, and religious news editors read theological publications. If theologians have any personal difficulties with church teaching, notes the "Instruction," they must not discuss them openly and must go instead to magisterial authorities and be counseled by them, but there are no structures within the church to permit this type of informed dialogue to occur.[42] In 2009 Örsy reiterated his concern that creative theologians were in constant danger of being silenced and emphasized the dangers this presented to the church's future: "Creative thinkers are one of the greatest assets of our church: they let the internal riches of the evangelical message unfold."[43]

The guidelines of the "Instruction" are a formula for theological mediocrity, arid pastoral reflection, and the stifling of any realistic effort to dialogue with today's complex world and create vibrant Catholic identities. McCormick and McBrien quoted Avery Dulles SJ, who said that the effort to crush dissent "inhibits good theology from performing its critical task, and is detrimental to the atmosphere of freedom in the Church."[44]

42. See Ladislas Örsy, "Magisterium and Theologians: A Vatican Document," *America* 163, no. 2 (14–21 July 1990): 30–32.

43. Ladislas Örsy, *Receiving the Council*, 103.

44. Avery Dulles, cited by McCormick and McBrien, "Theology as a Public Responsibility, 186–87. John Thiel, president of the Catholic Theological Society of America (CTSA), when commenting on the CDF's criticism of Sister Margaret Farley's 2006 book on sexual ethics, noted that the criticism "seemed to understand that the role of authentic Catholic theologians was simply to repeat what the magisterium teaches." The board of CTSA stated that the role of

Cardinal Joseph Ratzinger (later Benedict XVI), then-prefect of the CDF, following publication of the "Instruction," expressed the wish that it "will help create a climate of reduced tension in the Church."[45] The coercive power of Rome over the church worked effectively without the faithful questioning its correctness only so long as the latter were aware of only the pre–Vatican II model. With the council we know that there are alternative models of being church, and since people are now living according to these models, tensions between them and Rome have greatly intensified since the publication of the "Instruction" in 1990. In brief, the task now assigned to theologians is increasingly that of explaining the authoritative pronouncements of the official church. This is a return to pre–Vatican II practice.

Theologian Father Charles Curran, evaluating in 2012 the ever-increasing censuring of theologians and anyone who questions Rome's top-down decision making, concludes that Rome is now only interested in establishing and maintaining the boundaries of "a remnant church—a small and pure church that sees itself often in opposition to the world around it." This model of the church, he argues, "is opposed to the best understanding of the Catholic church." He continues: "The church embraces both saints and sinners, rich and poor, female and male, and political conservatives and liberals. Yes, there are limits to what it means to be a Catholic, but the 'small "c" catholic' understanding insists on the need to be as inclusive is possible."[46]

---

theologians is far more than this. They must be prepared to "give voice to the experience and concerns of ordinary believers, raise questions about the persuasiveness of certain official Catholic positions, and offer alternative theological frameworks as potentially helpful contributions to the authentic development of doctrine." Reported by Joshua J. McElee at www.ncronline.org/news/faith -parish/theological-society-backs-vatican-criticized-nun, accessed 11 June 2012.

45. See McCormick and McBrien, "Theology as a Public Responsibility," 184.

46. Charles Curran, at www.ncronline.org/news/condemnation-just-love-not -surprise-day-and-age, accessed 7 June 2012. John L. Allen thinks that Benedict XVI no longer believes in the notion of a "remnant church," that is, a church that is smaller in order to be more pure. To support his view Allen cites the pope's commitment to a New Evangelization, which aims to draw lapsed Catholics back to the church in the Western world and to reach out to others who feel alienated by postmodernity. At www.ncronline.org/blogs/all-things-catholic/benedict-xvi-pope -ironies, accessed 1 May 2012.

Narratives of Disconnection[47]

In narratives of disconnection leaders proclaim that policies of their institutions are true to their founding myths, but in fact this is not the case. For example, in 1948 the National Health Service (NHS) in Britain made healthcare a right, state-funded and free for all, and no longer something that could be bought or sold. The rich and the poor are to receive the same benefits free. Since the 1980s, however, successive governments have increasingly opened the NHS to market economics, which marginalizes the poor. But Ministers of Health continue to state that their policies are true to its founding myth.[48]

An example of a similar disconnection is to be seen within the church. In 2000, Pope John Paul II wrote that in the conclusions of Vatican II "we find a sure compass by which to take our bearings."[49] That is, he insisted that the fundamental mythological theological shifts, such as collegiality, would be adhered to. However, that was not to be.[50] In 1991 the bishops of the United States approved a new Lectionary that favored the use of inclusive language, but approval was suddenly revoked by Rome in 1994. Texts retaining many of the most controversial uses of masculine vocabulary were reintroduced by a small group meeting in Rome. Its members had minimal experience of the American culture, no women were involved, and only one member had a graduate degree in Scripture.[51] Nathan Mitchell of Notre Dame University critiques this form of intervention: "Fueled by fear, fantasy and misinformation, stalwarts in the Roman dicasteries seem to feel they can bully both bishops and believers into submission [in liturgical matters]."[52] Rome subsequently asked that members of the International Commission on

47. See Gerald A. Arbuckle, *Refounding the Church: Dissent for Leadership* (Maryknoll, NY: Orbis Books, 1993), 72–97.

48. See Gerald A. Arbuckle, *Humanizing Healthcare Reforms* (London: Jessica Kingsley, 2012), 96.

49. John Paul II, Apostolic Letter *At the Beginning of the New Millennium* (Sydney: St Pauls Publications, 2001), 75.

50. Bishop Fellay, superior general of the traditionalist Society of St Pius X, reportedly stated that accepting the council's teaching is no longer "a prerequisite for the canonical solution" of the status of the society. At www.cathnews.com/article .aspx?aeid=31699, accessed 8 June 2012.

51. See John L. Allen, "On the Lectionary, Eleven Men Made a Deal," *National Catholic Reporter* (25 September 1998): 3–5.

52. Nathan D. Mitchell, "Troubling Assertions from Rome about ICEL," *America* 195, no. 7 (1 July 2000): 20–21.

English in the Liturgy (ICEL), appointed by the episcopal conferences of English-speaking countries, require its *nihil obstat*—an action in defiance of the powers of local churches.[53] In 2001 Rome issued a document, *Liturgiam Authenticam*, reaffirming a ban on gender-inclusive language, without consultation with the episcopal chairman of ICEL.[54] The document asserts that Rome has the right to intervene in liturgical matters. This evoked strong reactions from commentators. For example, John Allen writes: "[The document] strikes at the heart of Vatican II ecclesiology by centralizing power in the curia and by insisting that local cultures adopt an essentially Roman style of worship."[55] And intervene it did, with a vengeance! Recently (2010) Rome imposed a new English translation of the Roman Missal on the English-speaking world.[56] Not only is the language exclusive, but the translation slavishly follows the Latin style of long sentences broken up into numerous clauses. The language is often archaic and at times unintelligible.

Narratives of Denial

Narratives of denial are stories based on the manipulation of history and there is usually a conscious unwillingness to correct the narratives. The present Chinese government has made the Opium Wars (1839–1842 and 1856–1860) into a founding myth of the nation's struggle for modernity. Chairman Mao deliberately blamed Western aggression at the time of the Opium Wars for China's decline as an empire, and so emerged the narrative of China as victim. This still remains an important tool of government propaganda against the Western world. However, Westerners, though they have good reason to be ashamed of their treatment of China in the nineteenth century, "administered the final blows to an empire that was already on the brink."[57]

---

53. See Donald W. Trautman, "Rome and ICEL," *America* 195, no. 3 (4 March 2000): 7–11.

54. See *The Tablet* (12 May 2001): 704–5.

55. John L. Allen, "New Document Replaces 35 Years of Liturgy Work," *National Catholic Reporter* (25 May 2001): 13.

56. See Philip Endean, "Worship and Power," *The Tablet* (28 August 2010): 8–9; Peter J. Cullinane, "Liturgy and the Role of Bishops," *The Tablet* (30 July 2011): 17–18; Seasoltz, *A Virtuous Church*, 200.

57. *The Economist* (29 October 2011): 87; see Julia Lovell, *The Opium War: Drugs, Dreams and the Making of China* (London: Picador, 2011).

Patriarchy is a social system in which the male gender role represents the primary authority and power figure at the heart of all social relations, and in which fathers have authority over women, children, and property. Integral to patriarchy is the assumption that men must rule and maintain female subordination. Within the church the insistence that exclusive or patriarchal language still be used in the liturgy is a narrative that denies the findings of contemporary scriptural research, the facts of history, and the insights of contemporary social movements for gender equality.[58]

As regards gender equality in the New Testament, two traditions are represented. The first appears in writings *attributed* to St. Paul and affirms patriarchal values and women's inferiority as accepted in the wider secular culture of the times (1 Cor 11:5-10; Eph 5:22; 1 Cor 14:34-35). The second tradition in other writings of St. Paul and in the gospels is often overlooked. This tradition emphasizes that an egalitarian emphasis in ministry was common in the early Christian communities (Gal 3:28; Rom 16:1-6).[59] In the gospels Jesus also strongly stresses the egalitarian approach of love and ministerial service in words and actions, not the culture of patriarchy (John 20:11-18; Luke 18:1-8).[60] Thus in pre-Pauline and Pauline Christian communities women appear to have acted in almost identical ways to men.[61] As Maureen Fiedler records, "Women led eucharistic worship in house churches, preached the gospel, went on missionary journeys, and filled leadership functions in early Christian communities."[62] All this was to change with the Peace of Constantine (313 CE), and persecutions against Christians ceased. From then on the church's leadership embraced the patriarchal values and structures of contemporary Roman culture. As regards the position of women, by Roman civil law a woman was under the control of her father before marriage and under her husband's authority after marriage. A woman had no

58. See Arbuckle, *Violence, Society, and the Church*, 39–43, 69–72.

59. See Elisabeth Schüssler Fiorenza, *In Memory of Her: A Feminist Reconstruction of Christian Origins* (New York: Crossroad, 1983), 205–41.

60. See Francis J. Moloney, *"A Hard Saying": The Gospel and Culture* (Collegeville, MN: Liturgical Press, 2001), 3–34.

61. See Valerie Abrahamsen, "Women," 806–18, in *Oxford Companion to the Bible*, ed. Bruce M. Metzger and Michael D. Coogan (New York: Oxford University Press, 1993), 816.

62. Maureen Fiedler, "Gender Equality: Theory and Practice," *Rome Has Spoken*, 121–22.

legal protection; her status was that of physical and mental weakness. All this negatively affected the status and role of women in the church. Even some early fathers of the church in their theologizing about the role of women in the church uncritically absorbed the contemporary cultural views about the gender superiority of men. For example, Tertullian in the third century declaimed that women are dangerous to men: "You are the devil's gateway . . . you are the deserter of the divine law."[63] Because women, according to the culture of the time, were considered in some way impure they had to be excluded from direct involvement in liturgies. The Synod of Laodicea in the fourth century declared: "Women are not allowed to approach the altar."[64] The Synod of Paris in 829 told women not to press around the altar or touch the sacred vessels.[65]

The distressing patriarchal influence is also obvious historically in the way in which women's religious congregations evolved. From the fourth-century onward, restrictions on women ministering in the church intensified. But there is evidence of communities of consecrated virgins even before the time of St. Benedict (ca. 480–547). Some argue that they were formed as a protest against the exclusion of women by the increasing patriarchy in the church. However, after the time of St. Benedict women's religious congregations emerged as counterparts to the men's orders and were dependent on them in various ways. The patriarchal culture of church and society effectively stifled efforts by women to act alone in devising new forms of religious life. As the centuries passed the enclosure of religious sisters became stricter, and their habits and veils more copious. Extremely brave and prophetic women like St. Angela Merici (1474–1540), the founder of the Ursulines, and Mary Ward (1586–1646) attempted to dispense with the cloister and habit and become more directly engaged in ministry to people, but without immediate success. One of the faults of human cultures is the unquestioning assumption that contemporary values and customs had legitimacy in the distant past. Since the church has a culture, it must always be examining itself to see whether or not it has absorbed values that contradict Tradition. Patriarchal values still haunt our worship and behavioral patterns.

63. Tertullian, quoted in ibid., 114.
64. Synod of Laodicea, in ibid., 115.
65. Synod of Paris, in ibid., 116.

Narratives of Mobilization

Narratives can mobilize others to act for progressive social and institutional change. Significant resistance movements of the twentieth century, such as civil rights, feminist, and ecological movements, developed because individuals congregated and told stories of injustices. They discovered commonalities in their stories that energized them to develop collective action.[66] Within the church, for example, there has been a global reaction to the dismissal of Bishop William Morris in Australia; people have come together in various ways such as through the use of social media to share their concerns about the perceived inadequacies of the dismissal process, including the need for more transparency in the authority structures of the church.

Narratives of Refounding

Paul Ricoeur writes that a narrative can encourage people to "try new ideas, new values, new ways of being-in-the-world,"[67] and consequently new identities. The reader's world is suddenly questioned by the narrative. New and imaginative possibilities of being and acting are presented to them; what is found in the story's plot has the radical ability to "disturb and rearrange"[68] the reader's own relation to life. Listeners or readers are drawn into the raconteur's experiences; they are invited to enter the narrator's perspective of life and to participate in profound individual and cultural changes. Examples of superb Christian narrators are St. Augustine (345–430) with his *Confessions*, and St. Teresa of Avila (1515–1582) with her autobiography; readers can feel disturbed enough by their stories to radically change their own lives. With the *Confessions* begins the tradition in the church in which people tell how their own journey in life interacts with the story of God's ever-loving and forgiving presence. Then there is the subversive humor in J. R. R. Tolkien's immensely popular narrative, *The Lord of the Rings*. The theme is the evil of the misuse of power and the eventual triumph of good. The unlikely main hero in the saga, Frodo Baggins,

---

66. See Catherine K. Riesman, *Narrative Methods for Human Sciences* (Los Angeles: Sage, 2008), 9.

67. Paul Ricoeur, "The Function of Fiction in Shaping Reality," *Man and World* 12 (1979): 123–41, at 134.

68. Paul Ricoeur, "On Interpretation," 1–20 in idem, *From Text to Action: Essays in Hermeneutics II*, ed. Kathleen Blamey and John B. Thompson (Evanston, IL: Northwestern University Press, 1991), 6.

is the symbolic antithesis of corrupting power. He is the embodiment of St. Paul's famous biblical self-discovery of the founding myth of the incarnation (John 1:10-13), namely, that God chooses those who are foolish in the world's assessment in order to shame the wise (1 Cor 1:27). The subversive and socially incongruous lesson of the narrative is clear: every individual, provided she or he is selfless, can resist evil and consequently be of help to others.[69]

A narrative of refounding is a story that radically encourages people "to try new ideas, new values, new ways of being-in-the-world." Refounding is the process whereby people relive the founding mythology of a group and are so inspired by the experience that they imaginatively and creatively search for thoroughly new ways to relate it to contemporary life (see chap. 4). When Saint Mother Teresa told of her care of dying individuals she would return to the founding mythology of her faith—a story of Christ's compassion for people on the margins of society. This motivated her to change her own life. Many observers have been so disturbed by her stories that they also felt impelled to alter their own lives and challenge society's neglect of disadvantaged people.

Happy Feet: A Narrative of Refounding

As I have said, people are often helped to create identities by listening to the stories of other people; they imaginatively identify with and learn from the experiences of other people or events. The film *Happy Feet* broke records worldwide at the box office, charming audiences with the comic story of Mumble, the tap-dancing penguin. Mumble had a terrible singing voice, so he was considered odd in his community. He felt lonely, isolated, misunderstood. Noah the Elder, the stern conformist leader of Emperor Land, finally expels little Mumble from the community, believing his unorthodox behavior is the cause of the lean fishing that threatens their livelihood. Mumble stumbles on another community of decidedly

---

69. See Gerald A. Arbuckle, *Laughing with God: Humor, Culture, and Transformation* (Collegeville, MN: Liturgical Press, 2008), 106.

un-Emperor-like-penguins, the friendly Adelie Amigos who happily enjoy his dancing gifts. And by Mumble's creative, collaborative leadership and bravery the people are able to discover the fundamental cause of the famine, namely, excessive fishing by humans. Mumble begins to teach everyone that uniqueness and questioning the status quo are no burdens, but are gifts to be treasured. The myth that energizes the Mumble narrative is built on the need to respect the dignity of all and the message that diversity can be a communal blessing. But there is a second myth to energize audiences to challenge the status quo: the need to respect the environment. At the film's end we see a group of researchers filming the colony of dancing emperor penguins. The message is clear: Mumble and his friends tell us to stop commercial overfishing of the Antarctic.

Narratives of Grieving

Narratives of grieving remain an essential precondition for the successful creation of new identities and are an integral part of every narrative of refounding. Grieving is a process whereby loss is formally acknowledged and allowed to slip into the past; then the future can be slowly and more or less confidently embraced with all its uncertainties, fears, and hopes. In both Old and New Testaments (see chap. 5) we see many examples of people who, once they begin to recount the story of their grief, are able to discover new hope, new visions of society, and new identities. For example, in the Lament Psalms the twofold dynamic of grieving is forcefully expressed. First, there is the public declaration before God of loss, with its crushing sadness, and then the energizing identification of what is surprisingly new and hopeful in the experience of individuals or the nation, however faint this might be.[70] The public proclamation of grief can, however, be silenced; people may be too crushed to recount their sadness, or oppressive political powers fear that the public narratives of grief will threaten their own stability. Tyrannical governments particularly fear the

---

70. For an understanding of the significant relationship between ritual and cultural change see Gerald A. Arbuckle, *Grieving for Change* (Sydney: St Pauls Publications, 1991); *Refounding the Church: Dissent for Leadership* (Maryknoll, NY: Orbis Books, 1993), 180–200; *Healthcare Ministry: Refounding the Mission in Tumultuous Times* (Collegeville, MN: Liturgical Press, 2000), 271–341.

public display of grief at funerals of their victims, for it is there that the narratives of sadness can energize people to further resist tyranny.[71] For example, following the massacre of students in 1989 by the Chinese military in Tiananmen Square, Beijing, the government prevented any media coverage of their funerals. Yet unarticulated grief remains like a powder keg waiting to be ignited into all kinds of individual and community-destroying behavior. Ovid, the first-century Roman poet, well described the reality of unnamed grief: "Suppressed grief suffocates."[72]

Today the church is overloaded with grief as a consequence of repeated loss. The departure of people in their thousands from the church, the closure of parishes often without consultation, sexual abuse scandals, questionable liturgical changes, the failure of Rome and bishops to consult, witch-hunting of theologians, lack of due process in ecclesiastical trials,[73] discouragement of responsible dissent even to the point of public excommunication[74]—these are some of the issues that have caused, and continue to cause, so much unresolved grief. Restorationists discourage or prevent narratives of grieving. Instead, they are reviving the narratives of the pre-conciliar church to block people from creating narratives that would vibrantly relate the council's theology to contemporary pastoral issues. Little wonder that the church is increasingly seen as irrelevant in today's secularizing and postmodern world.

Summary

* Identity is a process of "self-or-institution-engaging-with-context." As the context changes, there is potentially a new identity. Strictly speaking, a person or institution has many identities and which one is chosen at a particular time will depend on the context.

---

71. See Walter Brueggemann, *Hope within History* (Atlanta: John Knox, 1987), 72–91.

72. Ovid, *Tristia* V, Elegy 1, l. 63.

73. For example the dismissal of Bishop Bill Morris of the Toowoomba diocese, Australia, in 2011. He has never been told the names of his accusers or what he was formally accused of, nor has he seen the official Vatican visitor's report. See Michael Kelly, "Rites and Wrongs," *The Tablet* (21 January 2012): 4–5.

74. For example, the excommunication by Bishop Thomas Olmsted of Phoenix, Arizona, of Sr. Margaret McBride in 2010 for having made, according to reputable moralists, a justified decision to save the life of a pregnant woman. She was accused of permitting abortion. See Roberts, *The Emerging Catholic*, 151–53.

- An institution requires four qualities to maintain its identity: a founding story that defines how it is to engage with the context; clearly defined symbolic and ritual markers that identify its unique story; ability to encourage responsible dissenters who are prepared to propose and live out new narratives of thinking and acting, because no institution can survive and remain effective unless it fosters a space and freedom in which people can be creative; and formal and informal educational programs that ensure its members remain in touch with the founding story.

- Through self-narratives or storytelling, individuals and institutions[75] are able to write and rewrite their identities; this is a process of negotiation through which they determine what they consider to be acceptable identities in particular contexts.

- Identities can be clarified either deductively or inductively; if deductively, identities are imposed from outside, with little or no involvement of recipients; if inductively, people are intimately and imaginatively involved in negotiating their identities.

- Myths are stories that make life intelligible in the past, and narratives are the retelling of these stories in light of present needs. One reason for the collapse of institutions is their inability to refound themselves through imaginative and creative narratives in light of radically new needs. There is a failure to accept that narratives successful in the past are no longer relevant because the context and needs of people have changed.

- Sometimes storytellers consciously or unconsciously refashion narratives in ways that contradict or modify their original founding myths. For example, fundamentalist narratives often are narrow reactions to the disruptive consequences of rapid social, economic, or political change. Identities are defined in simplistic and absolutist terms. Catholic fundamentalists, for example, reduce Catholic identities to a singular identity, namely, "orthodoxy," that is, the unquestioning or uncritical obedience to hierarchical statements, even if these statements are contrary to Vatican II and Tradition itself.

75. See Mary Jo Hatch, *Organization Theory: Modern, Symbolic, and Postmodern Perspectives* (Oxford: Oxford University Press, 2013), 176–82.

- The church is both divine *and* human. As the esteemed theologian and historian Henri de Lubac wrote: "Like all human institutions, the Church has her exterior façade, her temporal aspect, often ponderous enough—chancelleries, code of law, courts. There is nothing 'nebulous and disembodied' about her—far from it. . . . [It is] no 'misty entity.'"[76] That is, the church is not a pure spirit. It does form a human culture that must constantly be critiqued by the values of authentic tradition and the Gospel. However embarrassing the findings, this critique of its mythologies and narratives must be undertaken with deep faith and humility. For example, the refusal to use inclusive language in our worship demands such a critical cultural and historical review.

- The following chapter further explains that before Vatican II Catholic identities were relatively static and imposed from two sources: internally by Rome and externally as a result of social and political discrimination against Catholics. Vatican II rightly undermined the mythology of the fortress church, but it left Catholics without satisfying narratives; in light of the resulting widespread confusion this has resulted in many different sociological definitions of Catholic identities.

76. Henri de Lubac, *The Splendour of the Church* (London: Sheed and Ward, 1956), 114.

Chapter Two

The Catholic Story: Identities' Crisis

You must bear in mind that, if I speak strongly in
various places . . . against the existing state of things
[in the church], it is not wantonly, but to show I feel the
difficulties which certain minds are distressed with.[1]
(John Henry Newman)

I sink in deep mire,
where there is no foothold . . .
I am weary with my crying;
my throat is parched.
My eyes grow dim with waiting for my Lord . . .
Do not let the flood sweep over me . . .
or the Pit close its mouth over me. (Ps 69:2-3, 15)

This chapter explains that:

- over the last fifty years sociological and theological changes have led to very different definitions of Catholic identities, from static to dynamic

- from the Reformation until the Second Vatican Council the indicators of Catholic identities remained significantly stable throughout the church

1. John Henry Newman, letter to John Keble (6 September 1843), cited by José Ignacio Gonzalez Faus, *Where the Spirit Breathes: Prophetic Dissent in the Church* (Maryknoll, NY: Orbis Books, 1989), 103.

- in this period these indicators of Catholic identities were imposed by two factors: external discriminatory forces and a defensive hierarchy
- the rigid cultural boundaries of this global church under siege collapsed under the combined pressure of several movements: the success of Catholic education, Vatican II, and postmodernity
- in the second decade of the twenty-first century there are many different sociological expressions of Catholic identities

The purpose of this chapter is to describe the significant changes since the early 1800s in what it means to be a Catholic. Once "Catholic identities" were assumed to be collectively static. The universal Catholic culture was expressed as a unitary and homogeneous entity, a community of universally shared, unchanging customs and experiences, with any internal complexity and diversity denied. Then the Vatican Council of 1963–1965 undermined the unity and continuity of the worldwide Catholic culture that had prevailed for several centuries.

This momentous event in the church evoked, and continues to arouse, a widespread identities crisis among Catholics. A sense of collective "sameness and historical continuity"[2] has been lost, leaving many feeling confused and rootless. No longer can the implications of the phrase "being a Catholic" be universally clear. This identities' crisis was signaled by widespread rejection of the 1968 encyclical *Humanae Vitae* and has been further intensified by the publicity surrounding the sexual abuse scandals within the church, by liturgical changes introduced without sufficient consultation, by a more open and questioning approach to religious education, and by increasing hesitancy by Rome to encourage collegiality as mandated by the council. The credibility of the Vatican and the hierarchy is now questioned by many Catholics, something unheard of sixty years ago. The impact of postmodernity

2. Erik Erikson, *Identity: Youth and Crisis* (London: Faber & Faber, 1968), 22. Developmental psychologist Erikson created the term "identity crisis" to describe periods in people's lives when they must seriously seek answers to questions about their identity. Previous identities no longer give them a sense of meaning and direction. The term is now applied more widely to describe questioning crises in organizations.

and globalization on Catholics has further confused their traditional identities. Some bishops try to reassert their episcopal authority by loudly pronouncing on critical social and moral issues without adequate preparation and consultation. Their statements are immediately circulated on the worldwide web, thus further undermining the credibility of the hierarchy as a whole.[3]

Mission and Identities

In implementing the mission of Jesus Christ the church has three tasks: to ensure that God is worshiped, that the Gospel is proclaimed, and that the needs of those who are poor, ill, or marginalized are responded to. Parishes and Catholic schools in such countries as the United States, Canada, Britain, Ireland, New Zealand, and Australia primarily focus on the first and second tasks. Their explicit purpose is to form students in the knowledge of God and God's purpose in the world. The Gospel is to be openly proclaimed in all its radical message. Parents assent to this purpose by sending their children to the church's schools, and normally the church may require baptism as a condition of entrance. However, the explicit and primary purpose of Catholic social services and healthcare facilities is the third task listed above, namely, to serve the social, physical, and mental healing needs of people who are sick and often also marginalized, irrespective of whether they believe in God or not. Certainly the healing mission of Jesus Christ is to be proclaimed, but primarily through witness, not through words. Certainly God is to be worshiped, but in ways that respect the beliefs of caregivers and staff members who may not belong to the Catholic tradition.

Despite the different emphases in expressing the mission of Jesus Christ, Catholic institutions have one vital point in common: their effectiveness depends chiefly on staff members' personal knowledge of and commitment to this mission.[4] The mission is to be interpreted and lived in an identifiably Roman Catholic way. Otherwise these institutions will be Catholic in name only. But the difficult question is: what does *an identifiable Roman Catholic way* mean in today's context? As

---

3. See Tom Roberts, *The Emerging Catholic Church: A Community's Search for Itself* (Maryknoll, NY: Orbis Books, 2011), 147–59.

4. See Declaration on Christian Education 8–9, in *Vatican Council II: Volume 1, The Conciliar and Post Conciliar Documents*, ed. Austin Flannery (Northport, NY: Costello Publishing Company, Inc., 1996).

we will now see, there have been significant sociological shifts since the early 1800s, but especially since 1965, in the way Catholic people, and others, have answered this question.

Identities Defined

Identities, as explained in chapter 1, are a *process* of the "self-or-group-engaging-with-context."[5] Who we are individually or culturally is to be found primarily in the way we live day by day within a particular cultural context or environment, not just in how we regard ourselves. This means, however, that to know a people's identities we must know the *context* with which they are interacting or engaging.

As a result of the profound sociological contextual changes both inside and outside the church, we can divide people's interpretations of what Catholic identities mean over the last two hundred years into two periods (see fig. 2.1). In the first period, the early 1800s to 1960, Catholic identities was reduced to something univocal and universal imposed on Catholics by the surrounding dominant antagonistic Protestant society and by a defensively protective hierarchy. In the second period, from 1960 to the present, what it means to be a Catholic has become increasingly a question of personal choice. In consequence there are widely different interpretations of Catholic identities by individuals and institutions.

Catholic Identities: Static and Imposed

The first period begins in the United States around the 1820s with ever-increasing numbers of European immigrants, the Irish in the lead. By 1850 Catholics had become the largest single religious group in the nation. The situation was similar in many ways in Australia, Canada, and to a lesser degree in New Zealand, which received only small numbers of Catholic immigrants.

---

5. Thomas K. Fitzgerald, *Metaphors of Identity: A Culture-Communication Dialogue* (New York: SUNY Press, 1993), ix.

   This rapid expansion of the Catholic presence inevitably evoked in the wider Protestant society significant religious and class prejudice against Catholics. Catholic immigrants, although still belonging to their traditional cultural groups, became in the eyes of this wider society a uniquely identifiable, all-embracing ethnic group that was defined in terms of religion. This form of ethnicity is termed *imposed ethnicity*, that is, particular people are branded as different and inferior by the dominant power bloc in society. The dominant group ("us"), often out of fear of losing its position of power, pejoratively stereotypes the marginalized group ("them"). The oppression is institutionalized so that in key areas of life such as housing, education, and social relations people who are negatively stereotyped are excluded from equality with the dominant group. The oppressed group must be submissive and accept its inferior position with patience. For example, Catholic immigrants to Australia in the early nineteenth century were looked upon benignly as long as they conformed "to Protestant expectations that their role in the community would be subordinate, inferior and passive."[6] Any attempt to change the *status quo* met with remorseless resistance and intensified discrimination. Even in the 1950s employers could let it be known explicitly or implicitly that employment opportunities were closed to Catholics.[7] Stereotyped as one socially and economically inferior ethnic group, they were considered dangerously unpatriotic since they were charged with submitting to a foreign, papal-ruled power and behaving in ways that insulted the American way of life.[8] They were even subjected to periodic verbal and physical attacks from a variety of extreme nationalistic movements such as the Know Nothings, the Ku Klux Klan, the American Protective Association, and Protestants and Other Americans United for Separation of Church and State.

   To protect the Catholic identities of poor immigrants trapped in this stigmatizing environment, ecclesiastical authorities reacted by building a unique Catholic cultural fortress. For example, while public schools were open to Catholics, it was taken for granted that

   6. Patrick O'Farrell, *The Catholic Community in Australia: A History* (Nelson: West Melbourne, 1977), 20.
   7. See Gerald A. Arbuckle, *Culture, Inculturation, and Theologians: A Postmodern Critique* (Collegeville, MN: Liturgical Press, 2010), 105–7.
   8. See James Hennesey, *American Catholics: A History of the Roman Catholic Community in the United States* (Oxford: Oxford University Press, 1981), 117–18, 246–47.

Protestant beliefs would be unquestionably pervasive. Defensive action against prejudice in its blatant and subtle forms led to the development of a wide range of institutions to safeguard the Catholic identities of poor immigrants: schools, recreational clubs for all ages, hospitals, orphanages, asylums, and even graveyards. In the United States in 1880 there were 2,246 parochial elementary schools and in 1910 there were 4,845; by 1900 there were sixty-three Catholic colleges.[9] Within the United States this defensive approach was so successful that by 1960 the church had become "the best organized and most powerful of the nation's subcultures—a source of both alienation and enrichment for those born within it and an object of bafflement or uneasiness for others."[10]

The more Catholics felt intimidated by prejudice and discrimination against them, the more they developed their own identifying symbols and rituals such as their schools and hospitals. The average Catholic hospital or aged-care facility resembled a traditional parish, often with its own priest-chaplain and a chapel for daily Mass, with morning and evening prayers, and with symbols of the Catholic tradition clearly visible. Detailed rules and laws were introduced by the church just to keep Catholics safe from the dangers of Protestantism and a world considered to be under the direction of evil or subversive forces. Catholics were not allowed to be present at a funeral, even of a family member or a friend, if it was to take place in a Protestant church. Even in a Catholic hospital Catholics could not invite a Protestant minister to assist a dying member of their denomination.[11] Catholics were regularly advised what films and books they should avoid. The Catholic Church became a proud, self-contained church under siege right through to Vatican II.[12] This was the pattern in many other First World countries. In Australia from the nineteenth century onward the development of the parochial school became the single most identifying feature of Catholicism.[13] In

9. Ibid., 187.

10. John Cogley, *Catholic America* (Kansas City, MO: Catholic America, 1986), 135.

11. See comments by John W. O'Malley in *Vatican II: Did Anything Happen?*, ed. John W. O'Malley (New York: Continuum, 2011), 9.

12. See Gerald A. Arbuckle, *Violence, Society, and the Church: A Cultural Approach* (Collegeville, MN: Liturgical Press, 2004), 62–73.

13. See Edmund Campion, *Australian Catholics: The Contribution of Catholics to the Development of Australian Society* (Sydney: Viking Press, 1987), 51–56.

1885 a plenary meeting of Australian bishops decreed that "parents who without cause or permission sent their children to a state school were to be denied absolution in the confessional."[14] I recall as a boy in New Zealand in the 1940s and 1950s it was taken for granted that Catholics would join exclusively Catholic recreational institutions such as debating and tennis clubs.

The development of a separate global, uniform, and unified Catholic subculture was further encouraged by the growing centralization of papal authority, a consequence of the Reformation, the French Revolution, and the Enlightenment. The church felt under siege by these external forces.[15] The French Revolution helped to destroy the stable sociopolitical order with which the church had been allied for centuries. Napoleon aimed to bring the church directly under the control of the state and thus to establish a new pattern of state-church relationships for the rest of Europe. Theologically and administratively the church could not accept this. The life of the church was further threatened by the Enlightenment and the Industrial Revolution with their "disturbing" values of naturalism, rationalism, secularism, liberalism, democracy, and their emphasis on the empirical sciences and their research methods. Pope Gregory XVI, who ruled the papal states from 1831 to 1846, condemned "the separation of the Church and state, denounced liberty of conscience as sheer madness, and referred to liberty of the press as abominable and detestable."[16] The more papal authority resisted the revolutionary insights and values emerging in the Western world, the more isolated the church became.

Thus the culture of the universal church became increasingly uniform, inward-looking, defensive, and protective of its members and its customs. Liturgies and many devotional practices were identical throughout the church. No matter where a Catholic went in the world, the symbols of Catholic culture were unchanging, similar, and very

14. Ibid., 65.
15. Sections of this chapter update material originally published in my *Refounding the Church: Dissent for Leadership* (Maryknoll, NY: Orbis Books, 1993), 36–97.
16. Thomas Bokenkotter, *A Concise History of the Catholic Church* (New York: Doubleday, 1990), 267. Gregory refused to accept railways in the papal states, claiming "with sublime incomprehension of modernity, [that trains] led only to Hell." R. J. B. Bosworth, *Whispering City: Modern Rome and Its Histories* (New Haven, CT: Yale University Press, 2011), 69.

visible. At the same time, Rome fostered a form of scholastic philosophy, neoscholasticism, that provided the church with a coherent deductive intellectual framework. Yet this philosophy had one serious disadvantage: it was so self-contained that its supporters saw no need to listen to, or even learn from, other philosophies and the rapidly developing social sciences.

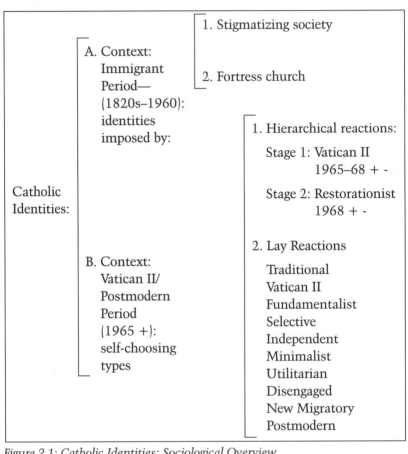

Figure 2.1: Catholic Identities: Sociological Overview

Hierarchical officials—pope, bishops, priests—held considerable position power over the faithful in this significantly uniform culture of the universal church. As the essential ritual intermediaries between the laity and Christ, they could threaten not to provide their services, even to the extent of excommunicating people from the body of the church. If laypeople dared to smudge the boundaries there were powerful symbols to indicate that they had moved to the edge of the group life and were risking their salvation. Thus, for example, for a Catholic to marry a non-Catholic within the church the ceremony had to be held in the sacristy, an uncomfortable and impersonal adjunct to the main church building. The group itself also exerted powerful informal coercive conforming power over individuals; the Catholic community was so strongly bonded that one would fear to break the rules lest one become a subject of gossip, ridicule, or even ostracism.[17]

Static Identities Shattered: Cultural Chaos

The static cultural boundaries of the siege church collapsed with remarkable speed under the combined impact of a number of forces in the 1960s: the success of Catholic education, Vatican II, the widespread rejection of *Humanae Vitae*, and the impact of the expressive revolution and its postmodern consequences.[18] The diocesan educational systems had become so successful that Catholics were able to move up into economic, social, and political positions of power that had been closed to them during the immigrant period. By the early 1980s, for example, in the United States the Irish had become the most financially successful of all non-Jewish ethnic groups.[19] The descendants of two centuries of immigrants were no longer outsiders.[20] Catholics as an identifiable, unified, involuntary ethnic group had ceased to exist. Sociologically they had become "indistinguishable as a group from their fellow citizens in terms of ethical values, social mores, and cultural tastes."[21] The remaining section of this chapter will concentrate on how Vatican II and postmodernity have radically affected how Catholics define their identities.

17. See Arbuckle, *Refounding the Church*, 82–84.

18. See Arbuckle, *Violence, Society, and the Church*, 157–73.

19. See John A. Coleman, *An American Strategic Theology* (New York: Paulist Press, 1982), 168.

20. In 2012 in the United States, Catholics form 29% of the Congress, a much higher percentage than any other denomination, and hold seventeen of fifty governorships—a sign of the changing status of Catholics. See Richard E. Pates, "In This Together," *America* 207, no. 4 (2012): 11–13, at 12.

21. Mark S. Massa, *Catholics and American Culture* (New York: Crossroad, 1999), 10.

Vatican II caused a profound mythological revolution, and this fact continues to be poorly understood by ecclesiastics, as is evident in the culturally insensitive manner in which recent liturgical changes have been introduced in the church. So to appreciate the dramatic nature of the cultural and personal turmoil that the council evoked, it is first necessary to grasp the nature and power of a culture and what happens when suddenly, for whatever reason, it disintegrates.

Culture and Change: Theoretical Reflections

1. Culture Defined[22]

A culture consists of symbols, myths, and rituals that inculcate how people should feel, think, and act. The emphasis is first on *feeling*. A culture provides people with a much-needed sense of purpose, order, and belonging because the human person is most uncomfortable with change and especially chaos. As explained above, critical to understanding the model is an appreciation of the meaning and power of *culture*. All cultures (or subcultures) contain three elements: symbols, myths, and rituals. A *symbol* is any reality that by its own power directs us to think about, imagine, make contact with, or move toward another more profound and often mysterious reality through sharing in the inner energy that the symbol presents, and not necessarily by stated or extra explanations. [23] A symbol has two particular qualities of *meaning* and *emotion*. The meaning dimension conveys a message about something; it causes me to react with negative or positive feelings. The photograph of my mother makes her present to me and I experience sadness because she is no longer alive. *Myths* (and *mythologies*, which are networks of interrelated myths) are symbols in story form (see chap. 1), for example, the creation stories in the book of Genesis. Through myths we know that we fit into a particular part of the world and that there are ways we must organize our lives to avoid falling into the frightening state of

---

22. The nature and power of culture are more fully explained in my book *Culture, Inculturation, and Theologians* (Collegeville, MN: Liturgical Press, 2010), 19–48.

23. Jean Daniélou writes that "the real significance of symbols [is] to afford us access through the visible world into a higher transcendent plane of being," idem, *The Lord of History* (London: Longmans Green, 1958), 135; Gerald A. Arbuckle, *Earthing the Gospel: An Inculturation Handbook for Pastoral Workers* (Maryknoll, NY: Orbis Books, 1990), 21–34; F. W. Dillistone, *The Power of Symbols in Religion and Culture* (New York: Crossroad, 1986), 7–29, 99–116.

chaos. *Rituals* are the visible acting out of the myths, and these are as many and as varied as human needs.

Of the many types of mythologies, creation myths are of particular importance to this book. Creation myths speak about first causes. In them people express their primary understanding of humankind, the world, or the particular part of it in which they live. The Exodus story, for example, tells the Israelites how they were formed and for what purpose. As with all creation myths, the more frequently the Israelites recount the myth through narratives (see chap. 1) the more they become aware of its profound meaning and its demands on them. Myths, like all symbols that form them, are storehouses of memory, linking people to the past and providing them with identities and impetus to face an uncertain future. Myths also give legitimacy to a culture's economic, social, political, and legal structures. Hence, demolish a group's creation mythology and inevitably they are destroyed as a people. No wonder the Israelites in exile felt so utterly lost; their three pivotal institutions—the temple, Jerusalem, and the kingship, all of which signified for them their election by God as the chosen people—had been destroyed: "By the rivers of Babylon we sat and wept at the memory of Zion" (Ps 137:1).

2. Myths: Polarities and Consequences

A remarkable quality of both symbols and myths is that they contain within themselves polar opposite meanings. The color white cannot really be described without reference to its opposite, black. So in the symbol of the color white there is contained also the symbol of blackness; one connotes the other. Thus the founding myth of the United States contains several sets of polar opposites: the dignity of the individual and his or her freedom, and at the other pole the rights of the community over individuals. On the organizational side there are the rights of sovereign states over against the rights of the federal government. However, creation myths, and narratives that apply the myths to the particular contexts in which people are living, do not spell out how the polar opposites are to be balanced. Thus there is a built-in ambiguity or vagueness in all creation myths that inevitably leads to tension.

Factions can form around both polar opposites in the myths, one faction claiming that it has the correct understanding of the myths and demanding respect for its position; the faction around the other polar opposite can do the same. In practice, one pole tends to dominate to the detriment of its opposite. This causes ideological polarization within a group, evoking bitterness, even at times violence. Such is the case in

the United States when the rights of the individual become so emphasized that community rights are repeatedly neglected. For instance, the
individual has an unqualified right to own guns despite the enormous
tragic consequences for the community. Likewise, the overemphasis on
individual rights continues to make it difficult to introduce universal
healthcare. A similar distortion exists in the secularized version of the
Genesis creation story: liberal capitalism stresses the rights of the individual to an extreme degree over those of the community; the opposite
is the case in Marxism. For the contrary demands of the polar opposites
to be kept in some balance, considerable wisdom, trust, and a spirit of
discernment, or at least an openness to bargaining or negotiation, are
required on the part of the parties involved. If not, the group will tear
itself apart. It is an ongoing struggle for people to maintain the balance
between the polar opposites of a mythology because some ambiguity or
vagueness always remains.

3. Culture Change: Model
Interference with or destruction of the inner mythological framework of cultures, even when there is conscious and intellectual assent
to what is happening, destroys the stable, deep-rooted sense of people's
felt belonging. They are apt to experience periods of intense loss and
confusion. The more rapid the change, the greater the cultural chaos,
that is, the radical breakdown of felt order, and its symptoms are many
and persistent, including anger, rage, a sense of drifting without purpose,
or a dreaded feeling of "lostness," depression, paralysis, the going-it-alone
of individualists, witch-hunting, dreams of a messiah, a yearning for a
utopian past or for quick-fix solutions.[24] The signs may also include
denial that there are problems at all, bullying, breakdown of trust, feelings of powerlessness, nostalgia for the past (the assumed golden age),
unreal optimism about the future, excessive concern for order, weariness
and cynicism, feuding and breaking up into power blocs, and marginalization of innovators.

Figure 2.2 is a model that describes what happens to a culture
and people's identities when their mythological creation stories are
questioned, threatened, or destroyed.[25] Of course, any model has its
weaknesses. Cultural change is far more messy, complicated, and acri-

24. See Arbuckle, *Refounding the Church*, 42–55.
25. Ibid.

monious in practice than any diagram can possibly portray. For example, people individually or collectively do not necessarily move automatically through all the stages. Although some may make the transition, others can become lodged in a particular stage and never move forward to a new cultural consensus. Still others may retreat to an earlier stage. Stage 1 of the model shows how the *status quo* is generally accepted; there is general consensus about collective identities. In stage 2, internal and/or external forces threaten to break up the group's mythological consensus. Some people may initially enjoy the changes, while others begin to fear for their cultural and personal identities and security. As the unease or stress increases, authorities move to freeze the changes through new policy decrees and/or to reimpose former structures of identities (stage 3). Some are relieved that authorities have reacted in this way; they feel these official rulings or legislative decrees from on high will contain or stop the anxiety-evoking changes. But there are others who believe that further imposed decrees will not by themselves alter anything, because along with structural change must go the more difficult attitudinal conversion or adjustment. Still others become disillusioned or resentful when change decreed from above is imposed on them. At this point the fourth and most disruptive stage, *chaos*, emerges (stage 4). At the beginning of the *Divine Comedy*, the poet Dante Alighieri (1265–1321) describes the fear-evoking nature of chaos, particularly the feeling of utter loneliness and loss of direction, and his words apply as much to the experience of groups as to individuals caught in the turmoil and uncertainties of dramatic change:

> Midway upon the journey of life
> I found myself within a forest dark,
> For the straightforward pathway had been lost.
> Ah me! how hard a thing it is to say
> What was this forest savage, rough, and stern,
> Which in the very thought renews the fear.
> So bitter is it, death is little more.[26]

26. Dante Alighieri, *Divine Comedy*, trans. Henry Wadsworth Longfellow (New York: Charles Bigelow, 1909), 15.

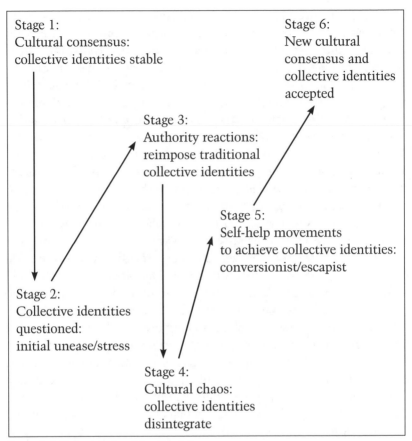

Figure 2.2 Cultural/identities Breakdown

Stage 5 offers two significant options, *conversionist* and *escapist*, for those who recognize that nothing can be done about the chaos unless *they* are prepared to act themselves. In the *conversionist* option people understand that realistic cultural change is slow and at times filled with uncertainty, demanding tolerance, patience, an ongoing struggle for inner and outer conversion and an openness to alternative or imaginative ways of doing things. For conversionist people, chaos is not something negative. They view it as a potentially liberating experience, the opportunity to create radically new and transformative ways of acting. On the other hand, when people take the *escapist* option they anxiously attempt to flee the frustration of chaos by retreating as individuals or groups into a comforting world of unreality and denial, building a powerful wall of intolerance around themselves; they remain attitudinally rigid, seeing the world in oppositional terms (either/or) and deeply fearful of the new. The culture they form is neurotic, out of touch with reality. In this atmosphere all kinds of fundamentalist sects, cults, and fads erupt, as was evident during the enormous cultural upheavals within the Western world in the late 1960s and early 1970s and globally as a consequence of the terrorist attacks of September 2001 and disastrous continuing economic crises.

Vatican II: "Mythical Earthquake" and Ongoing Consequences

Writers who assess the history of the impact of Vatican II on the life of the church rarely appreciate the fact that its documents would inevitably be the catalyst for continuing cultural chaos.[27] There is a failure to understand the fact that the church is itself a culture. It is not some ethereal, non-human reality that is unaffected by the largely unconscious and pervasive forces of culture. Consequently, inaccurate perceptions of and defective attitudes toward culture have led, and continue to lead, to bad theology as well as faulty pastoral policies and practices.[28]

The cultural consequences of Vatican II continue to have a profound impact on traditional symbols of Catholic fortress identities. The council was long overdue, but the suddenness and radical nature of the theological changes it initiated altered the entire mythic structure of the church. The revolutionary mythic changes[29] of this kind were bound to evoke culturally catastrophic consequences. Skilled leadership is always required to turn the chaos, that is, the radical breakdown of predicable order, into positive experiences; since the culture of the church had for centuries remained static it inevitably lacked personnel trained to lead the church through the resulting turmoil.

For centuries Catholics had been treated like dependent children, instructed by their clerical leaders on exactly how to win salvation by obeying detailed rules or "how-to's." Suddenly the council announced that they had to stand on their own feet and make decisions for themselves

---

27. An interesting exception to this is the work of Jesuit philosopher B. R. Brinkman, "Due Veduti di Roma," *Heythrop Journal* 3 (1996), 176–92.

28. See Arbuckle, *Culture, Inculturation, and Theologians*, xix–xxiv.

29. The dramatic quality of the theological and cultural changes introduced by Vatican II are further explained in chapter 6. John W. O'Malley agrees that the council is in profound continuity with the Catholic tradition, but as a historian he cogently argues that there are equally deep discontinuities. See his *Vatican II: Did Anything Happen?* (n. 111 above), 52–91.

in light of the needs of the world, as well as the Gospel and Tradition. The world was no longer to be seen as evil in itself and Catholics must now dialogue with people of goodwill, even with those who profess no faith at all. For centuries the belief that the church did not, and could not, change had been successfully instilled in the flock. Now no longer could they identify themselves, or be identified by others, by rigid unchanging symbols of a ghetto culture. The council fathers did not foresee that cultures, especially a deeply embedded, long-standing, highly centralized and authoritarian culture like that of the pre-conciliar church, do not change smoothly just because a document says they should. Then came the widespread withdrawal of people from the priesthood and religious life; outbursts of dissent and criticisms against the pope and episcopal hierarchies; and, in more recent years, the withdrawal of increasing numbers of laity from the church. The revelation of sexual abuse among the clergy and the coverup by ecclesiastical authorities has only added to, and dramatically intensified, the chaos. However, to add to the turmoil Rome decided in 2011 to introduce entirely new and often unintelligible liturgical changes. Chaos upon chaos! Catholics had enough chaos to cope with without having more added.

In summary, from a theological perspective I applaud the mythological changes of Vatican II, but as an anthropologist aware of the need to be sensitive to the complexities and uncertainties of cultural change I remain deeply saddened.[30] The resulting turmoil should have been expected and better catechesis prepared to explain the inevitably chaotic yet potentially creative consequences of the council's decisions.

---

30. See Arbuckle, *Culture, Inculturation, and Theologians*, 36.

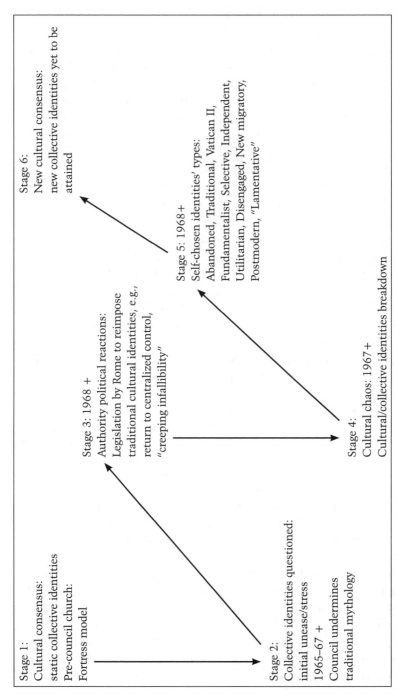

Figure 2.3: Cultural Reactions to Vatican II

Stage 1:
Cultural consensus:
static collective identities
Pre-council church:
Fortress model

Stage 2:
Collective identities questioned:
initial unease/stress
1965–67 +
Council undermines
traditional mythology

Stage 3: 1968 +
Authority political reactions:
Legislation by Rome to reimpose
traditional cultural identities, e.g.,
return to centralized control,
"creeping infallibility"

Stage 4:
Cultural chaos: 1967 +
Cultural/collective identities breakdown

Stage 5: 1968+
Self-chosen identities' types:
Abandoned, Traditional, Vatican II,
Fundamentalist, Selective, Independent,
Utilitarian, Disengaged, New migratory,
Postmodern, "Lamentative"

Stage 6:
New cultural consensus:
new collective identities yet to be
attained

Figure 2.3 summarizes what has occurred, and continues to occur, within the church since Vatican II. In stage 1 the prevailing creation mythology of the pre-conciliar church is: the church is a fortress, the perfect society, built and constantly reinforced to withstand the attacks of the external enemies: Protestants, heretics, and the evils of the Enlightenment. The boundaries of the fortress church are sharply marked out and effectively patrolled lest people attempt to break in or out. Stage 2 is the mixture of euphoria and initial unease. In three short years the traditional creation mythology is radically undermined in the council's documents. For example, the principle of collegiality runs like a thread through the documents at the level of the universal church (synods and episcopal conferences) and in dioceses (priests' and parish councils). Individual bishops are no longer to be mere lieutenants of the pope, but leaders of their dioceses in their own right. Pastors are to give greater recognition to the gifts of believers and seek their cooperation. In brief, the council aimed to bring a balance back to the centuries-old creation mythology of the church. However, the documents are filled with ambiguities and tensions resulting from the reintroduction of the polar opposites of key myths within the creation mythology. Gone are the many certainties of the pre-conciliar apologetics constructed on the assumption that theological opposites did not exist. Here are some of the mythic ambiguities contained in the documents:

> The church is universal, *but* it is to be incarnated within local churches to reflect their diversities of culture.
> The church is an institution under the leadership of the bishops who are committed to maintain order and unity, *but* it is also the People of God who as pilgrims are not concerned about rank.
> The pope has full, supreme, and universal power over the church, *but* the bishops collegially govern their dioceses with authority proper to them.
> The aim of liturgy is to help us adore God our Creator, *but* it must reflect the needs and customs of different peoples and cultures.

Nowhere in the documents does the council spell out precisely how these polar opposites are to be balanced in real life. In fact, it simply could not do so. Rather, it rightly challenged all members of the church to struggle to develop a living balance between the opposites through charity, ongoing mutual respect, and dialogue. People who had been used to being told in detail what to do in the church became confused. They opted with growing emotional intensity for one pole or the other in the myths, with the appearance of opposing sides that ceased to trust one another. In stage 3 (1968 +), as chaos threatened, Rome reacted in an increasingly restorationist style (stage 4), for example, episcopal conferences and synods of bishops have lost the power to act given them by the council; the Roman Curia is becoming more and more directive, and bishops continue to be appointed without proper consultation of local churches; control over liturgy given to bishops by the council is now firmly in the hands of Rome (see chap. 1). In other words, in the above list of complementary mythic oppositions the pendulum has swung firmly in favor of the first of the polar opposites.[31]

The council failed to remind Catholics that the implementation of its decisions taken in the spirit of *aggiornamento* would be a really messy, painful, and grief-evoking process. And Rome is also seriously at fault in failing to provide professionally sensitive follow-up leadership. It merely opted for a return to its authoritarian style of old. The fact is that the council radically altered the mythic structure of the church without taking into account that no such fundamental change, no matter how well-intentioned, is possible without being catastrophic for the people involved. If bishops at the council had been more open to the social sciences they would have been more sensitive to, and better prepared for, the explosive cultural implications of their documents when they returned to their dioceses. Cultures, and especially the centuries-old culture of the pre–Vatican II church, do not accept change smoothly simply because a document or authoritarian leaders say they should. The resulting turmoil should have been expected and better catechesis prepared to explain the inevitably chaotic yet potentially creative consequences of the council's decisions. Rome's intensified restorationist style tragically illustrates that it has still not learned how to lead cultural change. It openly supports the escapist and fundamentalist movements in the church (see stage 5), readily searching out and condemning creative, prophetic people yearning to apply the principles of Vatican II.

31. See Gerard Mannion, *Ecclesiology and Postmodernity: Questions for the Church* (Collegeville, MN: Liturgical Press, 2007), 43–74. Mannion uses the term "neo-exclusivism" as a synonym for "restorationism."

Example: Domestication of Prophetic Life

The following is an example of the inbuilt mythological tensions in the documents of Vatican II: The magisterium is the final authority in doctrinal matters, *but* prophetic thinking and action are crucial to the life and future of the church. No one is to be spared the prophetic critique of the Gospel, not even the institutional church. One of the main reasons why religious life developed historically in the church was precisely the need to respond to this challenge. "Religious orders," writes Johannes Baptist Metz, "are a kind of shock therapy introduced by the Holy Spirit for the Church as a whole. Against the dangerous accommodations and questionable compromises that the Church . . . can always incline to, they press for the uncompromising nature of the Gospel and of the imitation of Christ."[32] For instance, at the heart of the variety of identities of religious congregations is this call to be prophetic. Religious life, as an expression of the prophetic wing of the church, "while not entering into the hierarchical structure of the Church, belongs undeniably to her life and holiness."[33]

So often in history congregations have been founded at times in the church when it was making "dangerous accommodations and questionable compromises" and forgetting "the uncompromising nature of the Gospel." We have but to think of the prophetic mission of Saints Francis and Dominic and their followers in the thirteenth century who were concerned with the problem of wealth in the church and the abuse of power by feudal lords. In these circumstances itinerant preachers practiced extreme poverty.

However, historically whenever religious congregations fulfill their prophetic role it invariably leads to friction, even at times significant conflict, with hierarchical members in the church. Over the centuries Rome has repeatedly sought to domesticate congregations to prevent them from fulfilling their prophetic task. For example, the nineteenth century was a period of intense growth in the number of congregations, with over six hundred new communities being formed worldwide. Many founders opted for the apostolic model developed by St. Ignatius Loyola. This was possible even for women's communities, since Rome had finally acknowledged at the *theoretical* level that this model had validity for both men *and* women. In *practice*, however, Rome insisted that many

---

32. Johannes Baptist Metz, *Followers of Christ: The Religious Life of the Church* (London: Burns & Oates, 1978), 12.

33. *Lumen Gentium* 44 (Dogmatic Constitution on the Church), in Flannery, ed., *Documents of Vatican II*, 405.

inappropriate monastic and conventual customs had to be integrated into their constitutions, as if it still assumed that the ideal form of religious life was monastic and anything else was not quite authentic. This reflected the view that the world is evil and to be avoided; the changing world had to adapt to the church and not vice versa. Hence, as Father Avery Dulles, SJ, commented, the church's "narcissistic preoccupation"[34] discouraged any form of pastoral experimentation led by apostolic religious orders. Because of this inward-looking emphasis the prophetic purpose of religious life ceased to be its defining quality; instead, the vows became its primary focus. Theologian Jean-Marie Tillard writes:

> One becomes a religious for the sake of the Gospel, not strictly for the sake of the three classical vows. Although the vows represent elements that are specific to the religious life and therefore indispensable to whoever feels called to the life by the Holy Spirit, they are not the primary elements in the concrete life of grace of the religious.[35]

This means that a person could faithfully keep the vows but fail to be prophetic (contrary to a view that still lingers on in Roman documents).

Thus the dynamic founding energy of apostolic communities was quickly suffocated before Vatican II by rules, for example, the requirement of wearing habits and of maintaining at least a semi-cloister, which Rome decreed should be integral to all approved forms of religious life. The fossilization of apostolic life intensified after the publication of the 1918 Code of Canon Law; the practice of imposing structures inimical to the values of apostolic life was now fully supported by universal church law. In summary, the formation of mendicant and apostolic religious in this period reflected the prevailing attitudes of the institutional church: ghettoism, anti-world, anti-change stances or fear of prophetic questioning of the *status quo*, and nostalgia for monasticism as the ideal form of religious life. Candidates for ministry were trained as though the world did not exist. They had to become submissive to the ecclesiastical and pastoral *status quo*.[36]

---

34. Avery Dulles, "Vatican II and the Church's Response," *Theology Digest* 32 (1986): 985.

35. Jean-Marie Tillard, *A Gospel Path: The Religious Life* (Brussels: Lumen Vitae, 1975), 101.

36. See Gerald A. Arbuckle, *From Chaos to Mission: Refounding Religious Life Formation* (Collegeville, MN: Liturgical Press, 1995), 27–29.

Religious took seriously the mandate of Vatican II to return to the roots of their founding charisms and to relate them prophetically to contemporary pastoral needs.[37] Women religious especially rediscovered their prophetic foundations and committed themselves, often with limited financial resources, to the task of updating themselves in theology and professionally for ministry. I personally believe that religious women are among the most highly educated members of the church, for I see evidence of this in their massive contribution to healthcare, education, and the social apostolate. Their commitment to serve the needs of marginalized peoples, even in physically dangerous circumstances, continues to be an astonishing example of prophetic action.[38]

At the same time, however, the renewal of clerical education has lagged seriously behind that of religious, again especially that of religious women. This has resulted in a widening gap between the clerical and religious worlds and continues to exacerbate the inbuilt tensions between the magisterial and prophetic wings of the church. This is the most significant cause, for example, of the very public friction between Rome and the Leadership Conference of Women Religious in the United States (LCWR). The theological learning, professional training, and outstanding example of countless women religious that LCWR represents[39] present an unprecedented challenge to the power and authority of the hierarchy. Moreover, the general reluctance by Rome and many bishops to renew their administrative structures as Vatican II mandated, in vivid contrast to the renewal experiences of religious sisters in particular, is obvious to the church at large.

This is the background to the Congregation for the Doctrine of the Faith's (CDF) public admonition in April 2012 charging the LCWR with "serious doctrinal errors" and "doctrinal confusion" and demanding widespread changes to their administrative structures and proce-

---

37. See Decree on the Up-To-Date Renewal of Religious Life 2–3, in Flannery, ed., *Documents of Vatican II.*

38. In 1983 Rome, in a restorationist move, published a document called *The Essential Elements of Religious Life.* It sought to summarize the salient points of the church's teaching on religious life. In so doing, however, it aimed to reintroduce various attitudes and structures, generally referred to as monastic or conventual, into apostolic congregations that had removed them after Vatican II. See Arbuckle, *Refounding the Church,* 166–67.

39. The LCWR represents more than 80% of the 57,000 religious women in the United States.

dures. The document expressed deep concern that the LCWR was too committed to social service, that is, issues of social justice, "and not devoted to matters of interest to the CDF."[40] The admonition specifically mentions, for example, the organization's reluctance to be faithful to John Paul II's apostolic letter rejecting the ordination of women. In other words, the document is telling religious women that their task is not to be prophetic but to concentrate instead on teaching people to be faithful to the doctrinal statements of the magisterium. It is a call to return to the "domestication of religious life" that characterized the pre–Vatican II church.

The Rise of Postmodernity

At the same time as Vatican II became the catalyst for a cultural revolution within the church, the Western world was itself experiencing a most profound cultural shift from modernity to postmodernity; the visible sign of this dramatic cultural change was the expressive revolution of the 1960s (see fig. 2.1). A major document, "The Church in the Modern World" (*Gaudium et Spes*), called on Catholics to interact with the world's culture of modernity, a culture that was in fact already on the verge of dying. The expressive revolution[41] of the mid-1960s was a massive, well-publicized attack on all that had been held sacred by modernity since the sixteenth century. No value, custom, or institution remained unchallenged and unaffected. Naïve faith in science and technology disintegrated.[42] The expressive revolution was essentially an attack on boundaries of all kinds—gender differences, limits, certainties, taboos, roles, systems, styles, predictabilities, traditions. There was widespread erosion of the legitimacy of traditional institutions: churches, business, government, education, the family. In brief, traditions were devalued, censorship dismantled, churches deserted, schools degraded, the family derided. At the same time, in its embrace of modernity, the church failed to see that new and positive aspects of the expressive revolution could have been identified and welcomed. In the euphoria of any cultural revolution, such as the one Vatican II evoked in the church, people are apt to discard the past with little or no critical consideration. That is precisely what happened in our embrace of modernity. As early as 1973

40. See Phyllis Zagano, "A Very Public Rebuke," *The Tablet* (28 April 2012): 4–5.

41. See Arbuckle, *Violence, Society, and the Church*, 157–72.

42. See Hugh McLeod, *The Religious Crisis of the 1960s* (Oxford: Oxford University Press, 2007), 258.

an American Catholic sociologist, Father Andrew Greeley, could see that the church's uncritical accommodation to modernity was untimely.

> We abandoned concern about the sacred just when the sacred was being rediscovered. We stopped making our daily meditations and substituted group discussion just as the elites were rediscovering Zen. We completely forgot our own mystical past just when ecstasy was fashionable once again. . . . We entered the modern world just at the time when many of its elite members were preparing to leave it.[43]

The term "postmodernity" now connotes the epochal and complex cultural shift that resulted from the expressive revolution of the 1960s. Within this cultural shift three broad and identifiably different sets of reactions to the revolution emerged and continue to develop decades after the revolution: "pro-order," "anti-order," and "paramodern." The last two sets are particularly relevant to the themes of this book. The three types of reactions are not mutually exclusive. Thus a person or institution may exemplify qualities of all three sets, depending on the particular situation in which the person or institution finds itself. "Pro-order reactions" indicate a yearning to return to the order and predictability characteristic of modernity; thus from the late 1970s there has been a revitalization of nineteenth-century capitalism under such titles as neoliberalism, economic rationalism, or neocapitalism. The recent global recession and continuing economic uncertainty have, however, weakened this trust that market forces will resolve national and world financial problems.

Postmodernity: Confusion of Identities

Because change in contemporary postmodern societies is so rapid, people are increasingly pressured to develop fluid identities noted for their lack of depth, unpredictability, and constant alteration. Individuals are encouraged to experiment with different identities, almost like so many new garments, to search for "role models" and engage in different behaviors

---

43. Andrew Greeley, *The New Agenda* (Garden City, NY: Doubleday, 1973), 291–92.

as the contexts change. There is an endless, exhausting, even manic hunt for personal identity, but one is always aware that even when it is temporarily achieved to some degree it remains a fiction because there is no way to prove its objective truth. The pop stars Madonna and Lady Gaga, well-known for their constant changes of images and identities, are symbolic of the postmodern person.[44] In traditional cultures this almost frenetic changing of identities marks a person as unreliable, even devious, but in postmodern societies this chameleon-like ability to adopt new identities at any moment is thought to be highly desirable. This type of pressure on young people is extremely demanding. Our postmodern society insists that individuals must be true to themselves, but when their social contexts are so changeable, how can young people be expected to decide easily what self they should be true to?

"Anti-order reactions" are characterized by the rejection of totalizing narratives such as Christianity, skepticism and cynicism toward human progress, and the assumption that individuals alone are important. Modernity assumes we can know reality, but postmodern groups reject this, claiming that we are all confused by illusions and hyper-reality. All forms of authority are rejected on the assumption that people in authority distort the truth in order to maintain their power. Also discarded is the belief in the power of reason, science, and human progress; objective truth is considered an illusion, a fantasy, and all "grand narratives," that is, big theories like Christianity and Marxism that claim to explain everything, are rejected. In a postmodern view of the world truth is what each person determines it to be; only personal narratives, rich in experience and intuition, have validity. Whereas in modernity people considered that each person has a fundamentally unified and unchanging identity, postmodernists claim that individuals have multiple and conflicting identities; they are able to change their identities whenever they feel bored or uncomfortable with the ones they presently possess. The heroes in modernity are successful businesspeople and political leaders, while by contrast in anti-order postmodernity they are

44. See Gerald A. Arbuckle, *Violence, Society, and the Church*, 165.

social and entertainment superstars, whose tastes and lifestyles become models for society.[45]

"Paramodern reactions" refers to the signs of a new culture model that is slowly and hesitantly emerging in which "we glimpse new ways of thinking about ourselves, new possibilities for coexisting with others—even more profoundly different others."[46] People are reacting, on the one hand, to the excessive optimism in modern culture that science could eventually solve all human problems and, on the other hand, the in-built pessimism of anti-order postmodernity. Among the characteristic qualities of paramodernity are the recognition of the vital importance of the imagination and intuitive knowledge, the inductive method of learning, storytelling, gender equality, the need for interdependence, collaboration, spirituality, and reconciliation.

Impact on Mainline Churches

Many mainline churches suffered a widespread malaise as a consequence of the expressive revolution and its anti-order qualities on their followers. Since the churches were thoroughly ill-prepared to respond to the spiritual and ideological upheavals of the time, they experienced a loss of institutional vitality and direction. Significant numbers of young people felt that these traditional churches had so compromised with secular values, or had become so bureaucratic and unfeeling, that they were unable any longer to provide the desired havens of understanding and meaning. Within the Catholic Church the publication by Pope Paul VI of the encyclical *Humanae Vitae* at the high point of the expressive revolution in 1968, condemning the use of artificial methods of birth control, including the pill, evoked further disillusionment. The negative reactions to the encyclical signified the dramatic nature of the breakdown of unified ethnic identity in the church, precipitating the most serious crisis for papal and episcopal authority since the Reformation. It came under attack not only from lay Catholics but also from leading theologians, clergy, and significant sections of the media. Even some national episcopates questioned the conclusions of the encyclical.[47]

45. See ibid., 155–73.

46. Walter T. Anderson, *The Truth about Truth: De-confusing and Re-constructing the Postmodern World* (New York: Putman, 1995), 11.

47. See comments by Mark S. Massa, *Catholics and American Culture* (New York: Crossroad, 1999), 5–6.

Overall there was a progressive movement away from Christianity and the mainline churches. In Holland, once a staunchly Christian country, the proportion of people registering no religion rose from 18% in 1960 to 28% in 1970.[48] In Australia one poll estimated that, in 1967, 3.1% declared having "no religion," but in 1979 the figure rose to 25.1%.[49] It became fashionable to attack Christianity openly, even to declare atheism as an esteemed value. In 1966, John Lennon, a member of the Beatles, the world-famous pop group, claimed that "Christianity will go. . . . We're more popular than Jesus now."[50] In 1971 he entreated his listeners in his song *Imagine* to embrace atheism and anarchy.[51] This militant support of atheism has become far more acceptable since the expressive revolution, with books from fierce atheists like zoologist Richard Dawkins now among the bestsellers.

In the decades since the 1970s the authority of the mainline churches has further dramatically weakened in many Western countries. In Britain in 2001, fewer than 8% of people attended Sunday weekly worship, less than 25% claimed allegiance to any church, fewer than 10% of children attended Sunday school, fewer than 50% of couples had been married in church, and cohabitation without marriage had become an increasing phenomenon.[52] The moral standing of the churches has plummeted, exacerbated in more recent years by well-publicized sexual and financial scandals involving the clergy.

Institutional religion is now seen as irrelevant to people's lives. So radical and rapid has been the decline in institutional religion that in some countries scholars now speak of the death of Christianity. The Church of Scotland has even calculated that in the year 2033 it will cease to exist as a result of membership decline.[53] It is, however, the Catholic Church that has experienced the most significant net loss. Most commonly the reason given for former Catholics in the United States joining a Protestant denomination is that the church has failed "to deliver what people consider fundamental products of religion: spiritual sustenance and a

48. See McLeod, *The Religious Crisis*, 212.
49. See Tom Frame, *Losing My Religion: Unbelief in Australia* (Sydney: UNSW Press, 2009), 90.
50. John Lennon, quoted in McLeod, *The Religious Crisis*, 212.
51. Ibid.
52. See Callum G. Brown, *The Death of Christian Britain* (London: Routledge, 2001), 3.
53. See ibid., 5.

good worship service."[54] Those who leave are more interested in spiritual sustenance than doctrinal matters. Mass attendance is down by at least 50% in Britain and the situation is worse in France, Holland, and Spain. Vocations to the priesthood and religious life have rapidly declined so that in Europe thousands of parishes are without a resident priest.[55] Religious congregations, with average ages of seventy and above, now face extinction. In the United States a recent Pew Forum study concluded that one in ten Americans is a former Catholic and that about one in three of those raised Catholic has left the church.[56] Sociologist Sister Patricia Wittberg, SC, points out that over the centuries women have manifested a greater religiosity than men, but in the United States fewer young women are practicing their faith. She fears that Generation X (women born between 1962 and 1980) and especially millennial Catholic women (women born between 1981 and 1995) who are interested in spiritual issues and religious practice "will seek an outlet for this interest outside the church." She cogently argues that unless more women from Generation X, the millennials, and subsequent generations are attracted to remain in the church it "could cease to be an influential voice in Western societies."[57]

Case Study: Australia

The decline of religious practice within Australia is disturbing. Approximately 26% of the population is Catholic, but in 2006 only 13.8% attended Sunday Mass, "and not all of those attend every week."[58] One in four parishes no longer has a

---

54. Thomas Reese, "The Hidden Exodus: Catholics Becoming Protestants," *National Catholic Reporter,* 18 April 2011, at www.ncronline.org/news/hidden -exodus-catholics-becoming-protestants, accessed 24 October 2011.

55. See Peter Doyle in J. Derek Holmes and Bernard W. Bickers, *A Short History of the Catholic Church* (London: Burns and Oates, 2002), 300.

56. See Jerry Filteau, "Saying Bishops 'Scared,' Panelists Urge Laity to Take Lead," *National Catholic Reporter,* 4 January 2011, at www.ncronline.org/news/account-ability; William V. D'Antonio, "Catholics in America," *National Catholic Reporter,* 24 October 2011, 1.

57. Patricia Wittberg, "A Lost Generation?" *America* 206, no. 5 (20 February 2012): 13–16.

58. See Stephen Reid, Robert Dixon, and Noel Connolly, *Catholic Religious Institutes in Australia* (Sydney: CRA, 2010), 2.

full-time resident priest; only about 600 locally born priests are likely to be available for parish ministry by 2025; in 2010 there were 5,565 religious sisters, down from 15,000 in 1966.[59] A survey of priests published in 2011 not surprisingly found that their morale was very low, due *inter alia* to overwork and the growing conservatism and centralism in the church.[60]

Overall in Australia, Christian affiliation is expected to drop below 50% around 2030 and the Christian churches will be marginal players in Australian life. Anglican theologian Tom Frame foresees that eventually the mainline churches that fail to provide an attractive and plausible alternative to the secular ethos will cease to exist. Frame's opinion is that the "left-leaning, cause-driven, liberal Protestant churches that lack doctrinal rigor and are preoccupied with the promotion of social justice and cultural inclusion will be the first to go."[61]

"Renewalist" Groups

An immediate effect of the decline of the mainline churches has been the rise of new religious movements, including Evangelical conservative churches like the Assemblies of God. In reaction to the chaos of the cultural revolution, these movements respond to deep human needs: desire for an experiential religion, that is, to feel God's love in the here and now; desire for an intimacy in community life through small-group activity; desire to be able to tell their own stories and be listened to; need for clarity of meaning and direction in life; need for therapeutic services, including solutions for addictions; young people's desire to assert independence from adult restrictions, expressed in joining cults or sects.[62]

59. See Peter J. Wilkinson, *Catholic Parish Ministry in Australia: Facing Disaster?* (Manuka: Catholics for Ministry/Women and the Australian Church, 2011), 3, 19.

60. See Chris McGillion and John O'Carroll, *Our Fathers: What Australian Catholic Priests Really Think about Their Lives and Their Church* (Mulgrave: John Garratt, 2011), 35–40.

61. See Frame, *Losing My Religion*, 99.

62. See Arbuckle, *Earthing the Gospel*, 120–27.

The term "renewalist" describes a form of Protestant Christianity that bypasses the traditional hierarchies and bureaucracies of the mainline churches. This model emphasizes direct access to God. John Micklethwait and Adrian Wooldridge describe renewalism as "a strange mixture of unflinching belief and pragmatism, raw emotion and self-improvement, improvisation and organization."[63] Today the growth of new religious or "renewalist" movements is markedly evident not just in Western countries, but also in Africa, Asia, and South America. The world of megachurches, "pastorpreneurs," and house churches is thriving everywhere. It is estimated that there are over five hundred million renewalists, including Pentecostals and charismatics, and they are increasing in numbers twice as fast as Catholics. About thirty years ago renewalists formed a mere 6% of the Christian population, but now they are 25%. In Australia, for example, attendance at Pentecostal services has increased 27% over the last ten years.[64] These renewalist groups owe some of their success to their ability to adapt to local cultures and needs such as people's search for identities through storytelling and imaginative and participative liturgies.

Self-Chosen Catholic Identities: Sociological Types

Among the consequences of the religious turmoil of the 1960s is the startling fact that affiliation with a particular religion is no longer generally an inherited reality. A surprising 44% of persons in the United States belong to a religion other than the one they were born into.[65] Thus "religious identities are becoming something that people craft rather than take for granted."[66] Sociologist Andrew Greeley in 1977 first described what he termed the "communal" Catholic, a phenomenon widely observed today. People still claim to be Catholic, but they freely choose for themselves what that means. Rejecting many of the traditional markers of Catholic identities, they refuse to take seriously the teaching authority of the church's hierarchy and selectively disagree with the church's dogmas or moral teachings, though they might continue

---

63. John Micklethwait and Adrian Wooldridge, *God Is Back: How the Global Revival of Faith Is Changing the World* (New York: Penguin, 2009), 218.

64. See ibid., 217–23.

65. See Austen Ivereigh, "God Makes a Comeback," *America* 201, no. 8 (5 October 2009): 11–14, at 12.

66. Micklethwait and Wooldridge, *God Is Back*, 357.

to send their children to Catholic schools. Many choose new religious forms that give them a more personalized experience of community and God. They move away from traditional Catholic recreational and social clubs in order to mix into the wider, less religion-based community,[67] thus further diluting the "Catholic" culture.

In 2005 the Gallup Organization published the results of a survey of what Catholics in the United States believe is central to their identities.[68] The survey correctly assumed that religious identities must always contain a central core of beliefs, so it was important to discover what respondents of all age groups considered to be at the heart of Catholic identity. "Helping the poor" and "belief in the resurrection of Jesus from the dead" tied for first place; in third place were "the sacraments, such as the Eucharist," and closely following was "the Catholic church's teachings about Mary as the Mother of God." However, most respondents considered the teachings on celibate priesthood, the death penalty, abortion, and same-sex marriage as more optional than essential. Sociologist Dean Hoge commented on the results: "Catholics distinguish basic creedal beliefs such as Jesus' resurrection and the nature of the sacraments from specific moral teachings about sexuality or the death penalty—they see the latter as less than central to their Catholicity." Regarding the way respondents perceive the boundaries of their faith, the survey revealed that 61% of Catholics aged sixty-five and over felt that "Catholicism contains a greater share of truth than other religions do," compared with 43% of those aged twenty-six or younger. Hoge concludes with this significant comment on the survey findings when compared with surveys in previous years:

> The main change is in the boundaries—they are now fairly vague and porous, and they are slowly becoming more so over time. Boundaries that make no sense to young adults cannot be maintained over the long haul. More meaningful boundaries need to be defined and explained.

67. See Andrew M. Greeley, *The American Catholic: A Social Portrait* (New York: Basic Books, 1977), 277.

68. Dean R. Hoge, "Survey of U.S. Catholics," *National Catholic Reporter*, 30 September 2005, at www.natcath.com/NCR_Online/archives2 /2005c/093005/093005k.htm, accessed 5 October 2011.

The following sociological types[69] describe eleven ways in which people express their Catholic identities.[70]

Type 1: Traditional Catholics	• attend Mass weekly and participate regularly in the activities of their local church; • do not question teachings of the pope and bishops; • concern for personal salvation with little commitment to social justice; • educated before the council; submit to liturgical changes but inwardly grieve for the past.
Type 2: Vatican II Catholics	• attend Mass weekly; • educated in and committed to the council's theology of church and world; • prepared, if necessary, to challenge the church and society to be true to this theology; • strong supporters of the council's emphasis on social justice inspired by a gospel-based spirituality; • although seriously committed to the council's theology, these Catholics no longer see their local parish as the center of their social and cultural life; dissatisfied with poorly prepared liturgies and homilies, they regularly search for more empowering services in other parishes; • shamed by sexual abuse scandals and cover-up; • deeply saddened by authoritarian/ bullying actions of members of the hierarchy.
Type 3: Fundamental- ist Catholics	• committed to the church but trapped in fundamentalist interpretations of Vatican II;[71]

69. A sociological type aims to illuminate complex social realities by highlighting emphases. Nuanced explanations or details are omitted to allow readers to grasp a little more clearly what in fact are highly complex situations. In practice the types are not necessarily exclusive of each other, though one type may tend to dominate.

70. Several of these models are adapted from descriptions provided by Chester Gillis, *Roman Catholicism in America* (New York: Columbia University Press, 1999).

71. See Arbuckle, *Refounding the Church*, 39–43.

(Type 3 cont.)	• fundamentalists[72] are of two kinds: "right" and "left," with little or no dialogue possible between the opposing "tribes"; • "right" fundamentalists are, e.g., anti-abortionists but unconcerned for other social justice issues, and actively promote pre–Vatican II symbols/ rituals, feel the church has been seduced by secular humanism; • "left" fundamentalists overemphasize social justice to the exclusion of other issues, e.g., neglect relationship with God in prayer.
Type 4: Selective Catholics	• attend Mass weekly and participate regularly in the activities of their local church; • reject some beliefs and practices of the church, e.g., practice birth control, consider abortion acceptable under certain conditions; • strong commitment at times to social justice.
Type 5: Independent Catholics	• attend Mass irregularly; • ignore teachings and practices that fail to make sense to them of what they consider irrelevant to contemporary life; • still consider themselves Catholic but choose to act independently of the church for the most part.
Type 6: Minimalist Catholics	• generally attend Mass at Christmas and Easter and possibly for specialized functions such as weddings and funerals; • claim to be Catholic but "generally they live their lives unaware, uninterested, or unaffected by the activities and teachings of the church."[73]
Type 7: Utilitarian Catholics	• minimalist in their commitment to Mass; • choose only those beliefs and practices not in conflict with mainstream values of their culture; • make use of Catholic institutions, e.g., schools, universities, provided they emphasize fashionable dominant values of their culture such as self-discipline, individualism, success in business or politics.

---

72. See Arbuckle, *Violence, Society, and the Church*, 195–214.
73. Gillis, *Roman Catholicism*, 18.

Type 8: Disengaged Catholics	• baptism alone identifies them as Catholic; they no longer follow Catholic religious teachings and practices; • possibly desire to be married in a Catholic church, even to have their children baptized and attend a Catholic school; • in reality "for all intents and purposes non-Catholic"; the church no longer has any relevance in their lives; • distrust ecclesiastical leadership; consider it hypocritical particularly in light of the sexual abuse scandals; • this type particularly characteristic of younger generations.
Type 9: New Migratory Catholics	• attend Mass at times according to pre-migration customs; • strongly devotional, even Pentecostal, and experiential in religious practice; • use local parish center for support and social activities.
Type 10: Postmodern Catholics	• may attend Mass at times, but seek, even earnestly, to construct from their own convictions an eclectic distinctive religious identity, drawing on Eastern religions, New Age practices, and fundamental Catholic beliefs such as the Eucharist, Mary, and pre–Vatican II liturgical styles and dress, though they cannot be classed as restorationist (see Type 1); • distrustful of "moralistic judgments" and inclined to accept cultural relativity as the only universal truth;[74] • born and educated after Vatican II; little knowledge of doctrinal beliefs and traditional Catholic cultural practices and prayers, e.g., Hail Mary, Sign of the Cross;

74. See the detailed analysis provided by William V. D'Antonio, James D. Davidson, Dean R. Hoge, and Mary L. Gautier, *American Catholics Today: New Realities of Their Faith and Their Church* (New York: Rowman & Littlefield, 2007).

(Type 10 cont.)	• customary categorization of Catholics as "liberal" or "conservative" makes no sense to them; • little interest in critiquing structures of the church and in social justice issues, though they are increasingly impatient with ecclesiastical patriarchy.
Type 11: "Lamentative" Catholics	• faithful to Mass and Vatican II theology; • strong spiritual interior life, focused on the Paschal Mystery; • feeling abandoned, betrayed, sad, and angry with perceived refusal by Rome to implement hierarchical administrative changes as mandated by Vatican II, and by the marginalization of prophetic people and movements in the church; • yearning for deep renewal and refounding of the church.

While types 1, 4, 5, and 6 could encompass pre-conciliar Catholics, most would at that time have identified with type 1. For example, in 1965 in the United States approximately 65% of Catholics attended Mass weekly and would have fitted into type 1, but by 2009 this had dropped to 36%.[75] Although statistics are not available, anecdotal evidence would suggest that following the council the significant shifts have been away from type 1 into types 3 to 7 inclusive, with a small but vocal group remaining in type 1. Type 8, New Migratory Catholics, is of course the result of significant migration of people in recent years from Asia and Latin America into the United States, Europe, and Australasia. Mass Vietnamese immigration to these countries began in 1975, following the end of the Vietnam war, so that in the United States today there are an estimated 100,000 foreign-born Vietnamese.

In the United States one-third of Catholics are now Hispanic. In 1990 it was estimated that there were 22.3 million Hispanics, but by 2003 this had risen to 39.9 million. Between nine million and eighteen million illegal migrants live in the country, most of whom are thought to be of Hispanic origin. The Georgetown study, published in 2006, concluded that about 70% identify themselves as Catholic, although only

75. See *The Cara Report* at www.cara.georgetown.edu/bulletin/, accessed 26 October 2009.

52% of these are registered with their dioceses or parishes.[76] While Hispanic cultures are diverse, they share fundamentally the same language and often have similar religious practices. In 2007 it was found that approximately half of Hispanic Catholics practice an identifiable type of charismatic Catholicism that includes speaking in tongues, miraculous healings, and prophesying. Among Catholics who are not Hispanic, only 12% embrace these practices.[77] Some Hispanics, or those deeply influenced by Hispanic traditions such as migrants from the Philippines, may place little emphasis on weekly Mass attendance but participate wholeheartedly in particular feast day celebrations. For example, it is a strong Filipino tradition, an integral part of their Catholic identities, to highlight Good Friday, the liturgy of Christ's passion and death, but not the feast of the resurrection of Christ.

In my opinion an increasing number of Catholics under forty years of age would identify with type 9: Postmodern Catholics. They have no personal knowledge of the pre–Vatican II church; at the same time, they experience the impact of the cultural revolution and its postmodern consequences. Chester Gillis, associate professor of theology and Catholic studies at Georgetown University, offered this sobering comment in 1999 on the level of commitment of the majority of Catholics in the United States: "Most Catholics like their Christianity to fulfill their spiritual needs but not at the cost of severely disrupting their lifestyle . . . [and] maintain a threshold that keeps them from embracing a radical commitment that would impinge on all areas of their lives."[78]

Summary:

- Sociological and theological changes in the Catholic Church since the Vatican Council have effectively undermined traditional perceptions of Catholic identities.

---

76. "Immigration: A Cause of Growth of the American Catholic Church?" at www.freerepublic.com/focus/f-news/1608763/posts, accessed 8 August 2011.

77. See Laurie Goodstein, "Hispanics Reshaping U.S. Catholic Church," *New York Times*, 25 April 2007, at www.nytimes.com/2007/04/25/us/25cnd-hispanic.html, accessed 8 August 2011.

78. Gillis, *Roman Catholicism*, 279.

- Before 1965 the markers of Catholic identities remained stable and universal for two reasons: hierarchical reactions to the Reformation and widespread social and political discrimination against Catholics.

- The theological and cultural boundaries of the fortress church were collapsing by the mid-1960s, leaving Catholics in a state of chaotic confusion regarding their religious identities.

- Vatican II encouraged Catholics to craft their Catholic identities on the basis of the Gospel and the church's Tradition; ill-prepared for this positive challenge, Catholics became and remain confused. Consequently, there are many different theological and sociological understandings of Catholic identities.

- The mission of the church is to engage with the postmodern world, to build on its strengths and weaknesses; evangelizers need to realize that in postmodern cultures "religious identities are becoming something that people craft rather than take for granted."[79] Moreover, most Catholics no longer relate to the church in the same ways as their grandparents or parents. However, this does not necessarily mean that the church is insignificant in their lives.[80]

- The next chapter examines the impact of this ongoing confusion on key ministries.

79. Micklethwait and Wooldridge, *God Is Back*, 356.
80. Gillis, *Roman Catholicism*, 22.

Chapter Three

Ministries: Crisis of Identities

[The] tensions over Catholic identity are now a defining feature of the landscape for Church-affiliated schools and colleges.[1] *(John Allen, Jr.)*

So set yourself to rest in this darkness as long as you can, always crying out after him whom you love. For if you are to experience him or to see him at all, insofar as it is possible here, it must be in this cloud.[2] *(The Cloud of Unknowing)*

This chapter explains that:

- while the church has extensive networks of schools and of social and healthcare services, their Catholic identities are increasingly uncertain
- the fundamental tension in these ministries is between "the mission" and "the business"
- when the emphasis is on "the business," the uniqueness of Catholic identities is under threat
- there is an urgent need to find ways to refound Catholic identities in these ministries

The previous chapter ended with an overview of Catholic identities as understood by individuals. This chapter concentrates on the Catholic

---

1. John Allen, Jr. *The Future Church: How Ten Trends are Revolutionizing the Catholic Church* (New York: Doubleday, 2009), 69.
2. *The Cloud of Unknowing*, ed. James Walsh (New York: Paulist Press, 1981), 121.

69

identities of institutional ministries. The first part presents a general review of the challenges facing the Catholic identities of ministries in the church; the second section focuses on particular ministries. What does it mean today to be a Catholic healthcare institution, a Catholic school, a Catholic college or university, a Catholic welfare agency? Would individuals and the institutional church identify them as Catholic?

As we will see, it is increasingly difficult to answer these questions in postmodern times. Difficulties about defining *and* maintaining Catholic identities in these ministries mirror the problems around identities in the church at large. This review will lead us to the conclusion that we face a pre-evangelization situation in our ministries. Old methods of formation for our ministries simply have little or no positive impact; rather, we need inductive methods that are able to evoke faith transformation. These methods are to be founded on the Scriptures and the storytelling style of Jesus Christ.

The Catholic Church has a very broad range of institutional ministries, including schools, universities, healthcare facilities, and welfare services. At present the church conducts the largest non-governmental school system throughout the world, with approximately 92,700 elementary schools and 42,000 secondary schools.[3] In the United States the church has the largest network of private schools: 6,386 elementary schools, 1,203 high schools, and 221 Catholic colleges and universities.[4] In Australia Catholics comprise 26% of the population, with 2,252 Catholic schools, from kindergartens to universities, and the Catholic education department is the biggest employer outside of the federal government. In England and Wales there are 2,257 Catholic schools, making up 10% of the total.[5] New Zealand has a population of four million, of whom a half million are Catholic. Despite the smallness of population and limited resources, the church there maintains 190 elementary schools and 47 high schools.

In the United States the church is responsible for 615 hospitals accounting for 12.5% of community hospitals, and over 16% of all hospital admissions. In addition, the Catholic healthcare network also includes 404 healthcare centers, 1,509 specialized homes, and 235 residential

3. See CARA (Center for Applied Research in the Apostolate) at www.cara .georgetown.edu/bulletin/2, accessed 20 August 2011.

4. See U.S. Conference of Catholic Bishops, www.usccb.org/comm./cip .shtml/6, accessed 24 August 2011.

5. See www.cesew.org.uk/, accessed 5 December 2012.

homes for children.[6] The church in Australia has the nation's largest nongovernment not-for-profit grouping of health- and aged-care services, with 75 hospitals and 550 residential and community aged-care services.[7]

As regards social services, in Australia the Catholic Church provides assistance to over a million people annually; in the United States there are approximately 1,400 local Catholic Charities organizations, which annually assist 9.5 million people with wide-ranging help.

Catholic Identities: General Challenges

While the above statistics are extraordinarily impressive, they conceal serious problems for the future viability of Catholic institutions. Before the mid-1960s all Catholic educational and healthcare facilities were staffed by religious and priests. No one needed to define the mission of these facilities, as the visible presence of priests, brothers, and sisters was enough to assure people that the pervading ethos was Catholic. But this has radically changed. These institutions are under so much pressure from internal and external sources that we rightly ask the questions: Are these institutions only Catholic in name? What must they do to maintain their Catholic identities? In a competitive world, can they even survive as institutions? The following points indicate the validity of these questions.

Staffing

It is increasingly rare for religious or priests still to be in charge of or staff these institutions. In Australia, for example, in 1959 there were 299 religious sisters staffing one large Catholic hospital. Today there are no sisters in the facility. In addition, staff members, including those who hold key administrative posts, are increasingly non-Catholics. For example, between 1974 and 1994 the percentage of non-Catholic teachers in Catholic elementary schools in England and Wales increased from 9.8% to 12.1% and in high schools from 35.6% to 41.1%.[8] The percentage would be far higher today; the situation is repeated in other countries. A further problem in Catholic ministries is the diminishing number of

---

6. See www.usccb.org/comm/cip.shtml/6, accessed 5 December 2012.

7. See www.cha.org.au/1, accessed 20 November 2011.

8. See Terence H. McLaughlin, Joseph O'Keefe, and Bernadette O'Keeffe, "Setting the Scene: Current Realities and Historical Perspectives," 1–22 in *The Contemporary Catholic School: Context, Identity and Diversity* (London and Washington, DC: Falmer Press, 1996), 13.

practicing Catholics available to fill positions. In the educational field this is seen by many observers as the greatest threat to the future of the schools. In a survey of Catholic schools in England and Wales in the mid-1990s the "difficulty of recruiting Catholic teachers is most apparent in the key posts for which the appointment of a Catholic is essential."[9] When Catholic people are available as teachers, few are either qualified or willing to enter the important field of religious education.[10]

Government Controls

The more governments are involved in financing Catholic ministries such as education, social services, and healthcare, the more difficult it is to maintain Catholic identities and resist the inroads of postmodern negative values. In many Western countries most of these ministries would be unable to survive without government financial support. But there are problems. For example, in New Zealand, although the government agreed that 60% of the teaching staff of junior schools must be practicing Catholics and at high school level 40%, these levels cannot be maintained when there is a shortage of qualified Catholic teachers. In England and Wales the government decided that the guardianship of the distinctive Catholic mission and ethos of a school should pass from the bishops to school governors and parents. However, as one commentator noted: "The long-term implications of this shift in power for the future direction and nature of Catholic schooling were clearly of great potential significance."[11] If governors fail to have a clear vision of what Catholic identities mean, the Catholic ethos of these schools is bound to suffer.

The consequences of government funding are especially evident in the sphere of social services. For example, Catholic Charities in Boston, Massachusetts, felt compelled to cease adoption services in April 2006 after it was refused an exemption from a state law requiring state-funded agencies to provide support to same-sex couples. One year later the En-

9. See Joseph O'Keefe and Bernadette O'Keeffe, "Directions for Research in Catholic Education in the USA and the UK," ibid., 297–310, at 302.

10. A study published in 2009 of principals of Catholic schools in Australia found that the majority of lay principals felt they had insufficient formation for the task and they lacked opportunities for reading. See Angelo Belmonte and Neil Cranston, "The Religious Dimension of Lay Leadership in Catholic Schools," *Catholic Education* 12 (2009): 294–319.

11. Gerald Grace, *Catholic Schools: Mission, Markets and Morality* (London: Routledge/Falmer, 2002), 37.

glish government legislated that private adoption agencies that refuse to serve gay and lesbian couples would no longer receive funding, resulting in the potential annual loss of about $9 million to Catholic social services. Several agencies have reluctantly agreed to abide by the legislation. The church argued that the legislation offended its moral teaching, that a traditional marital setting is better for children than placement with a same-sex couple, and that the rights of one social group, GLBT people, were being given priority over the rights of Christians. In the state of Victoria, Australia, the government effectively decriminalized abortion in 2008, introducing legislation that is among the most liberal in the world. Since Victoria has fifteen Catholic hospitals that account for approximately one-third of all births, this legislation threatens their existence. Archbishop Denis Hart of Melbourne warned that in the worst-case scenario, if a government is determined to enforce such laws the church might have to withdraw from hospital ministry altogether.[12]

Declining Resources

In the United States there has been a significant decline in the number of Catholic schools: in 1965 there were 13,000 schools enrolling 5.6 million students, but in 1995, despite the fact that the Catholic population had doubled since 1965, there had been a drop to 8,220, with a total enrollment of just 2.6 million students. By 2007 the number of schools had fallen to 7,500. Almost one in five Catholic schools has closed down in the last decade.[13] There are several reasons for this:

- As Catholics become increasingly mainstream they are less likely to send their children to parochial schools.

- Lay staffing costs have risen dramatically as religious depart from schools; in 1950, 90% of the teachers in Catholic schools in the USA were religious who received minimal financial payment for their work, but by 1967 the percentage had dropped to 58% and today it is 4%.[14]

---

12. See www.theage.com.au/national/catholichospitals-threaten-to-defy-abort-law-20080923-4, accessed 20 November 2011.

13. For an analysis of the problems confronting Catholic high schools in the United States see James L. Heft, *Catholic High Schools: Facing the New Realities* (New York: Oxford University Press, 2011), 5–14.

14. See Gilbert Cruz, "Looking for Solutions to the Catholic-School Crisis," *Time* (12 October 2009), at www.time.com/time/nation/article/0,8599,1929589,00 .html, accessed 21 November 2011.

- The decline is especially concentrated in inner-city urban areas where low-income, Hispanic, non-Catholic, minority families make up the school populations.

- There has been a decline in donations that traditionally helped subsidize poorer schools, sometimes due to disenchantment following sex scandals.

Joseph O'Keefe, SJ, of Boston College complained in 2005 that the traditional parochial school structure cannot meet the diverse, complex demands of the twenty-first century, at least in urban centers.[15] Parishes and dioceses are trying to run the schools according to structures that are now out of date; only innovative methods will save the schools in the poorer suburbs, but this policy is evoking significant resistance.[16] The increasing withdrawal of the church from the education of minorities in the poorer inner cities in the United States for financial reasons is extremely disturbing. Also, Catholic schools in England and Wales have been criticized for their hesitancy in facing up to the consequences of pluralism in its various forms: of Christian denominations, of religious faiths in society, and ethnic pluralism in urban areas.

Fundamental Tension

Figure 3.1 describes in diagram form the fundamental tension in all contemporary ministries between "the mission" of a Catholic institution and what can be termed "the business." The term "Catholic identities" means the church-*engaging*-with-the-contemporary-world, that is, the mythology of the life, death, and resurrection of Jesus Christ, engaging-with-the-world as *mediating* through such realities as the Scriptures, the church, its magisterium, authentic tradition, theology, sacraments, liturgies, moral and social teachings, "culture champions" such as institutional founders, refounders, and all values-committed people (chap. 4). The process of *engaging* and *mediating* is expressed in an ever-changing variety of Catholic identities. In Catholic institutions "the world" or "the business" consists of such realities as: people's needs, their cultures, institutional realities such as employer-employee relations, government

---

15. See Joseph O'Keefe, "How to Save Catholic Schools: Let the Revitalization Begin," at www.shc.edu/theolibrary/edu.htm, accessed 15 November 2011.

16. See comments by John Eriksen at www.time.com/time/nation/article /0,8599,1929589.00.html, accessed 12 December 2011.

standards, and funding requirements. The diagram demonstrates that it is "the mission" that should be the driving force, or the senior partner, in the tension. All decisions should be made in light of mission. However, there is constant danger that administrators will concentrate on meeting the challenges of "the business" side and be less concerned with the demands of "the mission," which are seen to be unimportant, "soft," unrealistic, or unworldly. Compared with the world of financial planning or the meeting of professional standards, the issues relating to "the mission" are viewed as rather quaint and irrelevant.

The Church engaging with . . . . "the business of" the World

Life, death, resurrection of
Christ as mediated through:

Scripture, e.g.:	People's needs
Good Samaritan parable values:	
respect/compassion	Postmodern culture, e.g.:
equity	individualism,
solidarity: option for poor	economic rationalism
community	
excellence	
Church magisterium/teachings/	Institutional cultures, e.g.:
tradition:	employer/employee
doctrines	relations
ethical principles	government policies
social teachings	
Symbols/rituals	
behaviors	
liturgies/sacraments	
"Culture champions," e.g.:	
institutional founders	
and refounders, values-	
committed persons	

Figure 3.1 Catholic Identities

Institutional "Splitting": Explanation

This process of branding one pole in the mission/business tension as "good" and the other as "irrelevant" is technically called "splitting," a fairly predictable symptom of organizations that are experiencing enormous pressure resulting from the speed of change. For example, in healthcare change "has become so rapid, so complex, so turbulent, and so unpredictable that it is sometimes called simply chaos."[17] But the human person or organization cannot live permanently in chaos. It is too terrifying. Hence they look for forms or frames to contain it.[18] In *splitting* people seek unconsciously to contain their anxieties in dysfunctional ways by projecting those anxieties and fears onto an external individual or group.[19] The projecting group judges itself to be "good" and the victim of the projection is judged to be "bad." The "bad" is assumed to be the cause of all the fears and "evils" being experienced.

That is, those who experience the "evils" are unable to cope with them personally (or as groups), so they take the easier option of degrading whatever they see as unimportant. They "split off" what is negative in their experience and project it onto others. This results in a form of fundamentalism in which complex issues and problems are reduced to simplified problems or causes (*"they* are to blame for *all* my problems"). The feelings are so high that normally reasoned arguments questioning the simplicity of the degrading process cannot be heard. The contemporary rise of extreme nationalism in Western democracies, with its anti-immigrant dynamic, is an example of splitting. In the midst of rapid social and economic changes people feel threatened; they want to feel good again, so the more immigrants are marked as "bad" or "useless for the economy" the more the locals feel good and in control of the threatening chaos.

It can also happen that "the mission" can be overemphasized to the detriment of "the business"; the language of mission can be used as a means to escape reality. It becomes the "good," and "the business" becomes an "evil of the profane world." The mission is spoken about and

---

17. W. Jack Duncan, Peter M. Ginter, and Linda E. Swayne, *Strategic Management of Health Care Organizations* (Oxford: Blackwell, 1995), 9.

18. C. Fred Alford, "The Group as a Whole or Acting Out the Missing Leader," *International Journal of Group Psychotherapy* 45 (1995): 125–42, at 133.

19. For fuller explanation, see I. M. Lyth, "A Case Study in the Functioning of Social Systems as a Defense against Anxiety: A Report on a Study of the Nursing Service of a General Hospital," *Human Relations* 13 (1960): 95–121.

praised for its inspiring beauty, as something "holy," not to be polluted through contact with the profane world of "the business." This false theology is as destructive as an overemphasis on business management, planning, or the achievement of academic acceptance. Anne Schaef and Diane Fassel have shown that the exaltation of the mission and the downplaying of business realities can be a form of addiction for a group. Administrators and employees can "become hooked on the promise of the mission and choose not to look at how the system is operating." The failings of the healthcare facility are dismissed "because [the latter] has a lofty mission."[20] The mission is used to camouflage injustices and bad business practices in the facilities. The fact is that both sides of the tension are necessary: "the mission" *and* "the business." But it is the mission that must be the senior partner in the tension, that which drives all decision making. The mission is not something to be considered from time to time; rather, it must permeate all decisions in "the business."

Particular Ministries: Identities' Challenges

Schools

The purpose of a Catholic school is to foster a learning atmosphere in which pupils can develop "an integration of faith and culture."[21] Given the summary of challenges listed above, this is not an easy task. Its enormity is further heightened by the fact that pupils come from a postmodern environment, with all its complex pressures. It is so easy for the schools to absorb in an unquestioning manner the negative values of the wider culture. Tertiary institutions such as universities, for example, are increasingly viewed by governments in utilitarian terms, that is, they are to be judged according to their contribution to the economic prosperity of their countries. The more they become engines of economic growth and technological advance the more money they will receive from governments and private donors.[22] Inevitably this market-oriented emphasis places growing pressure on all other Catholic

20. Anne W. Schaef and Diane Fassel, *The Addictive Organization* (San Francisco: Harper & Row, 1990), 123.

21. Sacred Congregation for Catholic Education, *The Catholic School* (Sydney: St Pauls Publications, 1977), 33.

22. See Stefan Collini, *What Are Universities For?* (London: Penguin, 2012), 3–19.

educational institutions, such as schools that prepare students for university education, to accept the same values, which are contrary to the Catholic tradition. As John Henry Cardinal Newman writes, the aim of university education is knowledge for its own sake: "a university training . . . aims at raising the intellectual tone of society, at cultivating the public mind, at purifying the national taste."[23] Drew Faust in her inaugural address as president of Harvard in 2007 echoes this view: "A university is not results in the next quarter. . . . It is about learning that molds a lifetime, learning that transmits the heritage of millennia; learning that shapes the future."[24]

Catholic Universities

The American politician and sociologist David Carlin believes that the Catholic identities of Catholic colleges and universities have since the 1960s "grown increasingly tenuous." He concludes that "Catholic colleges seem to be traveling the same road many Protestant colleges journeyed in the nineteenth and early twentieth centuries—a road leading to complete secularization, to complete loss of religious identity."[25] Peter Steinfels, former senior religion correspondent of *The New York Times*, writing in 2003, concluded that Catholic educators, in assessing the Catholic character of Catholic colleges and universities, either denied there is a problem or were overcome by fear if they openly emphasized "anything distinctively Catholic, or even generally religious, in recruiting a faculty, designing a curriculum, or regulating student life."[26] It was thought that if they did so they would jeopardize their reputation in the academic world. Philosophy departments, for example, anxiously avoided any positive references to the past achievements of Catholic philosophy or its connection with theology. Steinfels found

23. See John H. Newman, "Discourse VII: Knowledge Viewed in Relation to Professional Skill" (1852), in Ian T. Ker, ed., *The Idea of a University: Defined and Illustrated* (Oxford: Clarendon Press, 1976), 137–61, at 154.

24. Drew Faust, at www.president.harvard.edu/speeches/fausst/071012_installation.php, accessed 18 June 2012.

25. David R. Carlin, cited by Michael Buckley, "The Catholic University and the Promise Inherent in Its Identity," in John P. Langan, ed., *Catholic Universities in Church and Society: A Dialogue on* Ex Corde Ecclesiae (Washington, DC: Georgetown University Press, 1993), 74–89, at 75.

26. Peter Steinfels, *A People Adrift: The Crisis of the Roman Catholic Church in America* (New York: Simon & Schuster, 2003), 138.

that many institutions coped with the problem by relegating the institution's Catholicity to their theology departments or academically "safe" student activities such as liturgies, retreats, and other events arranged by campus ministry offices, or to the counseling offered in residence halls or psychological services. Many would avoid, mirroring society's postmodern suspicion of religious institutions, any reference to the fact that their universities were ministries of the institutional church. It was "safer" to emphasize instead a university's historical links with a particular religious congregational founder. The fundamental reason, Steinfels claims, why Catholic educators and administrators resist publicly stressing the Catholic identities of their institutions "arises from the assumption that there is really only one model for academic excellence and authentic inquiry, which is represented by the benchmark secular universities and liberal arts colleges."[27] It is assumed everything is open to question without any moral restraints or references to religion.

Father Edward Malloy, CSC, the former president of the University of Notre Dame, fears for the future of Catholic higher educational institutions, believing they may follow the example of the once faith-based universities of Harvard, Princeton, and Yale. These institutions rejected their religious identities as they became more academically sophisticated and mature. He argues that if "it happens, it will not be by way of a vote, but simply by default."[28] Malloy is deeply concerned about the issue of hiring faculty members and administrators. A Catholic university cannot maintain its Catholicity, Malloy explains, "in the absence of a core group of committed Catholic faculty."[29] It is difficult to obtain such a group. Not all faculty members who claim to be Catholic are in fact committed to the Catholic mission of the university. Some of the most dedicated members are in fact not Catholic. A further challenge to maintaining Catholic identities is lack of common knowledge of Catholic principles and practices among entrants to colleges and universities.[30]

Philip Gleason, professor emeritus of history at Notre Dame University, in his assessment of Catholic higher education in the United

---

27. Ibid., 141.
28. Edward A. Malloy, "The Religious Impact of Catholic Education: Is There a Gap between What Catholic Universities Proclaim and What They Practice?," 1–19, in Francis J. Butler, ed., *American Catholic Identity: Essays in an Age of Change* (Kansas City, MO: Sheed & Ward, 1994), 18.
29. Ibid., 13.
30. See ibid., 7–8.

States in 1995 found that only a small number of institutions had completely abandoned their Catholic character. However, he significantly commented that "the crisis is not that Catholic educators do not want their institutions to remain Catholic, but that they are no longer sure what remaining Catholic means."[31] John Wilcox, professor of religious studies at Manhattan College, wrote in 2000 that "many administrators, trustees, faculty, and students are still not sure what Catholic identity means and why it has become such an important issue."[32] Though these educational institutions have been fully "modernized in institutional terms," Gleason writes, the need to clarify their Catholic identities "presents itself more imperiously than ever."[33]

In their evaluation of Jesuit colleges and universities in the United States, Peter McDonough and Eugene Bianchi emphasize the consequences of depending on public funding. This "has inhibited and indeed prevented them from characterizing themselves as pervasively religious."[34] Since the 1960s their emphasis on secular excellence has affected the way these institutions have recruited faculty members, basing the choices on their academic qualifications without much consideration for their religious affiliation or commitment to the academic mission of the church.[35] Steinfels comments that the "question of Catholic identity is . . . inescapably linked to hiring policies. This is a point of enormous delicacy." He then quotes George Marsden, who has analyzed the secularization of America's Protestant colleges and universities:

> Once a church-related institution adopts the policy that it will hire simply "the best qualified candidates," it is simply a matter of time until its faculty will have an ideological profile essentially like that of the faculty at every other mainstream university. The first loyalties of the faculty members will be to the national cultures of their professions rather than

31. Philip Gleason, *Contending with Modernity: Catholic Higher Education in the Twentieth Century* (Oxford: Oxford University Press, 1995), 320.

32. John R. Wilcox, "Religious Identity: A Critical Issue in Catholic Higher Education," xv–xvi, in idem and Irene King, eds., *Enhancing Religious Identity: Best Practices from Catholic Campuses* (Washington, DC: Georgetown University Press, 2000), xv.

33. Gleason, *Contending with Modernity*, 322.

34. Peter McDonough and Eugene C. Bianchi, *Passionate Uncertainty: Inside the American Jesuits* (Berkeley: University of California Press, 2002), 212.

35. Ibid.

to any local or ecclesiastical traditions. . . . [It] becomes impossible to reverse the trend and the church tradition becomes vestigial.[36]

A comment of a Catholic layman, a professor of English at Boston College, is relevant: "There is great . . . failure of imagination about how to incorporate the non-Catholic world into the Catholic ethos, without watering down the latter, or distorting the former."[37] The consequence is that Catholic institutions lose all sense of religious uniqueness. Religious identity is reduced to "icons and symbols, rituals and barely tangible meanings—the atmospherics—whose consequences for action are elusive."[38]

In 2006 Melanie Morey and Father John Piderit, SJ, published their conclusions from the first in-depth cultural analysis of the Catholic character of Catholic universities and colleges in the United States. Their comments on the Catholic identities of these institutions are disturbing. While most identify themselves as Catholic in their mission statements, nonetheless there is "almost universal resistance to using rich Catholic language," which indicates "that institutional self-identification with Catholicism is still less than robust"[39] at many institutions. In interview conversations with senior administrators the researchers felt that they "were all using the same script when speaking about religious culture—a script that had been sanitized for the sake of offending no one."[40] They concluded that many senior administrators were "seemingly more committed to the religious sensibilities of non-Catholics than they are to reclaiming symbolic religious language that is clearly 'Catholic.'"[41] This timidity on the part of colleges and universities about identifying themselves in prophetic ways as Catholic does not augur well for the future.

This has also been the dramatic fate of numerous non-Catholic educational establishments, as Malloy has written. Universities such as Harvard, Yale, and Princeton no longer claim any relationship to their founding churches or denominations. In fact, at times these formerly

36. Steinfels, *A People Adrift*, citing George Marsden, "Catholic Identity," 152.
37. Steinfels, *A People Adrift*, 231.
38. Ibid., 233–34.
39. Melanie M. Morey and John J. Piderit, *Catholic Higher Education: A Culture in Crisis* (Oxford: Oxford University Press, 2006), 220.
40. Ibid.
41. Ibid., 221.

Protestant institutions of higher learning can be openly hostile toward their Christian roots. In effect, argues Marsden in his analysis of these institutions, nonbelief has been established as the only valid perspective.[42] Those familiar with the ancient colleges of the universities of Cambridge and Oxford will recognize the same drift away from their founding Christian roots. Significant colleges are blessed with deeply Christian names—Jesus, Christ, Corpus Christi, Trinity, Emmanuel, St John—but the titles have ceased to have any religious significance. From the Reformation to early last century most colleges were intimately accountable to the Anglican Church for their religious ethos. This is no longer the case.

Healthcare

At no previous time has health and care of the aged in the Western world faced a more chaotic and threatening environment. We struggle to move from a hospital to a community focus, from an emphasis on illness to wellness, from a biomedical to a holistic model of healing, from simple to complex technologies, from patient passivity to collaborative interaction, from once independent institutions to mergers with or acquisitions of former competitors in order to remain viable. Costs are escalating and populations aging, while people's expectations of healthcare facilities continue to rise. There are increasingly complex medico-ethical challenges. Then there is the administrative burden of coping with changes in funding sources and local and federal regulations.[43]

In the United States the healthcare systems that belong to the Catholic Health Association form the largest non-government non-profit healthcare sector. However, moral theologian Father Richard McCormick, SJ, contended in 1995 that many non-profit hospitals will

---

42. See George M. Marsden, *The Soul of the American Academy: From Protestant Establishment to Established Nonbelief* (New York: Oxford University Press, 1994), and idem and Bradley J. Longfield, eds., *The Secularization of the Academy* (New York: Oxford University Press, 1992). Marsden sees the same overwhelming forces in the academic world in general that are marginalizing Christianity and calls for Catholic education to make a major effort to examine the implications of faith today. The same challenge could be directed at Catholic healthcare. See also the comments by Charles E. Curran, "The Catholic Identity of Catholic Institutions," *Theological Studies* 58 (1997): 90–108.

43. See Gerald A. Arbuckle, *Humanizing Healthcare Reforms* (London and Philadelphia: Jessica Kingsley, 2013), 1–10.

find it harder to support themselves as competition for patients from for-profit facilities intensifies. He argued that it would be increasingly difficult to obtain funds to serve the poor because managed-care organizations (that is, healthcare insurance systems that control the costs and quality of healthcare) will resist subsidizing the uninsured, and cutbacks in Medicare and Medicaid may well continue. The situation has not changed much since he made these comments, though the health reforms introduced by President Obama may help to alleviate the situation somewhat. He ended with this challenging question: "How do we save the souls of these institutions as they maneuver through a competitive minefield?"[44] The fact that a significant number of mission statements in Catholic hospitals in the United States do not refer to Jesus Christ is a disturbing fact. A sample of twenty-five mission statements from Catholic hospitals and healthcare systems in the United States shows that only twelve specifically use the words "Jesus" or "Christ." Since the teachings and actions of Jesus Christ are foundational to the integrity of Catholic healthcare identity and mission,[45] it is not sufficient to use phrases like "carrying on the traditions of the Sisters." It is not the traditions of the Sisters that is to be the primary concern in Catholic healthcare, but the healing mission of Jesus Christ.

In healthcare facilities the critically important people are sponsors, trustees, directors of boards, CEOs, and other major executives. They not only need to be motivated by Catholic healthcare values in their personal and professional lives; they are required to have ready access to the fundamental theological information that is the source of these values. However, the success of a healthcare facility in these turbulent times depends more on the CEO's creative ability, competence, and drive than on the work of any other individual.[46] The CEO, as delegated by the board, has to ensure that the mission permeates all decision making and action. For this reason he or she must believe in the philosophy of Catholic healthcare. But the warning to Catholic healthcare facilities is the same as that given above to our educational institutions, namely, that as long as the hiring and orientation of key staff members imitate

44. Richard A. McCormick, "The Catholic Hospital Today: Mission Impossible?," *Origins* 24, no. 39 (16 March 1995): 648–53, at 653.

45. See Carol Taylor, "Roman Catholic Health Care Identity and Mission: Does Jesus Language Matter?," *Christian Bioethics* 7: 29–47.

46. See John R. Katzenbach and Douglas K. Smith, *The Wisdom of Teams* (New York: Harper-Business, 1994), 45.

secular standards and do not take into account the religious mission and vision of their Christian founding, the Catholic identities of these facilities will surely disappear. More will be said of Catholic healthcare facilities in chapter 7.

"The New Evangelization": Renewal or Refounding?

In the Old and New Testaments chaos is not once and for all dead matter or sterile nothingness. It is described in terms of confusion, darkness, weariness, emptiness, nothingness, but carries with it the notion of indeterminacy and potentiality (for example, see Gen 1:1 and Psalm 88). Creation in its entirety is pictured as being constantly in danger of falling back into destructive chaos; only God as Creator can ultimately control chaos and order. As God explains to Job, in life's journey as God's face turns away from us and we encounter the fear-evoking force of darkness and uncertainty we come into contact with the chaos out of which we were made and the lessons it symbolizes (Job 41). The primary motif or symbolic use of chaos is that through God's creative power and mercy radically new and vigorous life can spring up, but this cannot happen without human cooperation. To be creative, therefore, the experience of darkness must be openly acknowledged and personally/corporately owned. We cannot learn from this ordeal if we deny it is happening to us. That is, we can encounter afresh—if we choose to do so—the mythical roots of our being, namely, our own powerlessness, and at the same time the saving, re-creative, energizing power of God.

There is no doubting the increasing chaos in the contemporary church and its ministries, as chapters 1 and 2 of this book describe. This chaos, that is, the dramatic breakdown of order, can still be a catalyst for an immense surge of faith-inspired evangelization because it can force us to look for radically new ways to preach the Good News, as the old pastoral methods are simply no longer effective in this postmodern age. The Gospel must be drawn into a dynamic interaction with contemporary issues, for example, secularism, world poverty, ecological crises. We desperately need new organizations, structures, and methods of evangelizing a constantly changing world. So enormous is the task and so great are the risks involved that no longer is the phrase "renewal of the church" adequate to convey the immensity of the challenge confronting us. A fresh expression is necessary. Hence I speak of the process of *refounding* Catholic identities, that is, of finding and implementing *radically* new ways of evangelizing a rapidly secularizing world. This is more akin to the legendary phoenix—a rebirth—than the gentle, refreshing breeze that "renewal" has come to connote. Those who lead this rebirth I describe in the following chapter as refounding persons. These people are not anti-tradition. On the contrary, they recognize that the fundamental challenge confronting the church's leaders is to guide the awkward, uneven, and unending movement of adapting the Gospel message to an ever-changing society without at the same time brokering or blowing away the sense of continuity with the past that provides us with the mythological roots of our identity.

The focus of the synod of bishops in 2012 was "The New Evangelization," enthusiastically encouraged by Benedict XV1, and in brief this calls for the reawakening of the missionary heart of the church in the midst of the prevailing disarray. The *Lineamenta*, the preparatory document for the synod, describes the postmodern challenges the church must face, particularly secularism, "a mentality in which God is completely or partially left out of life and human consciousness,"[47] relativism, a hedonistic and consumer-oriented mentality, fundamentalism, sects, and the impact of globalization.[48] The language throughout the document is that of refounding, not renewal—for example: "The new evangelization is a frame-of-mind, a courageous manner of acting."[49] It means that Christianity needs "to show boldness . . .[50] requiring us to find new approaches . . . so as 'to be Church' in today's ever-changing social and cultural situations,"[51] to "go beyond boundaries and broaden horizons. . . . Today, a 'business as usual' attitude can no longer be the case."[52] There must be "a deliberative process of devising new models of 'being Church' . . . in today's post-ideological era, to continue to maintain the church's identity as missionary. In other words, in the variety of her models, the Church must not fail to be seen as a 'domestic Church' and 'The People of God.' "[53] There are three broad types of evangelization listed in the document, though "it is unthinkable to create barriers between them or to put them in watertight compartments";[54] they are:

---

47. *Lineamenta, "The New Evangelization"* (Nairobi: Paulines, 2011), 24.
48. See ibid., 24.
49. Ibid., 25.
50. Ibid., 27.
51. Ibid., 32.
52. Ibid., 34.
53. Ibid., 31.
54. Ibid. This is a quotation from John Paul II (*Redemptoris Missio* 34).

ongoing pastoral care of practicing Catholics; proclaiming the Gospel to people who are not Christians; and particular emphasis that must be given to those Catholics in the West "who lead totally unchristian lives and . . . [who] maintain some links to the faith but have little or poor knowledge of it."[55]

Refounding demands that we return to the very roots of the church's founding, with the focus on Jesus Christ. Thus we need "to create in every place and time the conditions for . . . personal encounter of individuals with Jesus Christ."[56] This means that we must "rekindle in ourselves the impetus of the Church's beginnings and allow ourselves to be filled with the ardour of the apostolic preaching which followed Pentecost."[57] Refounding that missionary zeal requires that we spread the Gospel "in conformity with magisterial teaching."[58] The process of evangelization will be characterized by dialogue,[59] "charity, witness, proclamation, celebration, listening and sharing."[60]

The document is inspiring, but there are very serious interconnected obstacles to its implementation. *First*, what ultimately is the ecclesiology that is to underpin the new evangelization: that of Vatican II or restorationism? Despite the emphasis in the document on Vatican II ecclesiology, in practice pre-conciliar restorationist ecclesiology is actively present in the contemporary church (see chap. 2). Restorationist theology does not encourage the listening and dialogue the document particularly emphasizes. *Second*, though the document strongly urges local churches and individuals "to show boldness" in finding new ways to evangelize contemporary cultures, restorationist forces aggressively resist such pastoral creativity. Fine rhetoric conflicts with reality. A climate of fear haunts the church, fear of being reported not just to one's local bishop but to Rome itself. This is not an atmosphere in which bold new pastoral innovation that goes to the roots of postmodern secularism and relativism can be fostered. That is, unless the institutional church is prepared to break the culture of fear and distrust in which we live, refounding the church, or in the words of the *Lineamenta* "devising

55. *Lineamenta*, 32.
56. Ibid., 38.
57. Ibid., 70.
58. Ibid., 12.
59. Ibid., 23.
60. Ibid., 40.

new models of 'being Church,'" so lauded in theory in the document, cannot be achieved.

Summary

- The chaos in the church is everywhere to be seen and our ministries mirror this. The self-confidence of Catholic bishops, priests, educators, school superintendents, and teachers has waned; they are no longer so sure that what they are doing is effective and valuable.[61] In the words of the late Cardinal Carlo Martini, "Our culture has grown old . . . the bureaucracy of our Churches is growing out of proportion, our liturgies and our vestments are pompous. . . ."[62]

- There are still people at all levels in the church who would deny this chaos and the depth of its seriousness. There are those who, while admitting the church is in chaotic times, still think that all that has to be done is to restore the structures and ministerial methods of the past and all will be well. Others, while affirming that inner personal and institutional conversion is necessary, uncritically turn to "new age"-influenced management theories and psychological studies to provide them with the "magic potion" to solve their institutional problems. When one potion fails they turn to another. And so it goes.[63]

- The prophets of the Old Testament warn against such denial. They also found people who wanted them to gloss over the gravity of what was happening to them; they wanted the prophets to flatter them, to tell lies to avoid the hard truths: "Do not prophesy to us what is right; speak to us smooth things, prophesy illusions" (Jer 30:10). If we deny the chaos in our ministries we are refusing to acknowledge that this can be a grace-filled chance to create radically new ways to evangelize in today's postmodern environment.

- The next two chapters explain the multidisciplinary refounding model and how it is to be applied to the contemporary needs of our confused church and ministries.

61. Andrew M. Greeley, *The New Agenda* (Garden City, NY: Doubleday, 1973), 266.

62. Carlo Cardinal Martini, in *The Tablet* (8 September, 2012), 8.

63. See John Micklethwait and Adrian Wooldridge, *The Witch Doctors: What the Management Gurus Are Saying, Why It Matters and How to Make Sense of It* (London: Heinemann, 1996), 365–74.

Chapter Four

Founding and Refounding Identities

The future of the Church cannot be planned and built
up merely by the application of generally recognized
Christian principles: it needs the courage of an ultimately
charismatically inspired, creative imagination.[1] *(Karl Rahner)*

I will open my mouth in a parable;
I will utter dark sayings from of old,
things that we have heard and known,
that our ancestors have told us.
We will not hide them from our children;
we will tell the coming generation the
glorious deeds of the Lord . . .
and the wonders he has done. (Ps 78:2-4)

This chapter explains that:

• culture is a process of struggling to contain the disruptive forces of chaos

• an experience of chaos is an essential precondition for innovative action

1. Karl Rahner, *The Shape of the Church to Come* (New York: Seabury Press, 1974), 47.

- refounding, in times of chaos, is a process of storytelling whereby the original founding myth is rearticulated and applied to contemporary needs
- refounding persons, with their collaborators, shape new identities
- refounding persons are significantly gifted with imagination, intuitive thinking, and courage to act; they are contemplatives who act

The ultimate foundation of all Christian identities is that we have been personally created in the image and likeness of God (Gen 1:26), redeemed by the suffering, death, and resurrection of Jesus Christ, and called into intimate friendship with our Savior. This gives us a dignity beyond anything the human mind could ever dream of attaining. The overriding purpose of all pedagogy, therefore, is to foster in ourselves and others a personal encounter and friendship with Jesus Christ. Through this we discover that God "loves us so much, we also ought to love one another" (1 John 4:11). Hence the overall aim of this and subsequent chapters is to discover imaginative and creative ways to foster and sustain this encounter within the contemporary turmoil in society and the church. "Being Christian," writes Pope Benedict XVI, "is not the result of an ethical choice or a lofty idea, but the encounter with an event, a person, which gives life a new horizon and a decisive direction."[2]

When, on 28 August 1963, Martin Luther King Jr. masterfully delivered his momentous "I have a dream . . ." speech he produced a superb example of the subversive power of narrative. In his call for racial equality and an end to discrimination King inspired people to transform their lives and the legal, economic, and political structures of the American nation. By brilliantly applying the biblical belief that all people are equal before God he called not for superficial changes to society but for its radical revitalization. This was a call for refounding, not for a shallow tinkering with existing laws and behaviors. This process of relating the founding myth to contemporary situations is the narrative of refounding, through which new institutional and personal identities emerge.

---

2. Benedict XVI, encyclical letter *On Christian Love* (Strathfield: St Pauls Publications, 2006), 5.

This chapter further develops, through a series of axioms, the theme of refounding in times of turmoil that was briefly explained in the last chapter.[3] As explained in chapter 1, narratives can evoke the revitalization of the moral imagination of people because of their singular power to re-vision reality. This is because particular narratives allow people to "try new ideas, new values, new ways of being-in-the-world."[4] The reader's existing world is suddenly challenged by the narrative; new and imaginative possibilities of being and acting are presented. The narrative's content has the radical ability to "disturb and rearrange"[5] the reader's own relation to life. The subversive dynamics of refounding narratives will be explained in this chapter through a series of axioms.

Definition

Refounding is the process whereby people, confronted by personal and/or institutional chaos, relive the founding myth of their group. They find themselves so inspired by their experience that they imaginatively and creatively search for radically innovative ways to relate it to contemporary needs, thus forming new identities. This search is conducted through narrative speech and action.

Axiom 1: *A culture is a process of struggling to contain chaos, yet an experience of chaos is an essential precondition for innovative action.*

A culture is a human creation that protects us from the fear-evoking dark abyss of radical disorder that is chaos. It is "an area of meaning carved out of a vast mass of meaninglessness, a small clearing of lucidity in a formless, dark, almost ominous jungle."[6] The author of Psalm 69 describes

---

3. This chapter expands and updates material I have published on refounding in *Out of Chaos: Refounding Religious Congregations* (New York: Paulist Press, 1988), *Refounding the Church: Dissent for Leadership* (Maryknoll, NY: Orbis Books, 1993), and *Healthcare Ministry: Refounding the Mission in Tumultuous Times* (Collegeville, MN: Liturgical Press, 2000).

4. Paul Ricoeur, "The Function of Fiction in Shaping Reality," in *Man and World* 12 (1979): 123–41, at 134.

5. Paul Ricoeur, "On Interpretation," 1–20 in idem, *From Text to Action: Essays in Hermeneutics II*, ed. Kathleen Blamey and John B. Thompson (Evanston, IL: Northwestern University Press, 1991), 6.

6. Peter Berger, *The Sacred Canopy: Elements of a Sociological Theory of Religion* (New York: Doubleday, 1969), 23.

in agonizing terms what he feels when the protective supports of his culture fall apart and he experiences the terrifying "ominous jungle" of chaos:

> I sink in deep mire, where there is no foothold; I have come into deep waters, and the flood sweeps over me.
> I am weary with my crying; my throat is parched . . .
> Do not let the flood sweep over me, or the deep swallow me up, or the Pit close its mouth over me. (Ps 69:2, 3, 15)

Change, at times even the faintest whisper of it, substitutes ambiguity and uncertainty for the known, but we yearn for the predictable that frees us from the fear of the unknown. As management consultant Margaret Wheatley comments, "We are not comfortable with chaos, even in our thoughts, and we want to move out of confusion as quickly as possible."[7] Yet chaos can be a freeing, though subversive, experience, for it breaks the crust of custom or habit, allowing the imagination[8] to dream of alternative or radically different ways of doing things. When members of a group own their own chaos, admitting their powerlessness, they are able to return to the sacred time of the founding of the group. Then they can ask fundamental questions about the group's origins, about what is essential to the founding vision and should be kept, and what is accidental and should be allowed to be discarded.

The poet John Keats correctly believed that the foundation of creativity is "negative capability . . . when a [person] is capable of being in uncertainties, mysteries, doubts, without any irritable reaching after fact and reason."[9] Saint John of the Cross would have agreed with this insight. In the first stanza of his *Canticle* he expresses his own experience of being thrown into the murky loneliness of his imprisonment at the abusive hands of his Carmelite confrères:

---

7. Margaret Wheatley, *Leadership and the New Science* (San Francisco: Berrett-Koehler, 1994), 149.

8. Walter Brueggemann writes: "Imagination is the peculiar province of . . . artists of all kinds; it is for that reason that artists are . . . always seen to be troublemakers whom establishment types view with suspicion. The vocation of the artist is to provide a *sub-version* of reality that insistently *subverts* the ordinary." *Disruptive Grace* (Minneapolis: Fortress Press, 2011), 296.

9. John Keats, quoted by I. Menzies Lyth, *The Dynamics of the Social: Selected Essays* (London: Free Association, 1989), 3.

Where have you hidden
Beloved, and left me groaning?
You fled like a stag
Having wounded me;
I went out in search of you, and you were gone.

Paradoxically, the more John pondered this personal encounter with incredible emotional and spiritual loneliness, the more creative his writings became.[10] Other medieval mystics share this common insight: the confrontation with one's inner darkness or chaos is the condition for creative discovery of life's meanings. Dante Alighieri, in his *Divine Comedy*, describes the imaginative moment that occurs once he has acknowledged the excruciating experience of personal chaos: "after I had reached a mountain's foot . . . which had with consternation pierced my heart, upward I looked. . . . Then was the fear quieted."[11] Psychoanalyst Wilfred Bion strongly advises his colleagues to admit at times in their clinical work that they do not know the answers to the problems confronting them. He tells them to sit patiently in the darkness of chaos, the darkness of *not-knowing*, waiting: a "very faint light" can only become "visible in maximum conditions of darkness."[12] In summary, culture is a process in which the inevitable disruptive experiences of chaos can be catalysts for radical cultural and personal changes, provided, of course, that there are people with the creative imagination and courage to take advantage of the breakdown of the status quo and to do so for the right ethical motives.

Axiom 2: *Refounding is a process of storytelling whereby imaginative leaders are able to inspire people to rearticulate the founding myth and apply it to contemporary needs.*

In cultural chaos people are left without familiar symbols and rituals. The only positive way out of this chaos is for them to reenter the sacred time of their founding with imaginative leaders who can rearticulate the founding mythology in narratives adapted to a changing world. The founding mythology again becomes generative, a process well described

---

10. See comments by Iain Matthew, *The Impact of God: Soundings from St John of the Cross* (London: Hodder & Stoughton, 1995), 10–13.

11. Dante Alighieri, *The Divine Comedy*, ed. James Walsh (New York: Paulist Press, 1981), 15.

12. Wilfred Bion, cited by P. J. Casement, *Learning from the Patient* (New York: Guilford Press, 1991), 358.

by anthropologist Bronislaw Malinowski as "a narrative resurrection of a primeval reality."[13] That is, inspired by the re-owning of the founding mythology, people can be motivated to develop "quantum leap" imaginative methods that apply the original founding experience to very different contemporary conditions. Anthropologist Mircea Eliade believed there is a creation aspect behind every kind of myth and narrative. Myth, he wrote, "is always the recital of a creation; it tells how something was accomplished, began to be. It is for this reason that myth is bound up with ontology; it speaks of realities, of what really happened."[14] For him "realities" means "sacred realities," and the sacred realities belong to sacred time, the time when creation took place, whereas in profane time people carry on their ordinary business of daily living.

The "recital" of the founding myth is aptly called a *regenerative ritual*. When a people's cultural identities disintegrate, or threaten to do so, in chaotic times, their experience of reliving the original founding story provides them with new energy to create new identities that are relevant to their situation. When African Americans feel oppressed, many still recite Martin Luther King's "I have a dream. . . ." speech. It helps them to be reenergized to overcome discrimination. Regeneration rituals are not commemorative. They are always foundational or *re-creative* in their demands on people. That is, people are expected to undergo a deep interior and exterior change or revitalization; they must experience a new creation out of chaos.[15] The escape into sacred time intimates immortality, or at least the chance to rediscover meaning in life. To use Eliade's language, in regeneration rituals sacred time breaks into profane time. Sacred time is ritual time. It consists of those rites in which people reenact the holy, aboriginal events of their culture, but these are now adapted to contemporary conditions never foreseen in the original founding times.

---

13. Bronislaw Malinowski. *Magic, Science, and Religion, and Other Essays* (Glencoe, IL: Free Press, 1948), 101.

14. Mircea Eliade, *The Sacred and the Profane* (New York: Harcourt, 1959), 95.

15. See Leonard J. Biallas, *Myths, Gods, Heroes, and Saviors* (Mystic, CT: Twenty-Third Publications, 1986), 24.

Examples

In late 2011 the events of Occupy Wall Street and its many supporting groups around the world were being reported. Television screens showed members of Occupy Wall Street at Zuccotti Park, New York, and groups of people huddled together under small, fragile tents outside St. Paul's Cathedral, London. In Zuccotti Park people had congregated on an inhospitable concrete space right in the middle of the nation's top financial district; St. Paul's is also close to London's financial center. It is easy to dismiss the protesters as impractical and unrealistic, but they were anonymously and collectively refounding people; their prophetic actions constituted a narrative that challenged the rich and powerful to cease neglecting society's poor and marginalized. In their narrative they returned to the Christian mythology that we must love our neighbor, especially the poorest. Reporters recounted how the homeless and mentally ill were attracted to join the protesters for free meals and company and one spokesperson commented: "We decided we would not marginalize these people like the rest of society does. I guess, we've created our own welfare state, and I mean that in the best sense of the term." She and others organized drug counselors and social workers to offer help for their visitors.[16]

Another collective narrative of refounding that is challenging the traditional greed of capitalism is taking place at an unexpected level of society. Among a small group of influential thinkers and business people there is a growing recognition that the primary purpose of business is not to make money—the more the better. They believe that in business institutions the interests of society and people are not just to be accidentally added to what the institution is doing but should be at the very center of its concern. Members of this group believe that their firms must be more than agents for creating profit. Rather, their core mission calls them also to be instruments for achieving positive social goals in their surrounding communities and for providing significant livelihoods for those who

16. See Michael Greenberg, "Zuccotti Park: What Future?," *New York Review of Books* (10 November 2011): 12–14.

work in their institutions. They are prepared to spend time, talent, and resources on national and community projects in which people are prepared to work together for the common good. Corporate social responsibility, in brief, is to be integral to all project planning and implementation. This is surely a quiet revolution. As in the case of Occupy movements, this revolution in thinking—technically termed "creating shared value"—finds legitimacy in the Good Samaritan parable. Examples of companies making efforts to create shared value are Google, IBM, Intel, Nestle, Unilever, Johnson & Johnson, and Procter & Gamble—and even Wal-Mart.[17]

When Saint Mother Teresa would tell of her care of dying individuals she would revisit the founding mythology of her faith, a story of Christ's compassion for people on the margins of society. This motivated her to change her own life and develop radically new ways to respond to the needs of dying people in India. Many observers were so disturbed by her stories that they also felt impelled to alter their own lives and challenge society's neglect of disadvantaged people.

While living in Paris in 1964, Jean Vanier became aware of the plight of thousands of people institutionalized because of their developmental disabilities. They were shut away and treated as worthless. The world of modernity, with its exaltation of human perfectibility, could not tolerate people who were branded as humanly defective. Vanier disagreed. He returned to the founding story of Christianity: that Jesus Christ has truly chosen the foolish and the weak of this world to confound the wise and the strong (1 Cor 1:27). It is they, the foolish and the weak, who come running to the wedding feast of the Gospel (Luke 14; Matt 22). It is over them that Jesus, moved by the Holy Spirit, cries out joyfully: "Blessed are you, Father, Lord of heaven and earth, for hiding these things from the learned and the clever and revealing them to little children" (Luke 10:21).[18]

17. See Mark R. Kramer, "Creating Shared Value," *Harvard Business Review* (January 2011): 62–77, and Rosabeth Moss Kanter, "How Great Companies Think Differently," *Harvard Business Review* (November 2011), 66–78.

18. See Jean Vanier, *Letter to My Brothers and Sisters in L'Arche* (Trosly, France: L'Arche, 1996), 7.

Vanier believed that people with mental disabilities have by "their very weakness and their call to friendship and communion the ability to touch the hearts of the powerful and strong, calling them to love and to a deeper recognition of their fundamental humanity. They possess thus a healing power, bringing people to unity, renewing the church and humanity."[19]

In August 1964 he invited two men, Raphael Simi and Philippe Seux, to leave their institutions and share their lives with him in a real home.[20] Now, nearly fifty years later, there are over a hundred L'Arche communities around the world in which people that society considers healthy and whole live with those who are often marginalized because of their mental disabilities. The latter are called "core members" and the former "assistants," to emphasize the fact that the primary teachers in these communities are the "little children" of God's kingdom. Wherever it exists in the world, the aim of L'Arche is to enable people with developmental disabilities to play their full part in society. L'Arche does this through creating outward-facing communities in which people with and without disabilities can share life, affirming one another's unique values and gifts. Whenever this happens, core members and assistants are collaboratively creating new and vibrant identities for themselves; at the same time people in the wider society are being challenged to reject the stereotype that people with developmental disabilities have nothing to teach us.

Today Vanier sees the constant need for refounding L'Arche communities, that is, the need to be constantly inspired by the founding mythology of Christ's loving concern for the marginalized; otherwise the mission will die. He writes:

19. Jean Vanier, *The Founding Myth and the Evolution of Community*, Prophetic Paper 2 (1993), 7. See also reflections by Hans S. Reinders, "Being with the Disabled: Jean Vanier's Theological Realism," 467–511, in *Disability in the Christian Tradition: A Reader*, ed. Brian Brock and John Swinton (Grand Rapids, MI: Eerdmans, 2012).

20. For more details see Kathryn Spink, *The Miracle, The Message, The Story: Jean Vanier and L'Arche* (London: Darton, Longman, and Todd, 2006).

The danger is that the [founding] myth disappears completely. The real meaning of a community, its raison d'être in the church and in the world may get lost [under the pressure of routine and the human difficulties of living with people who are disabled mentally]. . . . It is because of this danger that the specific myth of the community, its sacred story, needs to be announced over and over. Without it we can slip gently into the primacy of the need for security, comfort and the need for recognition. Without the myth [that is, the founding story] that awakens and stimulates hearts, galvanizing energies, we can quickly discover the demands of community life intolerable.[21]

Vanier recognizes the truth that even founders, including himself, must sometimes become refounders in their own lifetime. Speaking of L'Arche, he writes that:

Communities continually need to listen to the Holy Spirit welcoming new challenges. They need to be continually refounded. The essential founding myth remains but the way it is incarnated is called to change. That is where the presence of wise refounders is necessary. They are able to move ahead maintaining and deepening the founding myth, pruning and cutting away things which appeared to be essential in the early years but in reality were not.[22]

In summary, refounding persons know that to lose the founding story is to lose direction and energy for action. They therefore restlessly draw other people to share their excitement and pain; together they creatively struggle to find ways to build bridges across the chasm that separates the founding mythology from contemporary realities. Refounding leaders are dreamers who do, contemplatives who act. When leaders recount the founding story in a collaborative way, others are enabled to see how their own talents and journey in life can fit into the narrative of the organization in a mutually advantageous way, giving fresh energy and new identities to the organization.

21. Vanier, *The Founding Myth*, 8–9.
22. Ibid., 9.

Axiom 3: *Refounders are not loners; they need collaborators to help refine the insight, to plan, implement, and evaluate the project.*

A refounding person

- is one who, in imitation of the shock the original founding person experienced on perceiving the gap between deeply held values and the world of his or her time,
- acutely sees a like chasm between these values and their contemporary reality,
- and moves, through creative strategies, to bridge the gulf,
- while at the same time restlessly summoning others to undergo a similar conversion, to share in the vision, and to venture into the unknown in order to implement the strategies.[23]

Refounding persons are not loners in molding new identities for institutions amid changing contexts. The implementation of a refounding insight is extremely demanding of time and energy.[24] Refounders recognize their limitations and see the need for collaborators to sharpen their understanding of their creative vision, to plan and ensure its implementation. Refounding persons commonly begin with a vague intuition of what should be done. By involving others in the planning and implementation of a project the refounding persons are slowly able to refine their insights and strategies. Randall Stross points out that Steve Jobs of Apple, in his early inventing years, was unable to delegate and collaborate with others. His most creative breakthrough did not occur until he learned to plan and work with others.[25]

Refounders and fellow-collaborators in faith-based institutions cannot collaborate unless they admit to themselves their sense of powerlessness when confronted with their own inner wasteland of fears and imperfections. Vanier, in calling communities and members of L'Arche to undertake the journey of refounding, does not soften his words:

23. See Arbuckle, *Out of Chaos*, 89.

24. See insights by Vijay Govindarajan and Chris Trimble, *The Other Side of Innovation: Solving the Execution Challenge* (Boston: Harvard Business Review Press, 2010), 75–95.

25. See Randall Stross, "What Steve Jobs Learned in the Wilderness," at www .nytimes.com/2010/10/03business/03digi.html, accessed 4 October 2010.

> Chaos and divisions will arise. . . . Many communities have had to go through terrible crises because of their lack of openness; they were convinced that they were "the inspired ones of God." These crises bring about a necessary purification and bring the community gently or not so gently back to reality. . . . They discover humility and wisdom and are obliged to open up and seek help from others.

He writes that "in the founding of a community there is always a blind spot, a collective unconscious, which flows more or less from the unconscious of the founder and his or her very human need to control. This blind spot, this fear has to be purified if the community is really called to grow and deepen. The crisis is the purification of collective unconscious." Each member is called to the same inner purification as a condition for refounding communities:

> The blind spot in each person, those secret motivations not always visible to the eye, have to be identified, owned and purified in order to discover the community as the place where we are called to be united to Jesus in the "now" of everyday living and to grow towards a greater wholeness and maturity of love and compassion. . . . This purification comes most frequently in times of [chaos]. . . . It happens as we humbly accept help, as we discover we do not have to hide our weaknesses or prove we are right, but that God manifests his strength through our weakness.[26]

Axiom 4: *Refounding people are shocked by the gap between the founding myth and contemporary reality and feel impelled to bridge that gap.*

When people are passionately excited by the original founding mythology or story of an organization they experience a sense of intense shock when they contemplate the enormity of the gap between the ideals contained in the founding myth and the reality. The following simple secular example illustrates such an experience.

26. Vanier, *The Founding Myth*, 8.

Example

Egon Ronay (1915–2010), a famous British food critic, was greatly shocked one day in 1950 when he bought a simple cup of tea from the buffet at Victoria Railway Station in London. It came from a big tea-urn at the corner of the counter, supervised by a woman who pointed to the sugar, which was "heaped in a bowl, and dangling near the bowl was a spoon, which had somehow been tied to the ceiling with string so that customers would not steal it." The vision of the spoon was for Ronay a "Damascene moment." It summarized all the horrors of British cooking at that time. He could no longer stomach the pain of the gap between the ideal of railway food service and what the cup of tea signified, so he recruited a team of inspectors to survey the quality of British food preparation and he started his immensely successful publication, "Egon Ronay's Guide to British Eateries."[27]

Faith-filled people experience what can be termed a "faith shock" as they view the gap between the founding mythology of their beliefs and the reality of the world around them. This is evident in the lives of refounding people such as Jean Vanier, Saint Mother Teresa, and Cecily Saunders.

Axiom 5: *Refounding is not synonymous with renewal.*

Refounding is not synonymous with renewal. Renewal tackles only the symptoms of problems, but refounding seeks to make "quantum-leap" responses to their causes. A significant example is the problem of local or international poverty. Renewal responses aim to improve existing methods of poverty relief, such as expediting delivery of food supplies to the poor through more efficient and speedy transport services. Refounding, however, calls for radically innovative attacks on the structures of oppression, the paucity of educational facilities, and the corruption of officials.

27. *The Economist* (26 June 2010), 91.

For twelve years (1984–1996) Steve Jobs worked with some successes and failures just renewing or improving existing computer models. However, dramatic success came only when he realized that computing in the future would simply not resemble computing in the past. Then he truly refounded Apple with the invention of the immensely successful iPod, the iPhone, and the iPad. Future computing would not simply depend on renewing conventionally shaped computers.

So also, when thinking of the church's primary task of preaching the reign of God within an ever-changing world we need apostolic or pastoral creativity of quantum-leap proportions. In other words, renewal or the refurbishing of existing pastoral strategies is insufficient in a postmodern world. Rather, we require *radically* different, as yet unimagined ways to relate the Good News to the pastoral challenges of the world, including secularism, materialism, secularization, environmental destruction, political and social oppression. When this happens the church and its ministries will assume new identities.

Axiom 6: *Since founders and refounders have above-average gifts of intuition, empathy, imagination, and creativity, they prefer an inductive manner of thinking.*

Refounding persons, like creative people in general, are self-motivating, independent but collaborative, driven by their vision, task-focused, and action-oriented. That is, they contemplate *and* act. They begin with small steps and in the process focus their initial vision, which in the beginning can be quite vague. Jessica Livingston, after examining thirty-three founding persons in secular business, commented:

> The world thinks of . . . founders as having some kind of superhuman confidence, but a lot of them were uncertain at first about starting a company. What they weren't uncertain about was making something good—or trying to fix something broken. . . . If the founders I spoke with were superhuman in any way, it was in their perseverance. . . . [Founding a company] is a process of trial and error. What guided the founders through the process was their empathy for the users.[28]

28. "Introduction," in Jessica Livingston, ed., *Founders at Work: Stories of Startups' Early Days* (New York: Apress, 2008), xvi–xviii.

Founders' thinking is noted for its originality and the ability to see the forest beyond the individual trees. They are often more emotionally open and flexible than their less creative colleagues. They have the courage to be different, non-conforming, autonomous yet adaptive, and striving. Moreover, they have sustained curiosity, dedication, intuition, and willingness to be focused on what they do. Research shows that "morning, noon, and night are all the same to creative people; they don't work by the clock. Problems may take years to solve: time has a personal, not social meaning."[29]

Intuition and imagination are vital gifts for refounding people just as for all founders. Intuition is instinctive knowledge, that is, knowledge not gained by reasoning and intelligence but acquired by what can be called a "sixth sense." Unlike deductive thinkers, who see reality through preexisting principles, refounding persons are especially experience-oriented in their thinking, that is, they begin with the reality around them and work backward to conclusions. Jobs, in refounding his Apple empire, found that his success depended on intuitive thinking and knowledge, "a very powerful thing, more powerful than intellect."[30] He began to realize over time that "an intuitive understanding and consciousness was more significant than abstract thinking and intellectual logical analysis."[31] Intuitive thinkers just feel something is right. Empathy, the ability to recognize and to some degree share feelings being experienced by another person or group, is an integral quality of intuitive thinking.[32] Not surprisingly, therefore, Jobs emphasized the importance of empathy, an intimate connection with the feelings of the customer, in Apple's marketing.[33]

29. Michael K. Badawy, quoted in A. Dale Timpe, ed. *Creativity*. Art and Science of Business Management 4 (New York: Facts on File, 1987), 179–80.

30. Steve Jobs, cited by Walter Isaacson in *Steve Jobs* (London: Little, Brown, 2011), 48.

31. Ibid., 35.

32. Jessica Livingston concludes her study of thirty-three founders of businesses: "Starting [a business] is a process of trial and error. What guided the founders through this process was their empathy for the users. They never lost sight of making things that people would want," *Founders at Work*, xviii.

33. See Isaacson, *Steve Jobs*, 78.

Case Study: Jean Vanier, Founder of L'Arche

It is evident from the study of religious congregations that founders and refounders most often are unclear about the ultimate outcome of their efforts. They are so concerned about bridging the gap between the Gospel and the world around them that the details of what is necessary to achieve this in the long term do not concern them. They even hesitate to write rules because they are uncertain about the nature and shape of the organization that is emerging. They fear to "freeze" their movements into a rigid institutional status quo while their work is evolving. This can be immensely frustrating to deductive thinkers who would wish to have structures and rules immediately in place. These qualities of founding persons, for example, are evident in Jean Vanier's establishment of L'Arche, which is not a religious congregation. As Hans Reinders explains:

> When Vanier started up the first community of L'Arche, he had no idea what he was doing. He had no plan. . . . The only thing he had was a calling that committed him to the people he had seen in . . . a mental hospital. . . . L'Arche is lived rather than thought of, so that when in Vanier's work we encounter a profound Christian vision, it is important to realize that it is only in hindsight that this vision emerged. . . . In the beginning was the deed. . . . In other words, L'Arche had to be lived before it could be envisioned.[34]

Vanier himself describes what happened: "When I think of those [first] foundations, I see how everything was given: as sign or a gift led us to another sign, another gift. It was as if we were walking on a road without knowing quite where it was leading."[35]

---

34. Reinders, "Being with the Disabled," 469–71.
35. Jean Vanier, *Ark for the Poor: The Story of L'Arche* (Toronto: Novalis, 1995), 53.

Axiom 7: *Because refounding people are constantly in danger of being marginalized, they must be motivated by faith-based patience and courage.*

For centuries there has been a desperate need for refounding people in pastoral ministries and in the institutional church itself, but especially in chaotic times such as the present. Their task is to critique or responsibly dissent from the conventional and ineffective status quo. In faith-based situations refounding persons are those who acutely see the contemporary chasm between the Gospel and secularizing cultures. They imitate the "faith shock" and reaction of pastorally refounding people through the centuries, that is, of those who originally perceived the gaps between the Gospel tradition and the world of their time. Refounding persons and their collaborators in the church are people born anew by the power of Christ and by a reliving of the founding experience of church itself. Seized by the Spirit, they yearn to adapt the inner heart of the founding experience to the new pastoral and spiritual needs of today, and they invite others to join them in their task. They have a stubbornness in faith and a humility that comes from an awareness of their own failings and their utter dependence on God and that ultimately can carry them through inevitable periods of opposition, rejection, even marginalization.

Through creative pastoral strategies the refounding person in the church collaboratively moves to bridge the ministerial gaps between the Gospel and contemporary realities. Ultimately only a profound love for Christ and the church can sustain people in such a challenge, because their involvement in the refounding process commonly leads to its own particular type of suffering and marginalization. They are especially gifted, like their counterparts in secular organizations, with qualities of imagination, creativity, and courage, as were the original founders of institutions. Some openly challenge oppressive structures in the church, while others less dramatically foster pastoral refounding strategies in their local faith communities. As an example of the latter I think of a Marist colleague, chaplain to a Catholic high school of several hundred boys. At regular liturgical celebrations he is able to hold the attention of boys of all ages through his gift of storytelling. He empathetically connects with his congregation by being able to relate the postmodern needs of his listeners to the Gospel.

I have found countless examples of other people who have been or continue to be involved in refounding ministries, especially in the area of social justice and concern for people on the margin. They take the pastoral concerns of Vatican II creatively and seriously. Efforts at refounding or reforming the institutional church, however, are far more challenging. Reforms were introduced with considerable enthusiasm immediately after Vatican II, only to be followed by increasing signs of the return to the pre-conciliar centralized Roman administration.[36] As explained in chapter 1, the contemporary restorationist movements continue to make it extremely difficult to challenge the institutional church in charity to reform itself according to Vatican II documents.

It is inevitable that an innovator becomes the object of violence, scapegoating, or marginalization simply because she or he dares to disturb the orderly security of the status quo: "The individual who strays seriously from the socially defined programs can be considered not only a fool or a knave but a madman."[37] From experience we know that individually and corporately we so dread the pain of chaos that we commonly resist it. In theory we often proclaim we are open to change, but in practice powerful inner forces move us to resistance, even in matters of seemingly little importance. Founding and refounding persons, such as questioning theologians in our contemporary church, like the prophets of the Old Testament dare to tell the truth about reality. Walter Brueggemann, when reflecting on the role of these prophets (see chap. 5), writes:

> The prophetic antidote to denial is *truth-telling* . . . an act that is sure to provoke resistance and hostility among those in denial, because it requires seeing and knowing and engaging with that which we have refused to see, know, or engage.[38]

Socrates had the habit of consistently asking awkward, razor-sharp questions of his listeners. We know what happened to him. Extreme marginalization led to death! Refounding people are uncomfortable companions as they relentlessly question conventional wisdom for the sake of the mission. It is not just the prophetic person who suffers; for an organization that opts for the comfortable status quo there is an enormous cost to be paid. Tony Judt is correct: "A closed circle of opinion or ideas into which discontent or opposition is never allowed—or allowed only

36. See Gerald A. Arbuckle, *Violence, Society, and the Church: A Cultural Critique* (Collegeville, MN: Liturgical Press, 2004), 204–5.

37. Berger, *Sacred Canopy*, 23.

38. See Walter Brueggemann, *Disruptive Grace: Reflections on God, Scripture, and the Church* (Minneapolis: Fortress Press, 2011), 138.

within circumscribed and stylized limits—loses its capacity to respond energetically or imaginatively to new challenges."[39]

In summary, any organization that domesticates its rebels has acquired its peace but lost its future. Prophets of founding and refounding in the church commonly find themselves rejected by the very people who should be supporting them, simply because the vision they proclaim of a just world in union with God is too big, too terrifying. To realize this vision people must let go of cherished positions of control and power. All this is too disturbing to people set in their ways and who fear the unexpected. When Jesus foretold his suffering in Jerusalem, as had the messianic prophets, Peter would have none of it: "God forbid it, Lord! This must never happen to you" (Matt 16:22). Jesus refused to give in to Peter's fears; he scolded Peter: "Get behind me, Satan! You are a stumbling block to me; for you are setting your mind not on divine things but on human things" (Matt 16:23). Refounding people, as prophets of the Gospel message, are people of memory and imagination. They constantly and imaginatively recall Christ's mission to the world and its disturbing qualities for the comfortable. For this reason, and following prayerful discernment, they are loyal dissenters. Out of love for the Gospel message they dissent from structures and pastoral methods that are no longer relevant in the apostolate. For this reason they are often feared and rejected.

Rejection can lead to feelings of intense loneliness, a sense of abandonment. Recall the loneliness of the Old Testament prophets: "I did not sit in the company of merrymakers, nor did I rejoice; under the weight of your hand I sat alone" (Jer 15:17). The prophet is apt to alienate the wicked as well as the pious, cynics as well as believers, yet prophets cannot stop being who they are—those who challenge, defy despair or compromise, and push aside fear and numbness. The way to union in Christ is the road of suffering. Pride is the source of a deceptive experience of self-sufficiency. So for a refounding person a shattering failure or rejection can precede an ultimate leap into a more perfect faith, a faith that moves one into the darkness of belief and away from one's own false securities. The archetype of rejection and loneliness is Christ himself. He experienced in Gethsemane a mysterious and intense feeling

---

39. Tony Judt, *Ill Fares the Land: A Treatise on Our Present Discontents* (London: Allen Lane, 2010), 157.

of abandonment and incredible darkness: "A sadness came over him, and great distress" (Matt 26:37). Those who should have been closest to him, Peter and the two sons of Zebedee, had as yet no ability or grace to enter into the depth of Jesus' sadness. And in his abandonment Jesus turned to his Father in prayer.

We can be sure of this: If people are sincerely committed to refounding faith communities, God will invite them to walk with Jesus in their own Gethsemane. It will begin as they travel more deeply into their inner selves—a world of fears, prejudices, compromises, sinfulness, loneliness. This loneliness can at times be intense. Friends either disappear or, if they remain, are rarely able to empathize with the inner terrifying darkness. With Christ they will cry for deliverance: "Therefore I am content with weaknesses, insults, hardships, persecutions, and calamities for the sake of Christ; for whenever I am weak, then I am strong" (2 Cor 12:9-10). Recall a significant comment by Mark the evangelist when he reflected on the failure of the three disciples to support Jesus in his intense loneliness in the garden: "they did not know what to say to him" (Mark 14:40). They did not know how to help or what to say because they had not yet chosen, or been moved by the Spirit, to accept their own inner powerlessness and fragility. Without having made this inner journey, they could feel no empathy or compassion with Jesus in his suffering.

Refounding Religious Congregations: Reflections

This dynamic of marginalization is evident in the case histories of religious congregations. Marginalization of founding and refounding persons comes not just from ecclesiastical officials, but more sadly from members of their own congregations. Some members cannot abide the "boldness of initiatives [and] perspectives of newness"[40] of the apostolic initiatives that refounding people propose. Others who are trapped in the chaos themselves, especially if they have escaped into denial, do not always want to be reminded of their situation. They receive a twisted kind of identity from "enjoying the chaos."

---

40. Congregation for Religious and Bishops, *Directives for the Mutual Relations between Bishops and Religious in the Church* (Sydney: St Pauls Publications, 1978), 12.

For them the risks required of conversion and change are far more threatening than the existing problems around them. Others do not appreciate being challenged by people they feel they know so well; hence the words of Jesus: "Truly I tell you, no prophet is ever accepted in the prophet's home town" (Luke 4:24). Others are envious of his or her gifts and of the attention given that person, while others with no ill will just do not grasp or appreciate the qualities of the would-be refounding person and are understandably fearful of the uncertain world they are being called to enter.

Efforts at refounding religious congregations as institutions, especially those founded in the nineteenth and twentieth centuries, a period of intense growth, have often had limited success since Vatican II. These congregations were founded for specific pastoral needs of the time, for example, the need to educate and provide healthcare assistance to socially marginalized Catholics. Today these needs are mostly taken care of by government-supported institutions and these congregations, having lost their identity and lacking people of refounding gifts, have found it difficult, if not impossible, to focus in corporate ways on contemporary pastoral needs. Most now face an uncertain future, even extinction.[41] As these congregations struggle to survive, their leaders find their time and energy increasingly being consumed with managing the closures of ministries, mergers of provinces, and the care of elderly members. There is little strength left for creative ministerial direction of their congregations.

Moreover, a problem that many apostolic communities of this era face is that they were never founded. At first sight this statement may sound historically untrue. But, contrary to their founders' vision, these congregations were forced at birth into becoming precisely what their founders did not want, namely, highly structured, rule-oriented communities ill-equipped for apostolic mobility and creativity. Their prophetic vision was quickly smothered by the prevailing Roman vision of religious life, that is, that the ideal of religious life is monastic

---

41. For a thoughtful reflection on the future of religious life, see Gemma Simmonds, ed., *A Future Full of Hope?* (Dublin: Columba Press, 2012).

(see chap. 2).[42] Formation programs were aimed at crushing initiative and creativity, values so crucial for the refounding of congregations. Conformity to the status quo and Roman culture was the dominant value. So fundamentally it is not a question today of *refounding* but of *founding* these congregations for the first time. Yet as these same congregations have been forming candidates to be conformists and not people of refounding qualities, it is not at all surprising that there has been, and continues to be, a shortage of leaders with the courage and faith to undertake the radical changes demanded by refounding. They may use the rhetoric of refounding, but in fact they really mean renewal. They may depend too much on human techniques and gimmicky processes to stimulate radical revitalization, but no amount of merely human effort will bring about the refounding of any religious congregation.

Some congregations have also mistakenly thought that mission and identity are synonymous. They are not the same. Mission, no matter how inspiringly presented, is merely a *normative* statement about what people think makes them unique. *Dynamic* identity, however, is what people actually *do* (see chap. 1). Significant time and money will have been assigned to the study of the congregation's founding mission, but there are few significant corporate pastoral results. New histories of the founders are written, and more and more documents are produced, praising the exciting relevancy of the congregation's mission. But again nothing substantial eventuates. Why? Because the *dynamic* congregational identity is being neglected, that is, the immensely difficult and uncertain task of actually engaging the mission within the pastoral context. The latter demands an in-depth understanding of the fast-moving, contemporary world and thorough, professionally acquired skills of the sort that refounders possess. If these gifts are lacking, the institutional and personal transformation of congregations in a postmodern world cannot occur. A further factor inhibiting refounding is the failure to resolve in apostolic congregations the tension

---

42. See Gerald A. Arbuckle, *From Chaos to Mission: Refounding Religious Life Formation* (London: Geoffrey Chapman, 1995), 27–29.

between community, or belonging, and mission and ministry to the world. It is far easier to concentrate on community, and the requirements of being together at set times and places, than on ministry to a world in rapid change. Community must be at the service of the mission, not the other way around.

Refounding is primarily a faith journey in which there are no quick fixes. Rather, it demands that we individually and as institutions enter into a world of Gospel faith and, at times, agonizing darkness and chaos. Death, not survival, may be God's will. As congregations age and there are few, if any, new recruits, their administrations concern themselves with the inevitable problems of withdrawal from ministries and retirement programs. They look for simplistic and rapid solutions, even dropping their standards for recruitment and formation in desperate attempts to survive. Some established and new congregations, moreover, have adopted a restorationist stance, believing that because they attract recruits of conformist, but not prophetic, qualities they are truly refounding. New recruits are not an automatic sign of refounding.[43] Unless these recruits have the potential to prophetically challenge the church to be true to Gospel values, they have no capacity for refounding religious congregations.

Congregations desperate for candidates are constantly tempted to accept recruits with little or no potential whatsoever for refounding. The lowering of standards for entrance just so that a congregation will survive is a serious injustice to the church and to the candidates themselves. I heard one provincial say: "Whoever comes, the Spirit will work to transform them!" Many congregations hope to survive by recruiting in the developing world where there appear, for the moment, to be large reservoirs of candidates. However, unless these congregations are able to supply skilled formators and are prepared to train the candidates for ministries in an increasingly complex, globalizing world, they also commit grave injustices to the church and the personnel involved.[44]

43. See Arbuckle, *Out of Chaos*, 6–7.
44. See Arbuckle, *From Chaos to Mission*, 162–86.

Struggling congregations, in an effort to stave off death, are also commonly tempted to escape into "narratives of denial" (chap. 1). For example, they reconfigure or merge provinces without ever clarifying the reasons why. There is a belief that restructuring will automatically solve problems of diminishment; they are so frantic they fail to work through decision making based on vision, sound principles, and reality. Once they discover that the hoped-for revitalization fails to occur, congregational group depression is intensified.

In summary, congregational leaders of religious communities who commit themselves to the process of refounding in times of diminishment must be alert *inter alia* to the following points:

- Following the example of the biblical prophets, be truth-telling (chap. 5), that is, do not seek to hide the gravity of the challenges facing the communities internally and externally.

- Ensure that the vision is constantly and realistically clarified; it must be sharply focused. If it is not, strategic planning to realize the vision is fuzzy, whereas the vision must be inspirational or hope-raising to empower people to act.

- Congregational leaders must be aware of the distinction between the complementary roles of leadership and management; leaders challenge the status quo, but managers aim to provide order, support, and predictability. Managers must concern themselves with details; leaders, with creating and articulating the vision. Congregational leaders must not become unnecessarily involved in the tiring work of managing, though they will inevitably be tempted to do so. If they do, they will lose the capacity to create and sustain the vision and the ability to call people to be accountable to this vision.

- Be aware that structural changes, for example, those that occur in reconfiguring provinces, will not succeed if they ignore the realities of cultures. Organizational structures are visible formal directives that define positions of authority and actions that need to be followed. A culture (chap. 2) is much more complex, because it tells people how to view their world and, more important, how to experience it emotionally; a culture is the emotional bonding that holds a group of people, such as a province,[45] together. No matter how logically and rationally planned structural directives may be, the changes will not occur unless a people's emotional bonding is addressed. This will take significant time and much consultation.[46] This means that refounding is a collaborative process; there is no room in the refounding journey for authoritarian leadership.

- In order to be effective evangelizers in postmodern times, religious need to be academically and pastorally skilled; a commitment to study and ongoing training is a contemporary imperative.

- It is essential to maintain high standards for recruitment and formation, even though the congregation faces extinction.

In the first chapter I wrote that narratives of grieving remain an essential precondition for successful creation of new identities and are an integral part of every narrative of refounding; grieving is at the very heart of the message of the Old and New Testaments (see also chap. 5). The refusal to grieve over personal and institutional losses saps energy and there is little resiliency left to let ourselves be open to the creatively new.[47] I wonder at times if we religious, who should be at the service of the church in the scriptural art of grieving, are sufficiently aware at times of these imperatives. This was brought home to me rather dramatically in the late 1980s when I was leading a ritual of grieving for several hundred major superiors and their councils. They were invited in a faith atmosphere and in silence to spend a morning identifying losses in their lives and congregations. At noon they came together and I was to

---

45. See Gerald A. Arbuckle, "Merging Provinces," *Review for Religious* 53 (May-June 1994): 352–63.

46. See Arbuckle, *Humanizing Healthcare* Reforms (London and Philadelphia: Jessica Kingsley Publications, 2013), 14–15.

47. See Gerald A. Arbuckle, *Change, Grief, and Renewal in the Church* (Westminster, MD: Christian Classics, 1991), 61–160, and idem, *Refounding the Church*, 180–200. Shakespeare was right: "Grief makes one hour ten" (*Richard* II, I, 3, 261).

conclude their meditative reflections with a short ritual before inviting them for the rest of the day to identify signs of newness emerging in their experience. As I began the ritual, and to my immense surprise, I broke into tears and could not continue. Why did this happen? Later, as I debriefed, I realized that the men and women in front of me as congregational leaders had begun to experience the burdens of diminishing numbers and the pressures from bishops to continue staffing ministries. I also much later surmised that some had begun to deal with sexual abuse cases in their congregations. As I stood in front of these people, some of whom I could see had tears in their eyes also, I became the recipient of wave upon wave of grief. One biblical ritual of grieving could not possibly resolve people's sadness. Rather, such lamentation rituals must be an integral and regular part of all personal and community prayers because through them "the grief experience is made bearable and, it is hoped, meaningful."[48]

Axiom 8: *In the refounding process it is normally necessary to build structures that protect the project from unnecessary interference from existing organizational cultures.*

For the refounding process to succeed, people need to bypass existing organizational structures. Resistance kills change. Refounding or transformative people cannot waste time and energy, especially in the early stages of organizational change, on trying to win over people who significantly resist change. Their primary concern, in order to safeguard the integrity of the mission, is to identify and support other innovators and signs of life. They know that organizations survive and grow only if innovative people, including themselves, have the space and safety to think and act.

In order to be adequately supported, creative and innovative refounding persons may need to invoke the axiom "the new belongs elsewhere."[49]

48. Walter Brueggemann, "The Formfulness of Grief," *Interpretation* 31 (1977): 263–75, at 265.

49. See Jeffrey Cohn, Jon Katzenbach, and Gus Vlak, "Finding and Grooming Breakthrough Innovators," *Harvard Business Review* (December 2008): 62–69, at 65.

That is, when an existing organizational culture is resistant to change, a refounding person will bypass it by creating a new culture. This will allow innovative persons to have the space to act without undue interference from people resisting change. Change agents require simple and clear lines of accountability to the leadership of an organization—that is, a system uncluttered by traditional cultural attitudes and structures that impose on innovators unnecessary restrictions, supervision, and wearying defense of their creative actions. This does not mean that creative people are to be shielded from all conflict; indeed, creativity and adaptation are born of tension, passion, and conflict. Truly innovative people will have plenty of this anyway, but let us not burden them with unnecessary tension. It is a question of protecting them, as far as is possible, from unproductive and de-energizing conflict—that is, conflict that simply does not serve the mission. Tony Blair, when prime minister of Britain, wanted to refound the National Health Service, but he was hampered by the fact that his party was traditionally committed to the centralized control of the service. This stifled local responsibility. It was necessary to call his party back to its founding myth, namely, that the "state and social action [had to be] a means of advancing the individual, not subsuming them."[50] By establishing new structures to allow more local participation in the governing of the health service, Blair was able to bypass resistance from the centralized bureaucratic structure.

Case Study: Refounding Cooperatives

A cooperative is "an autonomous association of persons united voluntarily to meet their common economic, social, and cultural needs and aspirations through a jointly owned and democratically controlled enterprise."[51] It is of the essence of a cooperative that the people own it and officials are to be accountable to them for their actions. In the early 1950s in Fiji the British colonial government established a series of cooperatives among indigenous farmers, but they constantly

50. Tony Blair, *A Journey* (London: Hutchinson, 2010), 95.
51. Statement promulgated by the International Cooperative Alliance in 1995.

failed. Contrary to their founding democratic identity, the Fijian cooperatives were controlled by a paternalistic and centralized government-appointed administration. Officials preached democracy but did nothing to encourage it; the people felt ignored and prevented from being responsible for their own decision making. Consequently, the government-established cooperatives kept failing.

In 1953 Jesuit Father Marion Ganey was invited by the British government in Fiji to establish credit unions, a particular form of cooperatives.[52] A credit union is a group of people, united by a common bond, who save money together and make loans to each other at low interest. Structures must allow officials of credit unions to be accountable frequently and directly to the people who own them. Ganey accepted, but only on condition that the colonial government pass legislation to permit credit unions to be legally independent of existing organizations, particularly the Department of Cooperatives. He firmly believed that cooperative democracy is at the heart of credit union philosophy, but structures must allow it to exist and flourish. In the face of considerable opposition he was granted his request for legal protection and credit unionism was able to become the first successful, non-paternalistic self-help Fijian development movement. People in villages described to me their experience of church through credit union in this way: "Now I have dignity and self-respect because I am not being constantly told by others how to manage my own affairs." By returning to the founding mythological identity of cooperatives and building appropriate protective structures according to the principle "the new belongs elsewhere," Ganey identified the primary factor that prevented people from running their own affairs. This was an act of refounding, not renewal.

52. See Gerald A. Arbuckle, "Economic and Social Development in the Fiji Islands through Credit Unions," 90–108 in Neil Runcie, ed., *Credit Unions in the South Pacific* (London: University of London Press, 1969).

Refounding a Religious Congregation

It would be difficult to disagree with the view that St. Teresa of Avila (1515–1582) "was one of the greatest Christian women that ever lived."[53] Born in Spain in 1515, she entered a Carmelite convent in 1535, but eventually, following a radical personal conversion, she found the religious laxity in the congregation intolerable. Her mystic life, with divine conversations, her first ecstasy, and an intellectual vision of Christ started shortly after this conversion experience. Teresa became the first to give a scientific portrayal of the whole life of prayer, from meditation to the mystical marriage.[54] Threatened at times by the Inquisition and members of her own communities, she nonetheless persisted with her reform of the order and indirectly with the church itself, becoming one of the most influential figures in the post-Reformation Catholic Church. Her influence on religious life and society continues to this day. As one author writes, Teresa began "to adopt ascetical practices intended to simplify and focus her attention and to work against corruption and towards social justice in the Carmelite order and in the wider society."[55]

Gifted with practical as well as spiritual and intellectual skills, she recognized eventually that her order could not be reformed according to the radical demands of the Carmelite tradition. She finally evoked the axiom "the new belongs elsewhere." The existing congregational culture was so resistant to conversion that she decided to establish an entirely new congregation, the Order of Discalced Carmelites, but based on the original Carmelite founding myth. Her frustration is evident in her correspondence. She wrote in 1575:

---

53. Urban T. Holmes, *A History of Christian Spirituality* (New York: Seabury Press, 1981), 98.

54. See Thomas Bokenkotter, *A Concise History of the Catholic Church* (New York: Doubleday, 1997), 224; Cathleen Medwick, *Teresa of Avila: The Progress of a Soul* (New York: Knopf, 1999), passim.

55. Grace M. Jantzen, "Teresa of Avila," 698–99, in Adrian Hastings, ed., *The Oxford Companion to Christian Thought* (Oxford: Oxford University Press, 2000), 698.

> With regard to the Countess's convent, I hardly know what to say, for it is a long time since I was approached about it, and I must tell your Lordship that I would much rather found four houses with nuns—where those who are new to our method of life can pick it up in a fortnight, by simply doing as others do—than to have to initiate good ladies like these into our ways, no matter how saintly they may be.[56]

Thus later in that year she sought the aid of King Philip II of Spain in establishing an entirely independent congregation, as the survival of the reform of her convents was at stake: "I am quite clear that, unless the Discalced are made into a separate province and that without delay, serious harm will be done: in fact, I believe it will be impossible for them to go on."[57] Among her many gifts as a refounding person was her imaginative narrative skill in using everyday imagery in striking ways. In this she followed the example of the prophets of the Hebrew Scriptures and Christ himself. Not only did St. Teresa seek new identities for Carmelite sisters through refounding, but at the same time she helped to forge new identities for women in general. She astounded the male-dominated church with her extraordinary gifts and insights because it was thought, according to the papal bull of her canonization in 1622, that she had overcome "her female nature,"[58] that is, she had become the equivalent of a man. Tradition decreed that women could not do great things without the gifts of masculinity! In fact, St. Teresa refused to accept this identity based on prejudice. Rather, she sought through her example and writings to forge a new identity for women in the church.

56. Teresa of Avila, Letter to Don Teutonio De Braganza (6 January 1575), in E. Allison Peers, ed., *The Letters of Saint Teresa of Jesus* (Westminster: Newman Press, 1950), 169.

57. Letter to King Philip II of Spain (19 July 1575), ibid., 188.

58. Quoted by Cathleen Medwick, *Teresa of Avila: The Progress of a Soul* (New York: Knopf, 1999), 248.

Summary

- An experience of chaos is a precondition for radical individual and institutional creativity; chaos breaks apart a world of predictability. Refounding in times of chaos is a process of storytelling in which new identities are shaped, based on the original mythological truths and their application to contemporary situations. However, the process of refounding institutions very frequently fails mainly due *inter alia* to the resistances inherent in their cultures: The "stark reality is that few companies ever succeed in genuinely reinventing themselves."[59]

- People who are able to lead the refounding process require gifts of imagination, curiosity, creativity, collaboration, and immense courage to survive inevitable opposition; they are liminal persons, that is, they live on the threshold of order and chaos. Within the church there are many examples of refounding ministries by people deeply committed to Vatican II pastoral guidelines, but the institutional church is increasingly placing obstacles to this refounding dynamic; restorationism seeks to reinstate the pre–Vatican II narratives of hierarchical power and control.

- The fact that refounding people are highly intuitive immediately puts them on a collision course with abstract deductive thinkers who want precise answers based on observable facts. Refounding people are dreamers who act. But abstract linear thinkers and "quick-fix-action-people," who think structural change alone can be effective, see refounding persons as "flaky" and therefore dangerous and not to be trusted. They brand them as impractical and therefore to be ignored. Frequently, if the congregational prophet dares to persist in her or his vocation, the opposition turns to rejection, marginalization, or "banishment to the grim periphery" of the congregation.[60] Invariably, to the intense irritation of others, refounders refuse to give up, even if their reforming insights are repeatedly ignored.

- Despite all the initial enthusiasm and planning that religious congregations have committed to changing structures, the stark reality is that few, especially congregations founded in the nineteenth and twen-

---

59. Diane L. Coutu, "The Anxiety of Learning, an Interview with Edgar H. Schein," *Harvard Business Review* (March 2002): 100–107, at 100.

60. See comments by Peg C. Neuhauser, *Tribal Warfare in Organizations* (Grand Rapids, MI: Harper Business, 1988), 76–79.

tieth centuries, are succeeding in genuinely refounding themselves as institutions; the reasons for this are complex, but the institutional obstacles to refounding generally remain unchallenged. The next chapter focuses on some issues of refounding within the Scriptures.

Chapter Five

Founding and Refounding Identities: Scriptural Experiences

Telling stories is as basic to human beings as eating. More so, in fact, for while food makes us live, stories are what make our lives worth living. They are what make our condition human.[1] (Richard Kearney)

[It] is still possible to listen to the Parables of Jesus in such a way that we are once more astonished, struck, renewed, and put in motion.[2] (Paul Ricoeur)

[Parables] re-present a familiar or typified scene for the purpose of generating conversation about and stimulating the kinds of reflection that expose contradictions in popularly held beliefs or traditional thinking.[3] (William R. Herzog)

This chapter explains that:

- traditional pedagogical methods of evangelizing in the church have overemphasized cognitive conversion or coercion, but these approaches run contrary to the inductive refounding methods of the prophets of the Old Testament

---

1. Richard Kearney, *On Stories* (New York: Routledge, 2002), 3.

2. Paul Ricoeur, "Listening to the Parables of Jesus," in Charles E. Reagan and David Stewart, eds., *The Philosophy of Paul Ricoeur: An Anthology of His Work* (Boston: Beacon Press, 1978), 239.

3. William R. Herzog, *Parables as Subversive Speech: Jesus as Pedagogue of the Oppressed* (Louisville: Westminster John Knox, 1994), 26.

- the preferred pedagogical method of Jesus Christ in founding and refounding identities among his followers is the inductive or narrative method
- the narrative process of identification is particularly adapted to postmodernity

A fundamental theme of this book is that storytelling "is as basic to human beings as eating. More so, in fact, for while food makes us live, stories are what make our lives worth living."[4] This is especially obvious in every book of the Scriptures. In chapter 1 we saw that personal and institutional identities are socially constructed through a process of narratives. A narrative—oral or written—is created when "a teller motivated by unexpected events describes to a recipient of the story a sequence of purposeful actions with a plot (a beginning, middle, and end) set in a particular context and arranged according to a temporal structure."[5] The formation of identities through narratives uses items and experiences from all kinds of realities such as history, the environment, institutions, and group memory. Individuals and institutions select from this mass of material what they feel gives a sense of order and meaning, that is, identity, in their circumstances. Sociologist Manuel Castells, however, makes an important point when he argues that power is a critical factor in deciding the forms and origins of identity construction; whoever has access to power will ultimately determine in what ways identity is built.[6]

The first part of this chapter reflects on the ministry of the prophets of the Old Testament, the origins of their power as refounding figures, and the way they sought to involve the Israelites in shaping revitalized identities when relating to God. The second part of the chapter concentrates on the founding and refounding qualities of Jesus Christ and the evangelists. The Old Testament prophets, Jesus Christ, the evangelists, and St. Paul are pedagogical masters because they are inductive teach-

---

4. Kearney, *On Stories*, 3.

5. John D. Engel, Joseph Zarconi, Lura L. Pethtel, and Sally A. Missimi, *Narrative in Health Care: Healing Patients, Practitioners, Profession, and Community* (Oxford: Radcliffe, 2008), 6–7.

6. See Manuel Castells, *The Power of Identity* (Oxford: Blackwells, 1997), 7–8.

ers, avoiding abstractions, drawing on people's experiences of life, and involving them in stories abounding in metaphors and similes.

Prophets: Narratives of Refounding Identities

As explained in chapter 3, one of the most powerful symbols in the Scriptures is "chaos," which has many different expressions. It connotes confusion, darkness, emptiness, nothingness, loss of meaning, but it also can carry with it the notion of indeterminacy and potentiality. Almighty God, if people are willing to cooperate, can create a new people out of the chaos into which they have fallen.[7] The exodus out of Egypt, the core religious experience for the Israelites, forms the founding myth of how they were initiated as a people during chaotic times. In the wilderness they encounter not just the confusion of chaos but also dramatically repeated contact with God; the painful experience of the desert is at the same time remarkably creative because a new, intimate relationship and identity emerge between the people and God. The people are called to testify to this revitalized identity by placing God in the center of their worship, by humility, trust in God, love and justice toward their neighbor (Isa 1:16-17; 7:9; 30:15). Whenever the people forget these values they fall into chaos, becoming idolatrous and materialistic, suffering under foreign enemies, and being dragged into exile. The prophets are named by God to call the Israelites to join them in shaping a narrative of refounding the nation according to the values of the original covenant. Jeremiah is *the* prophet out of chaos, of life through death. He sees that the Israelite culture is to be reduced to the "primeval chaos from which God had originally redeemed it"[8]: "I looked on the earth, and lo, it was waste and void" (Jer 4:23). Yet God is forgiving, if the people repent of their ways. Thus Jeremiah foretells the eventual refounding of the nation's identity: "See, I appoint you . . . to build and to plant" (Jer 1:10).

---

7. See Walter Brueggemann, "Kingship and Chaos: A Study in Tenth Century Theology," *Catholic Biblical Quarterly* 33 (1971): 317–32, and idem, "Weariness, Exile and Chaos: A Motif in Royal Theology," *Catholic Biblical Quarterly* 34 (1972): 19–38.

8. Eric W. Heaton, *The Old Testament Prophets* (Harmondsworth: Penguin, 1961), 79.

Refounding Qualities

Among the key qualities of a prophet as a refounding person are his or her memory of God's mercy to the people and a vivid creative imagination that aids him or her in the task of challenging them to return to the Lord in the ways of justice and love. Frequently these prophets suffer harshly for their loyalty to God: overwhelming grief, social ostracism, physical pain, and even death are their lot.[9] For example, the prophet Jeremiah sees the coming doom of the Israelites as a consequence of their loss of God's friendship. The faith-shock of this vision, of the Israelites' loss of their God-given identity, causes him painful anticipated grief, which he graphically expresses in the lament style: "My anguish, my anguish! I writhe in pain! . . . Disaster overtakes disaster, the whole land is laid waste"(Jer 4:19-20). The consequent chaos is inevitable because their "sins are so numerous . . . [their] pain incurable" (Jer 30:15). Jeremiah, as God's messenger, calls the people to respond with narratives of lament: "call the mourning women . . . let them quickly raise a dirge over us, so that our eyes may run down with tears" (Jer 9:17-18). Jeremiah's cry is unambiguous. When the Israelites acknowledge their sinfulness in word and action God will listen and their covenant identity will be restored: "For I will restore health to you, and your wounds I will heal, says the Lord, because they have called you an outcast" (Jer 30:17).[10]

The prophets as refounding persons possess not just the gift of truth-telling (see chap. 4) but also the skill of grieving. This is the ability to call the people to name the pain of the chaos and myriad losses they have experienced. When the pain can be named it can be let go of in order to give space for the impossibly new to enter. As Claus Westermann writes, the cries of the prophets transform "the experience of chaos into a way of approaching God with abandonment that permits daring and visioning and even ecstasy."[11] We are called to search beyond the chaos to signs of newness God is offering us, not to deny or be paralyzed by it: "For thus says the Lord . . . who formed the earth . . . he did not

---

9. See Gerald A. Arbuckle, *Out of Chaos: Refounding Religious Congregations* (New York: Paulist Press, 1988), 62.

10. See Louis J. Stulman, "Jeremiah as a Messenger of Hope in Crisis," *Interpretation* 62 (2008): 5–20, and Kathleen M. O'Connor, "Lamenting Back to Life," *Interpretation* 62 (2008): 34–68.

11. Claus Westermann, *Elements of Old Testament Theology* (Atlanta: John Knox, 1982), 103.

create it a chaos. . . . I did not say to the offspring of Jacob, 'Seek me in chaos'" (Isa 45:18-19). Hope is integral to the call to grieve, to look beyond to the promises of God. Hope, of course, is not some nebulous "optimism or a generic good idea about the future but a precise and concrete confidence and expectation for the future"[12] that is founded in God's promises to the Israelite people.

The prophets' authority and power come directly from God, who personally selected them as the refounding instruments for the revitalization of the Israelite national identity. Several of the prophetic books explicitly contain "call narratives" in which the prophets record the fact that they have been personally summoned to prophesy (Isa 6; Jer 1; Ezek 1:1; 3:15; Amos 7:15).[13] Jeremiah recalls his experience: "Then the Lord put out his hand and touched my mouth; and the Lord said to me, 'Now I have put my words in your mouth'" (Jer 1:9).

The prophets are to be totally committed to God and the mission of refounding of the Israelite covenant way of life.[14] They are Israel's creative, dynamic and questioning memory, repeatedly returning in their narratives to the nation's original creation mythology and to the root causes of the people's miseries. The prophets reject the sinful behavior of the people, measured against the vision that can and should be realized, if only the Israelites would take their creation story seriously. God loves the people, but they must respond with sincerity of heart, worship, justice, and love, and they must be especially concerned for the needs of people who are poor and defenseless. Here is the narrative of the prophet Amos, drawing on his memory of the mythology of the founding of the Israelite people and condemning them for their culpable forgetfulness: "Hear this word that the Lord has spoken against you, O people of Israel . . . that I brought up out of the land of Egypt, . . . I sent among you a pestilence after the manner of Egypt . . . yet you did not return to me, says the Lord. . . . [P]repare to meet your God, O Israel" (Amos 3:1; 4:10, 12). We can feel the depth of Amos's faith-shock as he contemplates the enormity of the gap between God's loving gift of the covenant and the people's rejection.

---

12. Walter Brueggemann, *Reverberations of Faith: A Theological Handbook of Old Testament Themes* (Louisville: Westminster John Knox, 2002), 100.

13. See R. N. Whybray, "Prophets," 620–22, in Bruce M. Metzger and Michael D. Coogan, eds., *The Oxford Companion to the Bible* (New York: Oxford University Press, 1993).

14. See Arbuckle, *Out of Chaos*, 57–62.

Although each prophet calls for the same conversion, each directs the narrative to the particular needs of the time. Each uses different imaginative and innovative expressions that the people of their times would readily have understood. They break through the chaos of confusion, numbness and denial, by pointing out the particular way the people must journey to bridge the gap between their idolatry and injustices to the poor and God's call to live the covenant. Their exercise of creative imagination is possible, however, only because the prophets are compulsive listeners, that is, they are listening at the same time to God's covenant requirements and to the sinfulness and cries of the people. Despite their often gloomy, though realistic, condemnation of the Israelites' wayward ways, the prophets are optimistic, full of hope, and imaginatively creative about how the people are to return to their pilgrim road. No matter how dark and chaotic the world may be, God still loves them. This is why the prophets never give up; they have a faith-inspired stubbornness even in the face of their possible death at the hands of the people.

The prophets, like all authentic, faith-driven refounding people, are often marginalized by the very people they yearn to help. They are often verbally and physically abused and at times even murdered, because their message calling for personal and national transformation is unacceptable to people who have been seduced by worldly values. However, it is not just evil people who are rejecting the message, but the mediocre who feel affronted and annoyed that they should be told to live better lives. The people shout to Hosea: "The prophet is a fool, the man of the spirit is mad!"(Hos 9:7). Suffering is a mark of their authenticity as God's spokespeople. The painful rejection of Jeremiah is typical. Not only is he rejected by the people at large, but even his family and friends desert him (Jer 20:10), so he knows vividly the loneliness of marginalization: "I was like a gentle lamb led to the slaughter. And I did not know it was against me that they devised schemes, saying, 'Let us destroy the tree with its fruit, let us cut him off from the land of the living, so that his name will no longer be remembered!'" (Jer 11:19). Yet, despite the enormity of his torments, Jeremiah cannot desist from preaching unpalatable truths: "then within me there is something like a burning fire shut up in my bones; I am weary with holding it in, and I cannot. . . . But the Lord is with me like a dread warrior . . . ; my persecutors . . . will not prevail" (Jer 20:9, 11). Since truth telling is an integral quality of the prophetic ministry it inevitably results in resistance and persecution for people like Jeremiah.[15]

Evangelists: Narrators of Identities

The faith of Israel is articulated in many different ways: poems, prophecies, proverbs, laws. However, it is narrative that unites these different expressions to reflect the common identity of the Israelites. It is the story of God in their lives and how they react to this presence among them. In times of national turmoil the people respond to the fundamental questions of identity and meaning by retelling the mythology of their founding as the chosen people of God (Exod 12:26-27; 13:8, 14; Deut 6:20-25). This mythology gradually evolved into particular narratives such as those of creation, fall, promise, call, slavery, exodus, and covenant.[16]

So also in the New Testament the founding and legitimizing mythological identities of the Christian faith—the life, death, and resurrection of Christ—are told and retold in the narratives of the gospels. These narratives evolved as people in the early church wished to record their stories of the transforming power of Jesus in their lives. All four gospels have this in common: their project is to show that while the Christian message is linked to the Old Testament, nonetheless its legitimizing and unique founding identity is the person of Jesus Christ and his story. All gospels conclude with the account of Christ's resurrection, although Mark's ends with the finding of his empty tomb. Until the last quarter of the first century Christians lived within Judaism as just another group, but once they were expelled from the synagogues Christians needed to establish their unique identities in relationship to the communities that had marginalized them and to the wider multicultural Roman Empire. Through his life, death, and resurrection Jesus Christ condemns narcissistic worldly power and materialism, brings good news to people on

---

15. See Walter Brueggemann, *Disruptive Grace* (Minneapolis: Fortress Press, 2011), 138–45.

16. See Thomas H. Groome's excellent study of biblical inductive learning: *Sharing Faith: A Comprehensive Approach to Religious Education and Pastoral Ministry* (New York: HarperSanFrancisco, 1991), 140.

the margins of society, and reveals "a new Kingdom of truth and life, of holiness and grace, of justice, love, and peace."[17] While this is the fundamental narrative of all four gospels, nonetheless at the same time each gospel highlights different aspects of Christ's multifaceted identity simply because their contexts differ. That is, the intent of the evangelists was not to record as accurately as possible the exact words of Jesus but rather to reinterpret the narrative of Christ in different ways because the contexts of their faith communities were dissimilar.[18] Thus there are different accounts of the same parable in different gospels; similar parables occur in different contexts, aimed at different audiences, with consequently divergent meanings. So there is not just one Christian identity but many, depending on the contexts in which the evangelists are writing.

The plot of Mark's narrative is the unwillingness of people to accept the messianic identity of Jesus, resulting in his appalling death. So Mark emphasizes the "messianic secret" as the spectacular foundation of his narrative. Christians must accept the hard realities of the world in which they live, such as persecution, and cannot concentrate only on the wonderful truth of Christ's rising and exaltation.[19]

The plot of Matthew's account is the fact that Jesus as Messiah has established a new covenant with believers. Their communities of faith are now the rightful heirs to the promises made to them in the Old Testament (Matt 16:18; 18:17). They face rejection by the Jewish leaders who crucified Jesus, believing they were purging Israel of a deception (Matt 26:65-66; 27:63).[20]

The context of Luke's narrative, with its primary focus on the figure of Jesus, is the needs of a mainly Gentile Christian community. Both in his gospel and the Acts of the Apostles, Luke's narrative looks beyond Jewish hostility to the bringing of the Good News to the Gentile world. He describes what the content of the kingdom of God is to be: Jesus dead

17. See Daniel G. Groody, *Globalization, Spirituality, and Justice* (Maryknoll, NY: Orbis Books, 2007), 48.

18. See Barbara E. Reid, *Parables for Preachers: The Gospel of Mark* (Collegeville, MN: Liturgical Press, 1999), 15.

19. See Augustin del Agua, "The Narrative Identity of Christians according to the New Testament," 91–99, in Hermann Häring, Maureen Junker-Kenny, and Dietmar Mieth, eds., *Creating Identity, Concilium* 2000/2 (London: SCM Press, 2000): 91–99.

20. See Jack Dean Kingsbury, "Matthew," 502–6, in Metzger and Coogan, eds., *The Oxford Companion to the Bible*, 505.

and raised, his universal mission, and the power that this mission has to affect the lives of all peoples (Luke 4:14-44). He also wants to emphasize that Christianity has as much right to exist with its own unique identity in the Roman world as does Judaism. Much more than the other evangelists, Luke insists that the Spirit itself inspires the ministry of Jesus and also the fast-growing development of the faith communities in the Gentile world. For example, at least seventeen times in Luke's gospel and fifty-seven times in Acts the Spirit is depicted as inspiring the lives of Jesus and his supporters.[21]

In John's gospel the plot that draws the narrative together is not so much the kingdom but the need to reaffirm that Jesus, as divine and human, resolutely unites earth and heaven, thus "making it possible, even in this world, for every believer to share the life of eternity."[22] The context that made this emphasis urgent for John was the fact that members of his community were divided about the true nature of Jesus Christ, whose divinity and humanity needed to be resolutely defended. As people were divided over this critical issue, there were tensions within the communities. Hence, while restating Christ's dual nature in one person, John had to remind community members of the need for mutual love (John 15:12) and unity (17:11, 21-23).[23]

All four gospels are narratives about the person of Christ; the focus is on the experience of Christ, the revelation of God. People are called repeatedly to remember and retell the story of Jesus Christ and in so doing to develop a deep personal relationship with him. The more the early Christians pondered the story of Jesus in light of their own particular social, political, and economic circumstances, the more they could believe in Christ's loving concern for them as individuals and communities. It was not an abstract or academic knowledge of Christ, but a belief in a person who intimately cared for and loved them. To know Christ became for them "a dynamic, experiential, relational activity involving the whole person and finding expression in a lived response of loving obedience to God's will."[24]

---

21. See Joseph A. Fitzmyer, "Luke," 469–74, in ibid., at 474.

22. Stephen S. Smalley, "John," ibid., 373–77, at 373.

23. See ibid., 376.

24. Thomas H. Groome, *Christian Religious Education: Sharing Our Story and Vision* (Melbourne: Dove, 1980), 144.

Jesus Christ: Master Storyteller

Parables: Narratives of Identity

There is general agreement that we best discover Christ's teachings, as well as his fundamental pedagogy, in his parables, fictitious
stories Jesus tells in order to explain his teachings and mission.[25] As
John Donaghue, SJ, writes: "Among the many sayings in the Gospels of
Matthew, Mark and Luke, those which best embody the speech of Jesus
and which are most distinctive of him are the more than forty parables
attributed to him. . . . Through the language of Jesus we are in contact
with his imagination as it brings to expression his self-understanding
of his mission."[26] The emphasis on the parables does not exclude the
importance of the other recorded words of Christ or of his actions. On
the contrary, a better appreciation of the parables leads to a deeper understanding of his words and actions.[27] The parables are about ordinary
individuals and everyday events, but they are recounted in a way people
in every century can identify with. The parables together cover a wide
range of themes, revealing in colorful language the healing mission of
Christ. The parables fundamentally challenge his listeners to reorder
and remold their cultural and economic reality. Therefore we can speak
of the parables as subversive of a world that is unjust and lacking in
compassion. They call people to shape a world in which love and justice
prevail in human relationships, a world of inner and outer conversion
and reconciliation with one another and with our Creator.[28] There are
parables depicting

---

25. See Arland J. Hultgren, *The Parables of Jesus: A Commentary* (Grand Rapids,
MI: Eerdmans, 2000), 1.

26. John Donaghue, *The Gospel in Parable* (Philadelphia: Fortress Press, 1988), 3.

27. About one-third of the documented sayings of Jesus in the Synoptic Gospels
are in the form of parables. See Brad H. Young, *The Parables: Jewish Tradition and
Christian Interpretation* (Peabody, MA: Hendrickson, 1998), 7. The number of parables in the gospels is estimated to be as low as thirty-five and as high as seventy-two,
depending on the particular categorization.

28. One of P. G. Wodehouse's characters remarks: "A parable is one of those stories
in the Bible which sounds at first like a pleasant yarn but keeps something up its
sleeves which pops up and leaves you flat." Cited by A. M. Hunter, *Interpreting the
Parables* (London: SCM Press, 1960), 14.

- God's extraordinary forgiveness and grace, such as *The Lost Sheep* (Matt 18:12-14), *The Prodigal Son* (Luke 15:11-32)

- admirable behavior, for example, *The Good Samaritan* (Luke 10:25-37), *The Rich Man and Lazarus* (Luke 16:19-31), *The Pharisee and the Tax Collector* (Luke 18:10-14)

- the practical significance of wisdom, for example, *The Wise and Foolish Builders* (Matt 7:24-27), *The Unjust Manager* (Luke 16:1-8)

- how we are to relate to God, for example, *The Talents* (Matt 25:14-30), *The Barren Fig Tree* (Luke 13:6-9)

- the final judgment, for example, *The Weeds in the Wheat* (Matt 13:24-30), *The Final Judgment* (Matt 25:31-46)

- the happiness that results from discovering the message and mission of Christ, for example, *The Treasure in the Field* (Matt 12:44)

All the while in the parables Jesus is speaking of himself and how we are to relate to one another and to God. He does not give us dogmatic definitions of God, but "he entangles us as a narrator in the question of how we can interpret God's action."[29] For his followers down the ages who ponder the lessons of the parables and the actions of Jesus, his identity is never sealed once and for all but keeps expanding for believers through the interaction of their memory of him and the context of their daily lives. The identity of Jesus is shaped anew in every age and every culture. At one time Jesus becomes for individuals or groups the compassionate listener, the one marginalized and tortured, the companion in need, the wise judge.[30] Thus Jesus does not have one identity but many. As people ponder the parables and reflect on the lessons in light of their different needs, the parables become no longer narratives told by Jesus, but their own stories.

---

29. Hermann Häring, "The History of Jesus as the Foundation and Origin of Religious Identity," 100–12, in *Creating Identity* (see n. 19 above), 111.

30. Ibid., 107; see also Jaroslav Pelikan, *Jesus through the Centuries: His Place in the History of Culture* (New Haven, CT: Yale University Press, 1985), passim.

Interpretation

The interpretation of parables is a difficult task. Even though Jesus used well-known imagery, they remain mysterious and confusing.[31] In order to interpret the many meanings of the parables it is necessary at times to refer to their Old Testament roots and the way Catholic tradition has viewed them over the centuries. The parables take on new meanings and vitality when they are understood within the culture of their times. The stories are of varying length, containing a meaning or message over and above the straightforward and literal, with an element of metaphor. Of course the parables, like the rest of the gospels, come to us through the evangelists and the memories of the early Christian communities. This helps to further clarify the fact that the parables may have multiple meanings, depending at times on the particular needs of the people who related them. For example, for Matthew (Matt 18:12-14), the Lost Sheep functions to exhort church leaders to care for the weak in the community; in Luke it justifies Jesus' mission to the lost (Luke 15:4-7).[32]

Scholars do not agree on a common set of assumptions about parables or adhere to the same methods in explaining them.[33] For centuries parables have been interpreted as allegorical narratives that hid deeply important Christian truths. Thus St. Augustine, in explaining the parable of the Good Samaritan, considered the man who went down from Jerusalem to Jericho to be Adam and the robbers as the devil and his angels. Over the last century, however, several important new methods of interpretation have emerged. For example, Klyne Snodgrass aims to recover the original aims of Jesus and the evangelists through analysis of the parables. Thus he asks the question: "How did Jesus seek to change attitudes and behaviors with this parable?"[34] To emphasize the need to discover the historical Jesus speaking through parables, Snodgrass claims

---

31. See Barbara E. Reid, *Parables for Preachers: The Gospel of Matthew* (Collegeville, MN: Liturgical Press, 2001), 15–26.

32. See Charles W. Hedrick, *Many Things in Parables* (Louisville: Westminster John Knox, 2004), 100–104.

33. See ibid., xii–xv; Alison Jack, "'For those Outside, Everything Comes in Parables': Recent Readings of the Parables from the Inside," *Expository Times* 120/1 (October 2008): 8–15; Klyne R. Snodgrass, "From Allegorizing to Allegorizing: A History of the Interpretation of the Parables of Jesus," 3–29, in Richard N. Longenecker, ed., *The Challenge of Jesus' Parables* (Grand Rapids, MI: Eerdmans, 2000), 3–29.

34. Klyne R. Snodgrass, *Stories with Intent: A Comprehensive Guide to the Parables of Jesus* (Grand Rapids, MI: Eerdmans, 2008), 3.

that "any interpretation that does not breathe the air of the first century cannot be correct."[35] "Context," he continues, "is a determiner of meaning—in the end the only determiner of meaning, for words themselves have only possible meanings apart from context."[36] Parables should be read with the mission of Jesus primarily in mind, as "revealing the impact of Jesus' teaching about the kingdom."[37] In Luke, for example, Jesus uses parables to reply to the objections of people with whom he is conversing and dining.

By contrast, however, other scholars argue that readers or hearers also continue to have an important role in discovering the meanings within the parables, especially through the assistance of contemporary literary criticism and social scientific advances. For example, C. H. Dodd in 1935 claimed that parables are short metaphors for the kingdom of God. A metaphor is a figure of speech that describes one thing by speaking of something else. Dodd writes that in the parables Jesus reveals the meaning of the kingdom of God by describing qualities of the daily life of people at the time of Christ.[38] The kingdom has come, and through reflecting on the parables people can see its presence working today in their own lives.[39] Dan Otto Via later wrote of a different way of interpreting the parables, which he claimed were literary creations. Like any fictitious story, the parables have plots, characters, and drama, and are to be critiqued like any other literature. For example, he claims that the two fundamental types of plots in Western writing—comedy and tragedy—can also be found in the parables.[40]

William Herzog concluded in 1994 that the parables focus "not on a vision of the glory of the reign of God, but on the gory details of how oppression served the interests of the ruling class." They showed "how human beings could respond to break the spiral of violence and cycle of poverty created by exploitation and oppression." A parable was "a form of social analysis every bit as much as it was a form of theological

35. Ibid., 25.
36. Ibid., 26.
37. Ibid., 13.
38. See C. H. Dodd, *The Parables of the Kingdom* (London: Collins, 1961).
39. See ibid., 146–56.
40. See Dan Otto Via, *The Parables: Their Literary and Existential Dimensions* (Philadelphia: Fortress Press, 1967).

reflection."[41] Thus the parables have much in them to inspire and teach people today who are caught in poverty and oppression, because Jesus is depicted as a leader encouraging his peasant followers to revolt against the political, social, and economic oppression of his time. The primary aim of parables was not to "communicate theology or ethics, but to stimulate social analysis and change on the part of the hearers, whether the original hearers or later ones."[42] Mary Ann Beavis concludes that the parables need to be read in light of contemporary challenges, so the intentions of Jesus and the evangelists in creating them are irrelevant. For example, some parables can be read from a feminist perspective because they challenge patriarchal systems of power.[43]

Pedagogical Inductive Process

In using parables Jesus Christ shows himself to be a brilliant storyteller who aims to engage his listeners in reflective, inductive learning. At the same time his power as a storyteller comes from the Father (John 20:21). These are some key characteristics of parables that need to guide us when we use them as stories that can stimulate contemporary narratives of refounding pastoral ministries. Jesus demonstrates this in several ways:

1. Jesus uses parables as springboard stories

A springboard story assists learning, "not so much through transferring large amounts of information as through catalyzing understanding." It encourages listeners "to visualize from a story in one context what is involved in a large-scale transformation in an analogous context."[44] It is able to communicate new ideas in ways that help people to understand their complexity and encourage them to overcome their resistance to change by bypassing the normal defenses to people's feelings. Listeners are able to see that they can act in similar ways to change their environ-

41. William R. Herzog, *Parables as Subversive Speech: Jesus as Pedagogue of the Oppressed* (Louisville: Westminster John Knox, 1994), 3.

42. Alison Jack, "'For those Outside,'" 9.

43. See Mary Ann Beavis, "Introduction: Seeking the 'Lost Coin' of Parables About Women," 17–33, in eadem, ed., *The Lost Coin: Parables of Women, Work and Wisdom* (London: Sheffield Academic Press, 2002).

44. Stephen Denning, *The Springboard: How Storytelling Ignites Action in Knowledge-Era Organizations* (Woburn, MA: Butterworth-Heinemann, 2002), xix.

ment.[45] In the Old Testament, for instance, the prophet Nathan has to rebuke David for arranging the death of Uriah in battle so that he could marry Uriah's wife, Bathsheba (2 Sam 11:12). Instead of confronting David directly, Nathan tells a story about a rich man stealing a lamb from a poor man (2 Sam 12:1-25). David is enraged when he hears what the wealthy person has done—but he has unknowingly described himself. Then Nathan turns to David and says, "You are the man!" (2 Sam 12:7). David is mortified and repents.

Jesus Christ follows this tradition in his parables. Scriptural scholar N. T. Wright comments: "Stories are . . . peculiarly good at modifying or subverting other stories and worldviews. Where head-on attack would certainly fail, the parable hides the wisdom of the serpent behind the innocence of the dove, gaining entrance and favour which can then be used to change assumptions which the hearer would otherwise keep hidden away for safety."[46] Jesus in his use of parables was able to raise sensitive issues in an indirect manner that gave people freedom to apply the lessons to their own lives. The stories dispose them to listen; their defenses are down. Thus when Jesus is dining with Simon the Pharisee a woman of the city enters and covers the feet of Jesus "with kisses and anointed them with the ointment" (Luke 7:38). Simon is shocked. Rather than confront the prejudices of Simon directly and risk further alienation and anger, Jesus simply tells a parable about a repentant debtor (Luke 7:40-43). This gives Simon space to ponder and apply to himself the lesson of the parable. Likewise, down through the centuries the listener is "seduced" by the power of a good story, only to discover that the narrative leads him or her in unexpected directions or to unanticipated consequences. Paul Ricoeur writes that what is able to happen through the parables is the *recognition* of Jesus as being the Christ, "the communicating of an act of confession, a communication by means of which the reader in turn is rendered capable of performing the same recognition which occurs inside the text."[47]

45. See ibid., xv.

46. See N. T. Wright, *The New Testament and the People of God* (Minneapolis: Fortress Press, 1993), 40.

47. Paul Ricoeur, "The Bible and the Imagination," 49–75, in Hans Dieter Betz, ed., *The Bible as a Document of the University* (Chico, CA: Scholars Press, 1981), 68.

2. Jesus builds on the experience of his listeners

Good storytellers structure their stories in such a way that the language and concepts used are familiar and appropriate to their listeners. They begin with the known and gradually move to new insights. In doing this, accomplished storytellers ensure that each new insight is explained or described thoroughly to enable the listener to construct a meaningful figure.[48] Christ did this. His listeners could readily identify with the down-to-earth realities of the parables: the world of farming and fishing, of weddings and feasts, of rich land owners and restive tenants, of travelers banging on the front door at night, of a widow opposing a heartless judge. It is a world without superficial adornment in which even the hero of the parable can be a hard-headed schemer (Luke 16:1-8) or a seemingly impetuous landowner (Matt 20:1-16). But there is a particular quality to the parables not usually found in everyday stories; the insights contained in the parables are *dramatically* new. They turn people's expectations of the world upside down.

Thus the focus is not directly on the beauty and power of God but on the often brutal details of how secular and religious rulers exploited the powerless. In this sense they are a form of social analysis exploring how the powerless could break these exploiting forces, but in nonviolent ways and with compassion and reconciliation.[49] A parable is a process that begins not directly with the mysteries of God but with the perplexities of everyday life, and that draws listeners to discover a richer and deeper meaning in the midst of life's chaotic uncertainties.[50] In this, parables have qualities that resemble in significant ways the wisdom literature of the Old Testament. The unique quality of that literature is that while traditional methods of storytelling are used, books such as Job aim to uncover wise insights about life in view of what people are experiencing.[51] Jesus is the Sage seeking through storytelling to draw listeners to discover surprising meanings about the purpose of life and virtue in a meaningless and often unjust world. We live in an age of uncertainty and tumult akin to, but so much more dramatic than, the Old Testament and gospel times. Stories and parables engaged listeners in those

48. See Michael Kaye, *Myth-Makers and Story-Tellers* (Sydney: Business and Professional Publishing, 1996), 39–40.

49. See Herzog, *Parables as Subversive Speech*, 3.

50. Ibid., 266.

51. See Jill Y. Crainshaw, *Wise and Discerning Hearts: An Introduction to Wisdom Liturgical Theology* (Collegeville, MN: Liturgical Press, 2000), 161–91.

days; so the parables can hold the attention of contemporary seekers of meaning. People today yearn for the sayings and stories of wise people.

3. Jesus calls people to ask questions

Since the parables are so delivered that there is no one authoritative conclusion possible, Jesus is saying to his listeners: "Given the context in which you are living, what do *you* think about this situation?" Readers will make all kinds of interpretations and applications simply because the world in which they live is different.[52]

4. Jesus evokes personal and cultural transformation

The parables are not theological treatises but springboard stories that aim to engage listeners in discussions on critical points of everyday life, leading them at the same time to discover that there is a different and better way to live than through violence, injustice, and unkindness. It is through love, compassion, and mercy. People are to discover the answers themselves by pondering and repeating the stories. This is a respectful way of teaching. It is not a moralistic preaching process, for it allows hearers to exercise their own power of discernment and at their own pace.[53] But the parables are structured in such a way that the listeners must eventually make a choice—the way of love *or* selfishness, mercy *or* oppression, reconciliation *or* revenge. In short, parables call people to personal and cultural transformation.[54] People must make a choice. They cannot remain neutral when listening to the parables because the issues are starkly presented. Cultures of oppression must give way to justice. At the same time, individuals must be internally transformed. In this way parables can be a way to experience God through love. As St. Augustine wrote in the fifth century: "If you see charity, you see the Trinity."[55]

5. Jesus uses disarming humor

We surely should expect to find humor in the Scriptures, because this is one of the most effective ways to communicate and to convey

---

52. Charles W. Hedrick, *Many Things in Parables: Jesus and His Modern Critics* (Louisville: Westminster John Knox, 2004), 54–55.

53. See Donaghue, *Gospel in Parable*, 10–13.

54. See comments by Paul Ricoeur in "Biblical Hermeneutics," *Semeia* 4 (1975): 29–148, at 118 and passim.

55. Quoted by Benedictine XVI, *Deus Caritas Est* (Sydney: St Pauls Publications, 2006), 33.

profound truths in an appealing and respectful manner. In fact, comic incongruities abound in the Scriptures.[56] Jewish rabbis at the time of Christ also used parables as a teaching tool, but those of Jesus are extraordinary for their wit, terseness, pointed grasp of human behavior, and ability to convey profound truths in an ironic manner.[57] The humor he uses in some of the parables is relaxing. It is disarming for those listeners who would at times have violently resisted his teachings if they had not been "dressed up" in story form. As Robert H. Stein, a Scripture scholar, writes: "Often hearers could be challenged to pass judgment on a story before discovering that in so doing they had in fact condemned themselves."[58]

Consider, for example, when Jesus describes to his listeners the nature of the kingdom of God by likening it to a tiny mustard seed that, when planted, becomes "a tree, and the birds of the air made nests in its branches" (Luke 13:19). Again, the complacent, self-righteous Pharisee believes that he is superior to the publican, but Jesus condemns him for his arrogance and praises the humility and honesty of the publican (Luke 18:10-14). In the Prodigal Son story (Luke 15:11-32) the delinquent son, having lived in luxury, finds himself in an incongruous place, with the pigs so despised in Jewish culture. The incongruity is resolved through his conversion and decision to seek pardon from his father. Of course, the ultimate meaning, God's love and mercy for the repentant and outcast in society, is even more paradoxical. The tension between the demands of justice and mercy is resolved beyond human imagining in favor of compassion and mercy. Finally, there is a small aspect of the parable that would certainly have been seen as very funny by Jesus' listeners, that is, the father running to meet his son (Luke 15:20). Wealthy and powerful men never ran. Indeed, culturally it would have been a shameful thing to have done, something beneath a man's dignity. Jesus' listeners, especially those who were poor, would have chuckled to themselves at the thought of such a culturally topsy-turvy happening.

The humorous irony in the Good Samaritan story (Luke 10:29-37) is the fact that the priest and the Levite, professionally committed to

---

56. For a more extensive analysis of humor in the Scriptures see Gerald A. Arbuckle, *Laughing with God: Humor, Culture, and Transformation* (Collegeville, MN: Liturgical Press, 2008).

57. See John L. McKenzie, *Dictionary of the Bible* (London: Geoffrey Chapman, 1965), 635–36.

58. Robert H. Stein, "Parables," *Oxford Companion to the Bible*, 567–70, at 568.

maintaining Jewish religious traditions, fail in their duties of care for the severely injured victim of a robbery. The Samaritan, a non-Jew, spontaneously goes to the aid of the wounded person. Again, the deeper meaning of the story is one of divine humor. Jesus exemplifies the qualities of the Good Samaritan. He reveals God's preferential love for those considered socially or physically powerless.

6. Jesus describes the kingdom in "simple" language

The parables must be understood in light of Jesus' proclamation that the reign of God is inaugurated and realized in the person of Jesus. Jesus ties parables to the reign of God by using the former to describe the latter. The kingdom in Jesus' language is a symbol, not a concept. Its meaning is not specified or specifiable. Like all effective symbols, that of the kingdom, the reign of God, contains inexhaustible meanings.[59] The message of the parables is that the kingdom "is not merely imminent; it is here."[60]

7. Jesus uses a threefold ritual dynamic

There are three stages in the process of initiation rituals: separation, chaos/dislocation, and reentry.[61] In the separation stage participants are reminded that something important is about to happen, that predictable patterns of life are about to be challenged. For example, at the beginning of the parable about the sower Jesus abruptly interrupts conversation with the call "Listen!" (Mark 4:3). Something important is about to be said. In the chaos stage participants are thrown into confusion. They are startled by the surprising turn in the story and what it all means. Then, once they clarify the meaning, they must decide to embrace or reject the new mythology of life; in the reentry stage people return to daily life transformed by their decision in the chaos stage to move forward and change the world they live in. For example, in the Good Samaritan parable Jewish listeners would have expected a fellow Jew to come to the aid of the victim, but they are shocked into a state of chaos when they discover it is a hated Samaritan who is moved with compassion.

59. See Bernard Brandon Scott, *Jesus, Symbol-Maker for the Kingdom* (Philadelphia: Fortress Press, 1981).
60. See Dodd, *Parables of the Kingdom*, 40.
61. See Arbuckle, *Laughing with God*, 42–55.

Saint Paul: Refounding Christian Identities

In his missionary journeys St. Paul founded many churches, seeing himself as the chosen instrument to take the Gospel to the Gentiles, and aware that his power to do so comes from God (Gal 1:15-16; 2:7-8). By his letters and visits Paul is consciously calling these communities to revive the faith of their original founding. Each community faces different challenges, so that each has a different aspect of the Christian message.[62] He writes a furious and passionate plea[63] to a group of churches he had founded, whose members are mainly Gentile, not to abandon what he had taught them: "I am astonished that you are so quickly deserting the one who called you in the grace of Christ and turning to a different gospel" (Gal 1:6). In his role now as a refounder of these churches he calls them to return to the original identity he had so painstakingly fostered among them. They must resist the efforts of intruders who want them to conform to distinctive customs of Judaism such as male circumcision. These interlopers accuse Paul of heresy because the Jewish law was never abrogated by Christ. Moreover, they claim, Paul is not an authentic apostle, for he has never seen Jesus or been taught by him. The power to make these accusations, they assert, comes directly from the original apostles. Paul, however, vigorously disagrees. His legitimacy comes directly from God's revelation to him as well as his commission to evangelize the Gentile world, and not from any leaders in Jerusalem. He insists that Gentile believers have equal status with Jewish converts and castigates preachers who want to impose the opposite view. The Galatians must with determination rebuild communities that resist such false Christian beliefs. He forcefully writes: "There is no longer Jew or Greek . . . and if you belong to

---

62. Romano Penna writes of Paul's epistle to the Romans: "Far from being a speculative tract of theology, the Epistle loves to narrate. This genre is used on various levels according to different types. We have numbered six of them: the biblical kerygma, autobiographical elements of the sender, passages of theological biography of the readers, the theological narration, and the similes. . . . [The narrative style] confers upon the Epistle . . . a fresher and more concrete meaning; by making it more adherent to everyday life, narration renders the Epistle itself more vivid." "Narrative Aspects of the Epistle of St. Paul to the Romans," 191–204, in Clemens Thoma and Michael Wyschogrod, eds., *Parable and Story in Judaism and Christianity* (New York: Paulist Press, 1989), 202.

63. See Robin Griffith-Jones, *The Gospel according to Paul* (New York: Harper-One, 2004), 231–63.

Christ then you are Abraham's offspring, heirs according to the promise" (Gal 3:28-29). Both Jew and Gentile had been accepted by God because of their faith in Jesus Christ, not because of any law (Gal 3:1-5).[64] In brief, Paul's writing is *"of the essentially Jewish story,"* but *"now redrawn around Jesus* (italics original)."[65] The intruders, whom Paul adamantly condemns, refuse to redraw the Jewish story around the radical lessons of Jesus' life and teachings.

The personal shock and pain Paul experiences when he sees faith communities break away from the founding mythology is starkly evident in his correspondence with the Corinthian church. Its members are divided by personal loyalties to different religious teachers and by interpersonal tensions (1 Cor 1:10-13; 3:3; 11:18-19). Some had become arrogant and excessively self-confident (4:19; 5:2), probably because they thought they had special knowledge and spiritual wisdom (3:18; 8:1-2). They have failed to appreciate the significance of the Gospel in terms of Paul's own life; for this reason they have rejected him and his method of evangelizing. Listen to Paul's distress at what he sees: "We are treated as imposters, and yet are true; as unknown, and yet are well-known" (2 Cor 6:8-9). The gap separating them from Jesus Christ can only be bridged through rediscovering and reowning in their lives the narrative death and resurrection of Christ (Phil 3:10).

Summary

The lives of the prophets and of Jesus Christ highlight the qualities needed in contemporary refounding persons who are committed to the founding and refounding of faith communities:

- Refounders need to be people of immense faith, courage, and imagination, creatively flexible in order to relate to the different needs of listeners.

- Narratives that make sense to people, such as the narratives of the prophets and Jesus Christ, are those that arouse the senses from their slumber, that open the eyes and ears to the realities of life; these narratives have the ability down through the centuries to

64. See F. F. Bruce, "The Letter to the Galatians," 238–40, in *Oxford Companion to the Bible.*
65. Wright, *The New Testament and the People of God,* 79.

release the body from the constraints imposed by outworn ways of speaking, and hence to renew and rejuvenate one's felt awareness of the world."[66]

- The parables of Jesus Christ illustrate that one important aim of ministry is to enable individuals and communities to fashion narratives that weave together divine and human stories into a single fabric; parables evoke uneasiness in listeners, disturb their everyday assumptions about life, expose them "to the new, to a kingdom not yet experienced."[67]

- For the refounding of Catholic identities, we first need to invite people to rediscover, or discover for the first time, the person of Jesus Christ; the parables as springboard stories are ideally suited to our postmodern age which emphasizes storytelling as the means to achieve identities.

- To emphasize this conclusion, the next chapter explains why didactic or normative statements of Catholic identities have little or no impact on contemporary listeners.

66. David Abram, *The Spell of the Sensuous: Perception and Language in a More-than-Human World* (New York: Pantheon Books, 1997), 265.

67. Bernard Brandon Scott, *Hear Then the Parable: A Commentary on the Parables of Jesus* (Minneapolis: Fortress Press, 1989), 419.

Chapter Six

Catholic Normative Identities: A Critique

Our own time . . . must be increasingly marked by a new hearing of God's word and a new evangelization. . . . The greater our openness to God's word, the more will we be able to recognize that today too the mystery of Pentecost is taking place in God's Church.[1] *(Benedict XVI)*

This chapter explains that:

- over the centuries significant normative definitions of Catholic identities have developed
- it has been customary to impart these definitions in a deductive or "top-down" pedagogy
- unless people are themselves involved in an inductive manner, however, the deductive approach will remain ineffective in crafting Catholic identities
- since storytelling, a particularly positive quality of post-modernity, is the way people craft their identities, the process of crafting Catholic identities needs to be based on scriptural stories and parables

---

1. Benedict XVI, *Verbum Domini* (London: Catholic Truth Society, 2010), 139–40.

Martha Nussbaum, the celebrated philosopher of education, warns against the dangers of rote learning that results in uncritical thinking and at times disastrous behavior.[2] Thomas Groome is equally critical of the same pedagogy in faith education. Rather than "manipulation or indoctrination," he writes, "educators must re-present the Christian story and Vision in ways that are enticing and attractive to people's lives, that are likely to encourage them in personal conviction of its truths and values."[3] Neither critic condemns the importance of learning fundamental truths and values about life, but both are concerned about *how* this learning is to occur. Are people to be passive receivers *or* are they to be actively engaged in their own learning, involving imaginative and creative reflection on their own experience? As we saw in the previous chapter, Jesus Christ chose the second option.

This chapter summarizes in a series of models, followed by evaluation, what I call "normative Catholic identities." These models have been constructed and emphasized by church teaching authorities and theologians responding to changing times and needs. It is not that the norms enshrined in the models are wrong or right, but the question is: what model is the most suitable one to begin refounding evangelization in light of our postmodern age and the confusion that many experience about their Catholic identities. Readers may wish to review the sociological models of Catholic identities in chapter 1 before proceeding further. Several models specifically focus on Catholic healthcare institutions, but the insights are applicable to all Catholic organizations.

In evaluating the relevance of the models, therefore, I invite readers to bear these questions in mind:

- How are we to engage people in Catholic institutions, such as schools, universities, and healthcare, who are not members of the Catholic Church or, if they are Catholic, have little or no knowledge of the faith? What model is the most suitable to *begin* with?

- That is, how are we to "re-present the Christian Story and Vision in ways that are enticing and attractive to people's lives, that are

---

2. Martha C. Nussbaum, *Not for Profit: Why Democracy Needs the Humanities* (Princeton, NJ: Princeton University Press, 2010), 53.

3. Thomas H. Groome, *Will There Be Faith?* (New York: HarperCollins, 2011), 69.

likely to encourage them in personal conviction of its truths and values?"[4]

Model 1: Theological Identities

Theologian Richard P. McBrien writes: "There is no one characteristic, apart from the Petrine doctrine, which sets the Catholic Church apart from *all other* churches." The Petrine doctrine is the belief that the pope, as the chief shepherd and supreme authority in the church, is the successor of St. Peter. Beyond this Petrine doctrine,[5] however, McBrien adds that there are "various characteristics of Catholicism, each of which . . . Catholicism shares with one or another Christian Church or tradition" but that "a case can be made that nowhere else except in the Catholic Church are *all* of Catholicism's characteristics present in the precise *configuration* in which they are found within Catholicism."[6] That is, although Catholicism may to varying degrees share particular characteristics with other Christian traditions, their combination within Catholicism forms its individuality, its "Catholicity."[7] Certainly this "precise configuration" McBrien refers to is not static, but is constantly being molded by the Gospel, the official teachings and traditions of the church, and the reflective experience of members of Catholic ministries who must constantly make decisions in light of these foundational realities.

The particular unique *configuration* of characteristics within Catholicism that is not duplicated anywhere in the community of Christian churches is, according to McBrien, its "systematic theology; the body of doctrines; the liturgical life, especially the Eucharist; the variety of

---

4. Ibid.

5. Archbishop of Canterbury Rowan Williams, when describing the "distinctive constellation" of qualities that identifies Anglicans, omits any reference to the Petrine doctrine. *Anglican Identities* (London: Darton, Longman and Todd, 2004), 7–8.

6. Richard P. McBrien, *Catholicism*, vol. 2 (San Francisco: Harper and Row, 1980), 1172.

7. See Thomas H. Groome, "What Makes a School Catholic?," 106–24, in Terence McLaughlin, Joseph O'Keefe, and Bernadette O'Keeffe, eds., *The Contemporary Catholic School: Context, Identity and Diversity* (London: Falmer Press, 1996), 108.

spiritualities; religious congregations and lay apostolates; official teachings on justice, peace, and human rights; the exercise of collegiality; and, to be sure, the Petrine ministry." He then writes that "Catholicism is distinguished from other Christian churches and traditions especially in its understanding of, and practical commitment to, the principles of sacramentality, mediation, and communion. Differences between Catholic and non-Catholic (especially Protestant) approaches become clearer when measured according to these three principles."[8] In summary, he says, Catholicism "is a tradition that sees God in all things (sacramentality), using the human, the material, and the finite (mediation), to bring about the unity of humankind (communion)."[9]

Evaluation

McBrien's list of characteristics is fundamental in theologically defining the uniqueness of Catholicism. However, for staffs of Catholic institutions such as those engaged in education and healthcare it would need to be explained by a skilled theological educator over a lengthy period of time. Something simpler, directly related to the Scriptures and especially to the person of Jesus Christ is necessary in order initially to engage busy staff members whose knowledge of the faith may be extremely limited.

Model 2: Identity Indicators in Healthcare

The Catholic Health Association of the United States has listed in a policy statement five fundamental and positive tenets of Catholic healthcare practice.

- Healthcare is a service and never merely a commodity exchanged for profit, a service according to the mission of Jesus Christ.

- Every person is the subject of human dignity with intrinsic spiritual worth at every stage of human development.

- People are inherently social; their dignity is fully realized only in association with others. All must serve the common good; the self-interest of a few must not compromise the well-being of all.

8. Richard P. McBrien, *Catholicism* (North Blackburn: CollinsDove, 1994), 9.
9. Ibid., 17.

- A preferential option for the poor calls for commitment to the care of people who are poor and disenfranchised.

- Stewardship requires that we use natural and social resources prudently and in the service of all.[10]

The same document also emphasizes the need for holistic healthcare, including a commitment to pastoral care, adherence to the ethical teaching of the Catholic Church as found in the *Ethical and Religious Directives for Catholic Health Care Services*, ethical corporate policies, the proper treatment of employees, and the importance of the culture or ethos incorporating these values.[11]

Evaluation

This model is helpful inasmuch as it is a simple set of behavioral expectations that could be developed into evaluated policies. The list of the constituents of Catholic identities is short, but it suffers from the fact that it remains heavily theoretical or intellectually oriented. But its emphasis on the need for pastoral care and ethical corporate policies is timely. Reference is made to "the mission of Jesus Christ," but it remains a statement without any development. The fact itself is, however, a particularly positive point, especially since a significant number of mission statements in Catholic hospitals in the United States do not refer to Jesus Christ (see chap. 3 above).

In its excellent statement on ethical standards for Catholic healthcare facilities, Catholic Healthcare Australia provides this statement on Catholic identities:

> A healthcare organisation bearing the name 'Catholic' has a special responsibility to witness to the presence of Christ and to Catholic teachings about the value and dignity of the human person.
>
> Tangible signs of the Catholic identity of an organisation [include]: sponsorship, ownership, governance and/or management by the local church or by a religious congregation; recognition by the bishop of the diocese; priority given to pastoral care and mission integration; availability of the sacraments and the prominence of Christian symbols; acceptance of Catholic teaching and observances of canonical requirements.

10. Catholic Health Association, "How to Approach Catholic Identity in Changing Times," *Health Progress* (April 1994): 23–29.

11. Ibid., 24–28.

All who work in and for Catholic health care should be united by their adherence, not only to the ethical standards of their respective professions but also by a willingness to embrace the ethical standards of Catholic health care.[12]

Evaluation

The document begins, as does the American one, by focusing on the need to witness to the presence of Christ through our respect for the inherent worth of every person. It helpfully identifies some of the practical, measurable signs of Catholic identities within the Australian context, for example, priority of pastoral care and mission integration and willingness to embrace the ethical standards of the church. It was not the task of the document, however, to set out the processes that would lead to mission integration or people's willingness to embrace the church's ethical standards.

Model 3: "Catholic Identities" in Canon Law

Canonist Francis Morrisey, OMI, suggests two models for determining Catholic identities. The first can be called the canonical or traditional model and consists of three types: legal, doctrinal, and values-based.[13] For an institution to be legally[14] called Catholic it must demonstrate Catholic values, for example, fidelity to the Christian message as it comes through the church; be formally established and approved by the appropriate ecclesiastical authority and subject to the guidance of this authority, particularly the local diocesan bishop; be bound by canon law requirements regarding pastoral care and administration of property; and be subject to visitation by the diocesan bishop. From a doctrinal perspective an institution must conform to criteria such as maintaining a Catholic ethos by adhering to Catholic traditions, displaying religious symbols, and having a general apostolic purpose based on the personal commitment of those involved.

---

12. Catholic Health Australia, *Code of Ethical Standards for Catholic Health and Aged Care Services in Australia* (Canberra: Catholic Health Australia, 2001), 55.

13. See Francis Morrisey, "Catholic Identity in a Challenging Environment," *Health Progress* (November 1999): 38–45.

14. See Canons 216, 300, 803 § 3, and 808.

Morrisey has reservations about the canonical-based criteria because if they are applied to major organizations such as healthcare institutions, not all could pass. Hence he proposes a refinement to the canonical model by formulating criteria based on four interconnected themes: mission, sponsorship, holistic care, and ethics. The mission of the church is to reveal God's love for all peoples as expressed in the life of Jesus Christ. Because this is the mission of the church, Catholic institutions must necessarily be accountable for the implementation of this mission to the local diocesan bishop. Sponsors need to formulate non-negotiable values and behaviors for their organizations. Holistic healing necessitates concern for the whole person, including spiritual, physical, emotional, intellectual, and occupational aspects. Ethical behavior for members of a Catholic healthcare ministry means living one's life, while engaged in this ministry, according to the values of the Gospel and the church.

Morrisey points to three types of ethics: social, corporate, and clinical. Social ethics, particularly as defined by the social teaching of the church, require that we take into account the wider needs of the community; corporate ethics direct the healthcare ministry to act according to social justice in its relationship with employees; clinical ethics direct the ministry to respect the sacredness of life at all stages of development. Leonard J. Nelson concludes that some of these criteria are of little value in determining Catholic identities: "Mission can be stated at such a general level, i.e., providing care in a manner that is consistent with gospel values, that it may not constrain organizations in practice."[15]

Peter C. Phan,[16] Ignacio Ellacuría chair of Catholic Social Thought at Georgetown University, also questions the adequacy of the canonical definition of Catholic identity when this is confined to visible links with the church through formal baptism. Canon 205 reads: "Those baptized are fully in communion with the Catholic Church here on earth who are joined with Christ in his visible structure by the bonds of profession of faith, the sacraments and ecclesiastical governance." Phan notes that Catholic identities are defined, therefore, only in terms of three visible bonds, but the canon omits the all-important qualities of possession of the Holy Spirit and spiritual communion—qualities insisted upon

---

15. Leonard J. Nelson, *Diagnosis Critical: The Urgent Threats Confronting Catholic Health Care* (Huntington, IN: Our Sunday Visitor, 2009), 80.

16. See Peter C. Phan, "To Be Catholic or Not to Be: Is It Still the Question? Catholic Identity and Religious Education Today," at www.members.cox.net/vientrietdao /phancho/catholid.html, accessed 12 March 2007.

by Vatican II in the Dogmatic Constitution on the Church (*Lumen Gentium*) 8. He writes that the Code of Canon Law certainly gives a conceptually precise definition of what constitutes Catholic identity, with its emphasis on empirically verifiable criteria, but he finds a significant theological problem with this. The cost for canonical exactness is far too high, "since what is at the heart of Catholic reality, namely, union with Christ and other Christians in the Holy Spirit, is left aside. Indeed, Vatican II felt obligated to add to its description of Catholic identities the warning that even though incorporated into the church [that is, by formal baptism, GA], one who does not, however, persevere in charity is not saved. He remains indeed in the bosom of the church, but 'in body' not 'in heart' (*LG* 14). Clearly, for Vatican II the spiritual condition for full incorporation into the Church obtains primacy over the visible ones."[17]

Evaluation

Peter Steinfels notes that many North American Catholic schools have weakened their canonical links with the institutional Catholic Church. "What was stressed [in their self-description] was their city, region, history, or founding religious orders. . . . In a culture warm to vague spirituality but suspicious of institutional religion, it was evidently considered the better part of marketing to go lightly on the links . . . to a *church*—and especially one that was demanding and controversial."[18] Nevertheless, while accepting the criticisms of Morrisey and Phan, I believe that the canonical model has one distinctive benefit. It reminds Catholic facilities that they are ministries of the church: no institution may call itself "Catholic" unless it is in communion with the appropriate ecclesiastical authority, that is, the diocesan bishop.[19] Canon law sets out clear directives about the meaning of ecclesiastical accountability, for example, the use of properties and relationships with the local diocesan bishop. As laypeople become increasingly involved in the administration of Catholic institutions this point of accountability to the laws of the church needs to be frequently and unequivocally emphasized. For example, canon law states: "The Roman Pontiff, by virtue of his primacy of governance, is the supreme administrator and steward of ecclesiasti-

17. Ibid.
18. Peter Steinfels, *A People Adrift: The Crisis of the Roman Catholic Church in America* (New York: Simon & Schuster, 2003), 138–39.
19. See Morrissey, "Catholic Identity," 40.

cal goods" (Canon 1273). Therefore as such, Catholic institutions are subject to the requirements set out in Book V of the *Code of Canon Law*, "The Temporal Goods of the Church" (Canons 1254–1310). Because, for example, Catholic schools and healthcare services are ministries of the church, administrators are to be accountable for the use of ecclesiastical goods. They must also be accountable to the local bishop for the manner in which these ministries are conducted (Canon 678).

Model 4: An Outsider's View

A respected American Baptist theologian, Langdon Gilkey, distinguishes four notable qualities in the unique configuration of Catholicism:[20]

- Respect for tradition: tradition can act as both a memory of the past and a guide to the future.

- Positive acceptance of human nature: Catholicism emphasizes a realistic and optimistic understanding of people as capable of sin but essentially good.

- Sense of sacramentality: the belief that God's life and love comes to us, and that we go to God through the created order and everyday things of life.

- Commitment to rationality: Catholicism asserts the place of reason in life and in faith. People are encouraged to ponder the mysteries of their faith through rational reflection. Whatever is true, and whatever way it is acquired, for example, through the use of reason, is ultimately from God.

Evaluation

One weakness of Gilkey's theological model of identity clarification is that it can be used only by trained theologians and historians. However, it is an important model on the basis of which pastoral strategies should be constructed. Theologian Thomas Groome, in his commentary on Gilkey's model, explains that Catholic theology takes a middle position between extreme views on the role of the individual in seeking salvation. On the one hand there is the total self-sufficiency of Pelagius (ca. 400):

---

20. See Langdon Gilkey, *Catholicism Confronts Modernity: A Protestant View* (New York: Seabury Press, 1975), 17–22.

we can save ourselves without God.[21] On the other hand there is the Protestant reformer, John Calvin: we are a mass of sin, incapable of contributing anything to our salvation. Gilkey comments that Catholicism has "a remarkable sense of humanity." He writes that "consequently, the love of life, the appreciation of the body and the senses, the joy and celebration, the tolerance of the sinner, these natural, worldly and 'human' virtues are far more clearly and universally embodied in Catholics and Catholic life than in Protestants and Protestantism."[22]

Because of this optimistic but realistic acceptance of human nature, Gilkey speaks of "sacramentality," that is, the fact that God's love can be revealed through any human person, no matter what their religion or culture. Gilkey also includes respect for tradition and history as a distinctive quality of Catholic identity. By this he means that the Catholic story finds its roots in the Old and New Testaments and in the reflections on these roots by countless Catholics over the centuries. As Vatican II says: "The Tradition that comes from the apostles makes progress in the Church, with the help of the Holy Spirit. There is growth in insight into the realities and words that are being passed on."[23] Groome, when reflecting on Gilkey's emphasis on tradition and history, draws this important conclusion:

> The "Story" of Christian faith, then, includes: its scriptures and liturgies; its creeds, dogmas, doctrines and theologies; its sacraments and rituals, symbols, myths, gestures and religious language patterns; its spiritualities, values, laws, and expected lifestyles. . . . Any symbol that reflects and carries the historical reality of Catholic Christian faith is an aspect of Christian Story.[24]

Therefore traditional symbols such as the cross and statues of saints are external expressions of Christian identities. However, Father Avery Dulles, SJ, adds a much-needed distinction between tradition and traditionalism. "The acceptance of a divinely authoritative tradition is

---

21. See Groome, "What Makes a School Catholic?," 108–25.

22. Gilkey, *Catholicism*, 19. See Groome, "What Makes a School Catholic?," 110–12.

23. Constitution on Divine Revelation 8 (*Dei Verbum*), in *Vatican Council II: Volume 1, The Conciliar and Post Conciliar Documents*, ed. Austin Flannery (Northport, NY: Costello Publishing Company, Inc., 1996).

24. Groome, "What Makes a School Catholic?," 117–18.

characteristically Catholic, as opposed to Protestant. Yet the concept of tradition, like that of Catholicism, has varied over the centuries."[25] Traditionalism is not synonymous with tradition. Traditionalism would wrongly make tradition, and therefore Catholic identities, synonymous with such things as outdated teaching methods and styles of worship.[26]

Gilkey highlights the Catholic commitment to rationality. Catholicism avoids the excesses of fideism (i.e., blind faith) and rationalism (i.e., the self-sufficiency of reason). As Groome comments: "Catholicism has been convinced that understanding and faith, reason and revelation, need and enhance each other."[27] St. Thomas Aquinas described the relationship between reason and faith in this way: "Just as grace does not destroy nature but perfects it, so sacred doctrine presupposes, uses, and perfects natural knowledge."[28] It is this commitment to rationality that should encourage Catholics to have confidence in their discernment and decision-making processes. St. Ignatius Loyola (1491–1556) developed a particular form of reason-faith decision making called the "discernment model," which many religious congregations have adopted, and this needs to be maintained whenever laypeople assume control of their ministries.[29]

Model 5: Identities through Transformation

Sister Juliana Casey, IHM, a skilled educator in Catholic healthcare institutions, defines Catholic identities according to the "ancient characteristics, or 'marks' of the church."[30] These ancient characteristics, she writes, are repeated "whenever we say the creed: *one, holy, catholic,*

25. Avery Dulles, *The Reshaping of Catholicism: Current Challenges in the Theology of Church* (New York: Harper & Row, 1988), 75.

26. See ibid., 78; see also Francis A. Sullivan, "Catholic Tradition and Traditions," 113–33, in Michael J. Lacey and Francis Oakley, eds., *The Crisis of Authority in Catholic Modernity* (New York: Oxford University Press, 2011).

27. Groome, "What Makes a School Catholic?," 119; Benedict XVI's lecture at the University of Regensburg on 12 September 2006 was on the theme of the relationship between reason and faith.

28. Thomas Aquinas, *Summa Theologiae* I, 1, q. 8 ad 2.

29. For a description of this process of decision making, see John English, *Spiritual Intimacy and Community: An Ignatian View of the Small Faith Community* (London: Darton, Longman and Todd, 1992), 25–45.

30. Juliana Casey, "Holy Memory, Faithful Action: The Catholic Identity of Catholic Health East, Based in Memory, Has Important Implications for the Future," *Health Progress* (March 2000): 28–31, at 28.

and *apostolic*. . . . [Catholic Health East] is a specific manifestation of the call to oneness, for it is the fruit of many joining together in a common mission."[31] Speaking of the quality of "holiness," she comments: "A health system whose mission is to be a healing and transforming presence can carry that mission out only when its members themselves are transformed. Structures in the system must encourage the spiritual growth of caregivers and those served. The presence of God in all we do will be felt through prayer, celebration, reflection, and gratitude."[32]

Of the word "Catholic" she writes: "Its most basic sense is that of universal, or all-embracing. . . . To be catholic also implies a fidelity to the Catholic tradition in all of its aspects and fundamental expressions. . . . CHE . . . does not seek to convert others to the Roman Catholic tradition, nor does it apologize for its own identity as faithful to that tradition. Catholicity implies universality of welcome and collaboration for the sake of the ministry."[33] Of the fourth mark, apostolicity, she writes: "The term . . . refers to the church's grounding in the experience of the first witnesses to the resurrection. . . . To be apostolic is to be in communion with the tradition that began with the apostles and bear witness to that tradition."[34]

Evaluation

This is a model coming from a person well-versed in the Scriptures and theology, together with a wide personal experience of the ministry of healthcare. I repeat one of the key points in this model: "A health system whose mission is to be a healing and transforming presence can carry that mission out only when its members themselves are transformed." The implications of this statement are profound. For example, sponsors, board members, and senior executives cannot effectively be carriers of the founding story of Catholic healthcare *unless* they are willing to be transformed by the living presence and power of the Word of God. The challenge is: how is this transformation to take place? (see chaps. 5, 7, and 8)

31. Ibid.
32. Ibid., 29.
33. Ibid.
34. Ibid.

Model 6: Identities: Accountable Actions

This model (see fig. 6.1), constructed for Catholic healthcare ministries, is applicable, with appropriate modifications, to other ministries. Respect for the ethical teaching of the church is especially relevant when a Catholic facility is considering merging with or acquiring another facility that does not belong to the Catholic tradition.[35] The model also includes, *inter alia*, two further important qualities: excellence in ritual and respect for the particular founding charism of the facilities.

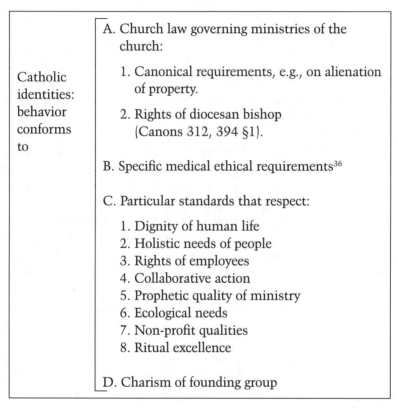

Catholic identities: behavior conforms to

A. Church law governing ministries of the church:

  1. Canonical requirements, e.g., on alienation of property.

  2. Rights of diocesan bishop (Canons 312, 394 §1).

B. Specific medical ethical requirements[36]

C. Particular standards that respect:

  1. Dignity of human life
  2. Holistic needs of people
  3. Rights of employees
  4. Collaborative action
  5. Prophetic quality of ministry
  6. Ecological needs
  7. Non-profit qualities
  8. Ritual excellence

D. Charism of founding group

Figure 6.1: Catholic Identities: Accountable Actions

35. See Gerald A. Arbuckle, *Healthcare Ministry: Refounding the Mission in Tumultuous Times* (Collegeville, MN: Liturgical Press, 2000), 281–91.

36. See Catholic Health Australia, *Code of Ethical Stardards* (Red Hill: Catholic Health Australia, 2001).

Evaluation

A charism is a gift of practical service for the common good of church and society. A congregational founder, for example, sees the gap between the Gospel and a particular need and moves to bridge that gap through creative pastoral programs such as healthcare and educational facilities for people on the margins of society, calling others to join with her or him in a collaborative way (see chap. 4). Normally the founding experience is officially recognized by the church; the task of members of this institution down through history is to keep the memory of this founding experience alive while adapting it to new circumstances.

However, emphasis on the charism of the founding group now requires significant caution for two reasons. First, many congregational founding stories developed during the nineteenth century with its distinctive, defensive Catholic culture. Catholics were educated into this culture and it formed a solid base upon which congregational founding stories could be constructed. With the breakup of this traditional Catholic culture and the impact of postmodernity, we can no longer assume that employees of Catholic institutions possess firmly established Catholic cultural roots (see chap. 2). The founding story of a congregation, divorced from the traditional Catholic culture, is left rather thin, in constant danger of losing its original prophetic emphasis. The second problem is the increasing pace of mergers of facilities with different founding stories. No one story should normally dominate the new organizational culture: hence the urgency to return to the primary story of Jesus Christ as, for example, healer or educator. This story is the ultimate root of all particular stories of facilities.

The model includes the need for excellence in ritual.[37] Ritual, a form of storytelling, is the stylized or repetitive symbolic use of bodily movement and gesture to express and articulate meaning within a cultural context.[38] Thus there are rituals in sport, dancing, traffic, politics, or any human interaction in which meanings that are encased in symbols and myths are visibly expressed and articulated. Ritual is the means by

---

37. See Gerald A. Arbuckle, *Earthing the Gospel: An Inculturation Handbook for Pastoral Workers* (Maryknoll, NY: Orbis Books, 1990), 96–111, and idem, *Culture, Inculturation, and Theologians: A Postmodern Critique* (Collegeville, MN: Liturgical Press, 2010), 81–98; Catherine Bell, *Ritual: Perspectives and Dimensions* (New York: Oxford University Press, 1997).

38. See Robert Bocock, *Ritual in Industrial Society: A Sociological Analysis of Ritualism in Modern England* (London: George Allen & Unwin, 1974), 35.

which we seek and establish orderly roles and boundaries for ourselves and for society. For example, if there were no rituals accepted by all players in a sporting tournament there would be total chaos. Ritual, for example, the set of rules that governs how traffic is to be organized and thus gives us a sense of safety when we drive, reassures us that we are in control in the midst of a chaotic world. Without ritual we would be unable to communicate with one another. In brief, ritual has the potential to transform people and their cultural environment; it can create a dedicated, collaborative employee or an office bully. Catholic agencies, such as parishes, schools, colleges, and healthcare facilities, need to symbolize their identities by such ritual symbols as crucifixes, chapels, statues of congregational founders, and ritual actions such as the celebration of Mass. Ritual actions, if sensitively prepared, have significant potential to involve participants in sacred storytelling.

Model 7: Identities: Norms Set by the *Catechism of the Catholic Church*

The *Catechism of the Catholic Church* was officially launched by John Paul II in late 1992 as "an organic synthesis of the essential and fundamental contents of Catholic doctrine. . . . It is intended to serve as a point of reference for the catechisms or compendia that are composed in the various countries."[39] This complex document is 904 pages in length, with 2,865 paragraphs.

Evaluation

This is not a document that is meant to be used as a direct source to *articulate* Catholic identities in any country. As Cardinal Joseph Ratzinger (later Pope Benedict XVI) stated: "It is clear from the start that this could not be . . . a manual to be used directly in parish or school-based catechesis. *Differences between cultures are too great for there to be any possibility of writing a single book of the teaching of the Universal Church; teaching methods need to differ in response to differing circumstances.*"[40] Because the document seeks to speak to the universal

---

39. *Catechism of the Catholic Church* (Sydney: St Pauls Publications, 2000), 9.
40. Cardinal Joseph Ratzinger, "The Catechism of the Catholic Church and the Optimism of the Redeemed," *Communio* 20 (1993): 469–84, at 473. Italics supplied.

church it is "a sprawling, unwieldy text."[41] It is written primarily for the bishops as teachers of the faith and pastors of the church.[42] It was assumed that each conference of bishops would then develop its own catechism, with this document as the background, in order to take into account local cultures and their particular needs. The instructions for the writing of the catechism significantly insist that the "presentation of the doctrine must be biblical and liturgical. It must be sound doctrine suited to the present life of Christians."[43] The biblical foundational emphasis is a particularly positive point,[44] but, as Jon Nilson notes, the scriptural references in the text do not always conform to the criteria of research methods and the language of modern thought.[45] Readers are given a wide range of quotations from historically authoritative theological texts without any interpretation or indication of how they connect with each other.[46] For this reason the *Catechism* at times requires theological scholars to interpret the meaning of its own text. But Pope John XXIII, in opening Vatican II, had stated: "This authentic doctrine has to be studied and expounded in light of the research methods and the language of modern thought. For the substance of the ancient deposit of faith is one thing, and the way in which it is presented is another."[47]

41. See Jon Nilson, "Book One: The Profession of Faith," *Chicago Studies* 33 (1994): 15–24, at 17; for other helpful comments see Johannes Baptist Metz, Edward Schillebeeckx, and Philip Hillyer, eds., *World Catechism or Inculturation, Concilium* 204 (Edinburgh: T & T Clark, 1989), 3–127.

42. *CCC*, 9.

43. "The Church, in the Word of God, Celebrates the Mysteries of Christ for the Salvation of the World," Final Document of the 1985 Extraordinary Synod, II. B. a. 4.

44. For this reason the *Catechism* stresses the Trinity as the central mystery of Christian faith and life and the trinitarian framework often shapes the analysis of key elements in the text.

45. For example, Nilson notes that the Genesis story has not been explained in light of contemporary scriptural studies: "Book One," 20–21.

46. For example, quotations are given from both St. Augustine (354–430) and St. Irenaeus (ca. 130–ca. 200), but their different approaches to theodicy (that is, that part of theology which is concerned to defend the goodness and omnipotence of God against objections arising from the existence of evil in the world) are not reconciled. See John Hick, *Evil and the God of Love* (New York: HarperSanFrancisco, 1966), 238–42.

47. Pope John XXIII, quoted by Peter Hebblethwaite, *John XXIII: Shepherd of the Modern World* (Garden City, NY: Doubleday, 1985), 431–32.

In summary, since the authors of the *Catechism* did not intend to present "the ancient deposit of faith" in "the language of modern thought," we cannot turn to the document for Catholic identities without expert assistance, both theological and pedagogical. In other words, it is a document that can never be imposed on people without the assistance of skilled interpreters and educators who can begin with the experience of listeners.

Model 8: Identities: Cultural Reactions to Vatican II[48]

A revolution is defined as a far-reaching and drastic change, especially in ideas and methods of behavior.[49] Vatican II definitely set in motion a timely revolution[50] in attitudes and structures as a response to its call to follow Christ's mission to evangelize "culture and cultures not purely in a decorative way as it were by applying a veneer, but in a vital way, in depth and right to their very roots."[51] The term "revolution" can correctly be applied to the cultural impact of Vatican II on the church, so dramatic were the mythic changes envisaged by the council. As John W. O'Malley, SJ, has written, the council "issued an implicit call for a change in style— a style less autocratic and more collaborative, a style willing to seek out and listen to different viewpoints . . . a style less unilateral."[52] Reflecting in 1971 on the impact of the council, O'Malley said that we "are not

---

48. For a fuller explanation of this analysis see Gerald A. Arbuckle, *Refounding the Church: Dissent for Leadership* (Maryknoll, NY: Orbis Books, 1993), 15–97, and idem, *Healthcare Ministry*, 97–107.

49. See William T. McLeod, ed., *The New Collins Dictionary* (London: Collins, 1987), 857.

50. I recognize that the word "revolution" as applied to Vatican II is now controversial, but anthropologically the term aptly describes the call of the texts for dramatic theological and therefore cultural changes. The movement from monarchical to collegial decision making and from esoteric liturgical rituals to celebrations in which "the faithful take part fully aware of what they are doing, actively engaged in the rite and enriched by it," is not evolutionary but revolutionary. Constitution on the Sacred Liturgy (*Sacrosanctum Concilium*) 11, in Flannery, ed., *Documents of Vatican II*. See John W. O'Malley, ed., *Vatican II: Did Anything Happen?* (New York: Continuum, 2011), 52–91, and comments above in chap. 2 n. 27.

51. Paul VI, *Apostolic Letter: On Evangelization* (Sydney: St Pauls Publications, 1975), 25.

52. John W. O'Malley, *What Happened at Vatican II* (Cambridge, MA: Harvard University Press, 2008), 307–8.

experiencing a 'reform' . . . understood as a correction, or revival, or even updating. We are experiencing a transformation, even a revolution."[53] Yet any radical disruption of a culture such as the one catalyzed in the church by the council, can be catastrophic at the personal and group levels even when people assent to it intellectually. In this statement we have the major clue to understanding the rise of different, often competing, identities within the contemporary church (see chap. 2).

There are three significant options for reacting to the uncertainties created by any revolution:

- First, there is the formation of new identities, with appropriate structures, based on the new or revised founding mythology. This is a long and often tortuous process demanding patience, experimentation, and the ability to live in the ambiguity of the here and now as the mythology is slowly and hesitantly owned and concrete structures are built on its value system.

- The second is a counterrevolution, the restoration of the old identities. O'Malley notes that "restorationists moderate excesses, but they do so by positing a dreamworld that artificially reconstructs the conditions of days gone by."[54] Often there are short periods of concessions to change in restorationist movements, then a growing rigidity, and insistence on widespread conformity to their values and decrees builds frustration to a breaking point.

- The third is the breakdown of the revolution into general disorder in which divers conflicting groups flourish, each claiming to interpret identities authoritatively. Others, weary of the infighting, withdraw entirely from the society in protest and go underground.

All three reactions to the council's revolution, especially the second and third, are evident today, so much so that there are at least three distinct, even at times radically different, ways of defining Catholic identities. Broadly speaking, three quite diverse types of institutions

---

53. John W. O'Malley, "Reform, Historical Consciousness, Aggiornamento," *Theological Studies* 32 (1971): 573–601, at 601.

54. John W. O'Malley, "Developments, Reforms, and Two Great Reformations: Towards a Historical Assessment of Vatican II," *Theological Studies* 44 (1983): 373–406, at 405.

identifying themselves as Catholic have emerged, depending on their theological view of the church.

First, there is the "collegial church" where the local church emphasizes a theology of Vatican II. For example, the United States Bishops Conference used this model of church on several occasions when constructing their pastoral letters to the faithful. This model assumes that the Holy Spirit resides in all members of the Catholic Church. Hence the hierarchy must listen to what the Spirit is saying to the whole church through appropriate consultative channels before making authoritative statements. John Paul II firmly reasserted his commitment to this model: "the Council documents have lost nothing of their value or brilliance. . . . [T]here we find a sure compass by which to take our bearings in the century now beginning."[55] Educational and healthcare institutions that accept this model of church will have a management style that emphasizes collaboration, consultation, dialogue with other denominations and faiths. Officials such as mission leaders in institutions commit themselves to an inductive approach and the use of the Scriptures in building Catholic identities.

A second type of reaction to the council is found in people and institutions that favor a restorationist church theology. These will avoid collaboration and dialogue with people and institutions that are not Catholic and will have a top-down management style. Restorationists seek to rebuild the pre-conciliar structures and values. Individuals and institutions of the third type of church, the "protest church," are unhappy with the pace of adapting the council's values and structures in parishes and dioceses. They wish to have as little contact with diocesan ecclesiastical structures as is possible. Followers of this identity model may themselves eventually succumb to fundamentalist sectarianism, for example, in their zeal some may reject everything of the pre-conciliar church, including the need for an institution to be the official carrier and guardian of the Gospel message.[56]

55. John Paul II, *At the Beginning of the New Millennium* (Sydney: St Pauls Publications, 2001), 74–75.

56. Michele Dillon, professor of sociology at Yale University, gives a nuanced and sophisticated expression of the "protest church" and its understanding of Catholic identity in her book, *Catholic Identity: Balancing Reason, Faith and Power* (Cambridge: Cambridge University Press, 1999).

Evaluation

This model is helpful for further understanding the dynamics of the cultural breakdown of the traditional ghetto culture of the church after the council as explained in chapter 2, but it also highlights the urgency and difficulties in building institutions founded on the mythology of Vatican II. Significantly, John Paul II restressed the critical emphasis in the council, namely, the need to begin with the Scriptures: "To nourish ourselves with the [Scriptures] to be 'servants of the word' . . . this surely is a priority for the Church. . . . [It] is inconceivable [to act] without a renewed listening to the word of God [in the Scriptures]."[57] In the same document the pope reasserts in strong language the need to commit ourselves to the guidance of the council in crafting Catholic identities: "I feel more than ever in duty bound to point to the Council as *the great grace bestowed on the Church in the twentieth century*: there we find a sure compass by which to take our bearings in the century now beginning."[58] Note that this statement in no way supports restorationist movements or the exclusivist tendencies found in the protest church.

Model 9: Identities through Models of Church and Mission

The well-known theologian Avery Dulles, SJ, in an early work described the church through the use of five different but interrelated models of identities: the church as institution, as mystical communion, as sacrament, as herald, and as Servant.[59] These models can be briefly summarized:

> **Church as Institution**
> The church has its distinctive form of government and organization, for example, pope, dioceses, bishops, as described in its legal text, the Code of Canon Law.

57. John Paul II, *At the Beginning*, 51–52.
58. Ibid., 75. Italics in original.
59. See Avery Dulles, SJ, *Models of the Church* (New York: Doubleday, 1978).

Church as Mystical Communion
All believers are bound together with the Holy Spirit in a communion of faith and love. This model is a source of encouragement to the ecumenical movement.

Church as Sacrament
The church is to be a sign and instrument of the union of the human family with God and with one another. God relates to us through visible realities, making human objects, signs, and symbols the bearers of God's loving presence.

Church as Herald
The church is called to proclaim by word the message of the Gospel.

Church as Servant
This model stresses the role of the church in holistic healing, particularly its focus on people who are marginalized in society.

More recently two prominent missiologists, Fathers Stephen Bevans, SVD, and Roger Schroeder, SVD, have identified four distinct models of mission, and therefore of identities, that are operative within the Catholic Church:

- Mission as participation in the mission of the triune God;

- Mission as liberating service of the reign of God;

- Mission as proclamation of Jesus Christ;

- Mission as prophetic dialogue.

It is this last model, the authors explain, that is a particular identifying feature of the contemporary church's ministry in the world.[60] A leading African missiologist, Father Francis Oborji, has also constructed a set of models of mission and identities:

---

60. See Stephen B. Bevans and Roger P. Schroeder, *Constants in Context: A Theology of Mission Today* (Maryknoll, NY: Orbis Books, 2004).

- Mission as conversion,

- Mission as church planting and church growth,

- Mission as adaptation and inculturation,

- Mission as dialogue with the religions,

- Mission as *Missio Dei* and service of God's reign, and

- Mission as ecumenical dialogue.[61]

Evaluation

Dulles emphasizes that the identity of the church is not restricted to his five models. Also, the models should be operating simultaneously. For example, if the institutional model is overlooked there will be no order or sense of direction in the church; that is, to obtain a sense of identity in the church, people must be aware of all models. This reinforces the point that there can be no one specific definition of Catholic identity (see chap. 1). The models of the church, together with the models of pastoral ministry as devised by Bevans, Schroeder, and Oborji, are especially helpful in describing theologically and in substantial depth the complexity of Catholic identities and the manners in which ecumenical dialogue and collaborative action can occur. Since the models require significant theological knowledge to interpret, they would not be suitable for initial workshops on Catholic identities in institutions such as schools and healthcare facilities. However, Bevans has an earlier book in which he helpfully identifies for the non-specialist six distinctive models the Catholic Church uses for theological reflection and identities: the translation model, the anthropological model, the praxis model, the synthetic model, and the transcendental model.[62]

Model 10: Identities through Catholic Social Teaching

The Catholic tradition of social ethics extends over two thousand years, but the main systematic developments only began with the publication of the encyclical letter *Rerum Novarum* by Pope Leo XIII in 1891.

---

61. See Francis A. Oborji, *Concepts of Mission: The Evolution of Contemporary Missiology* (Maryknoll, NY: Orbis Books, 2006), 59–180.

62. See Stephen B. Bevans, *Models of Contextual Theology: Faith and Cultures* (Maryknoll, NY: Orbis Books, 2002).

Since then the Catholic Church has produced an evolving and notable body of teaching on economic, political, cultural, and social matters. Although the meaning of the phrase "Catholic social teaching" may embrace the writings of theologians and ecclesiastical authorities on the local level, it normally is confined to a specific set of documents produced over the decades since 1891 by popes, the Second Vatican Council, and synods of bishops. The teaching has become a way for the church, as hierarchy and community of believers, to "re-vision itself as an actor and teacher in various social arenas and to express its understanding of how best to respond to the call of God and to the cries of divided, often desperate, societies around it."[63]

For many years this social teaching emphasized the negative consequences a market-centered economy can have on the human person, especially workers and people who are poor. Consequently, a particularly characteristic quality of the church's social teaching has been its constant criticism of uninhibited capitalism and state control. It has repeatedly emphasized the need to develop intermediate groupings or associations in political and economic life for the sake of the common good. In more recent times this emphasis on the common good has become popular in secular economic and political theory and has been termed "the third way" by sociologist Anthony Giddens: "The third way attempts to avoid an excessive domination of the state . . . but does not accept that the market can be left to its own devices."[64] Hence the importance the church gives to such institutions as Catholic educational and healthcare facilities in the life of a nation.

There are at least eleven fundamental, *interconnected* principles in this social teaching, namely:[65]

63. John P. Langan, "Issues in Catholic Social Thought," *Origins* 30, no. 3 (2000): 45–48, at 46.

64. Anthony Giddens, *The Third Way and Its Critics* (Cambridge: Polity Press, 2000), 13; Giddens's original text on this theme is *The Third Way: The Renewal of Social Democracy* (Cambridge: Polity Press, 1998).

65. See William J. Byron, "Ten Building Blocks of Catholic Social Teaching," *America* 193, no. 10 (1998): 9–12; for an overview of the major social encyclicals see Pontifical Council for Justice and Peace, *Compendium of the Social Doctrine of the Church* (Vatican: Libreria Editrice Vaticana, 2004).

- The principle of human dignity.
  This is the fundamental principle on which all the other principles are based. Because God has given all human beings dignity, every person has the right and duty to develop his or her life in a manner that promotes that gift.

- The principle of respect for human life
  Human life at every stage of development and decline is sacred and therefore worthy of respect.

- The principle of association
  By association with others, in families and other social groupings, persons achieve their fulfillment.

- The principle of participation
  People have the right to participate in those institutions that are necessary for personal fulfillment.

- The principle of preferential option for people who are poor
  This principle is clearly derived from the above four principles.

- The principle of solidarity
  We are one human family, committed to work for the good of all.

- The principle of stewardship
  We need to show respect for the Creator by using the gifts of creation, including one's talents, according to the mind of our Creator.

- The principle of subsidiarity
  No higher level of an organization should undertake any function that can be achieved efficiently and effectively at a lower level.

- The principle of human equality
  No one should hold a privileged position of power simply because of his or her wealth. All have the right to be treated equally in justice.

- The principle of the common good
  The common good connotes the social conditions that allow people to attain their full human potential and realize their human dignity.

- The principle of the preferential option for non-violence
  This principle is solidly rooted in Jesus' teaching and example.[66]

---

66. See the helpful analysis by Michael P. Hornsby-Smith, *An Introduction to Catholic Social Thought* (Cambridge: Cambridge University Press, 2006), 12, 302–17.

Evaluation

While not denying the critical importance of the church's social teaching, rightly dubbed "our best-kept secret," we can see that it has grave limitations as a primary source of Catholic identities. There are at least three noteworthy reasons for this. First, the focus of the social teaching has been limited. John Langan, SJ, holder of the Joseph Cardinal Bernardin Chair in Catholic Social Thought at Georgetown University, points to the failure of social teaching to address with sufficient seriousness critical contemporary issues like the oppression of women, the rise of nationalist and secessionist movements, the plight of refugees, and global warming. The scope of recent papal statements is too narrow. We need, he wrote in 2000, "a more sustained effort to understand the sources and the character of the evil which fractures and degrades . . . societies [that foster genocide within and across national borders]."[67] Catholic social teaching will become an esoteric language if it does not constantly address critical contemporary issues. Its principles will remain abstract and divorced from people's lives. Historian Richard H. Tawney, when reflecting on the decline of the Anglican Church in Britain in the nineteenth century, makes this relevant comment: "The social teaching of the [Anglican] Church had ceased to count because the Church itself had ceased to think. . . . Faced with the problems [of the contemporary world], it could do no more than repeat, with meaningless iteration, its traditional lore as to the duties of master to servant and servant to master."[68]

Second, sometimes the methodology used to formulate and explain the social teaching is too restricted. For the most part the principles of social teaching, especially before Vatican II, were founded almost entirely on the principles of the Catholic natural law tradition[69] "mediated

---

67. Langan, "Issues in Catholic Social Thought," 47.

68. Richard H. Tawney, *Religion and the Rise of Capitalism* (London: John Murray, 1943), 185.

69. Natural law in a theological context means the law implanted in nature by the Creator, which rational creatures can discern by the light of reason. The remote foundation of ethics based on this law is to be found in Greek and Roman philosophy and law. Aristotle (384–322 BCE) contrasted what is "just by nature" with what is "just by [human] convention," *Nicomachean Ethics* 5.7, 1134b18, trans. Martin Oswald (Indianapolis: Bobbs Merrill, 1962), 131; Stephen J. Pope, "Natural Law in Catholic Social Teaching," 41–71, in Kenneth R. Himes, et al., eds., *Modern Catholic Social Teaching: Commentaries and Interpretations* (Washington, DC: Georgetown University Press, 2005).

through Scholastic philosophy and theology."[70] Instead of repeating principles we need to begin inductively with the world as it is, with all its myriad hopes and sufferings, then rethink how these principles can be applied. Moreover, natural law theory has little acceptance outside the Catholic tradition, so it is difficult to make it a common foundation for dialogue beyond the boundaries of the church.[71]

Third, references to the Scriptures are limited. This is unfortunate because today they could provide a better foundation for dialogue on human rights than natural law theory. But until recent times the resurgence of Catholic biblical studies had a minimal impact on this teaching. The tendency has been to use Scripture as a support for theological arguments rather than the inspirational catalyst for reflection. Kenneth Himes, OFM, associate professor in the Department of Theology at Boston College, commented in 2004: "Whatever the intellectual power and depth of papal teaching, the encyclicals rarely touch the lives of everyday Catholics. *If Catholic social teaching is to form people's consciences, inspire their imaginations, and shape their lives, it must weave biblical theology into its presentations.*"[72] There are, however, some significant shifts in progress, inspired by Vatican II, in the presentation of the church's social teaching. John Paul II used Scripture in his encyclicals more significantly than his predecessors. In his encyclical One Hundred Years (*Centesimus Annus*, 1991), he built his claim of shared responsibility for all humanity on principles contained in the gospels of Matthew and Luke. There is a recent tendency, too, to formulate social teaching on the basis of love, as is evident, for example, in Pope Benedict XVI's inspiring gospel-based encyclical published in 2005, God Is Love (*Deus Caritas Est*). The primacy of love has three meanings: love is the foundation of justice and brings the actions of justice to their fullest potential and significance; love is the inspiration to be involved in justice; the fundamental commitment to love God leads to moral action.[73] The

---

70. John R. Donahue, "The Bible and Catholic Social Teaching: Will This Engagement Lead to Marriage?," 140 in Himes, ed., *Modern Catholic Social Teaching*, 9.

71. See, for example, the contribution by John Courtney Murray critiquing the social philosophy of John Rawls and the U.S. bishops' contribution to the welfare reform debate in Thomas Massaro, *Catholic Social Teaching and United States Welfare Reform* (Collegeville, MN: Liturgical Press, 1998), 189–223.

72. Himes, *Modern Catholic Social Teaching*, 11. Italics supplied.

73. See Edward P. DeBerri, James E. Hug, et al., *Catholic Social Teaching: Our Best Kept Secret* (Maryknoll, NY: Orbis Books, 2003), 14–17; Philip S. Land, *Catholic*

pope returned to the centrality of love in his social encyclical of 2009, On Integral Development in Charity and Truth (*Caritas in Veritate*).[74]

Model 11: Identities through Prophetic Dialogue

In 1968 the Latin American bishops met at Bogota and Medellin and laid the foundations for the church's first major contemporary local theology, namely, liberation theology, to be followed later, beginning in North America, by a major development in feminist theology that was much influenced by liberation theology. Liberation theology emerged in dialogue not with the nonbeliever but with "non-persons," that is, with people denied their rightful dignity by oppressive structures. While other theologies seek an understanding of revelation, this theology is praxis-oriented, that is, it actually aims to bring about the reign of God—a realm of peace and justice. It requires that evangelizers totally immerse themselves in the culture of people who are marginalized; otherwise dialogue and action are impossible. The theology assumes that the church itself belongs to the culture of the elite or oppressing class, and it is for this reason that the first act of liberation must be to liberate the church itself. For example, tradition in the church has effectively blocked any role for women in building faith communities. For the most part church history was a male narrative told almost entirely by males. Through the impact of liberation theology people are becoming increasingly aware of this prejudice and the need to purify tradition.[75]

Liberation theology became a powerful catalyst for the contemporary pastoral emphasis on the role of the church as an agent of prophetic dialogue. Pastoral life must be *"prophetic* because the church is obligated to preach always and everywhere . . . the fullness of the gospel in all its integrity. And it must be *dialogue* because the imperative—rooted in the gospel itself—is to preach the one faith in a particular *context*. Without dialogue, without a willingness to 'let go' before one 'speaks out,'

Social Teaching: As I Have Lived, Loathed, and Loved It (Chicago: Loyola University Press, 1994), 124–33.

74. See the analysis by J. Brian Benestad, *Church, State, and Society: An Introduction to Catholic Social Doctrine* (Washington, DC: Catholic University of America Press, 2010), 447–66.

75. See Lawrence S. Cunningham, *The Catholic Experience* (New York: Crossroad, 1989), 140.

mission is simply not possible."[76] The church's pastoral life, therefore, will have the following principal characteristics: presence and witness; commitment to social development and human liberation; liturgical life, prayer, and contemplation; interreligious dialogue; and proclamation and catechesis.[77] In 1990 Pope John Paul II identified similar prophetic qualities that should characterize the church's pastoral action: witness, proclamation, inculturation, interreligious dialogue, collaborative involvement in development, and charitable works.[78]

Evaluation

This model of crafting identities emphasizes the church not so much as an institution but more as a prophetic agent of evangelization. People become church, as it were, by living the life of Christ in their own cultures, challenging those cultures with gospel values by example, proclamation, and dialogue. Since this process emphasizes the importance of the Scriptures as *the* way to discover the radical or prophetic nature of Catholic identities, it is a less academic and theoretical way to construct those identities than other models so far analyzed. This rebirth of the prophetic nature of the Christian vocation can lead, as it has in the past, to tensions between the prophetic and institutional elements of the church. There is no way to resolve the tensions other than through faith-based dialogue. Most of today's Catholic social, educational, and healthcare ministries began through the prophetic action of members of religious congregations. It is imperative that this prophetic foundation in these ministries be maintained now and in the future.[79]

Model 12: Catholic Identities in Universities

In 1990 Pope John Paul II promulgated an Apostolic Constitution on the importance of maintaining Catholic identities in Catholic universities, titled *Ex Corde Ecclesiae* (From the Heart of the Church).[80] The

---

76. Bevans and Schroeder, *Constants in Context*, 350.

77. Vatican Secretariat for Non-Christians 1984, cited by Bevans and Schroeder, *Constants in Context*, 350.

78. See John Paul II, *Encyclical Letter: Mission of the Redeemer* (Boston: St. Paul Books, 1991), 57–79.

79. See Gerald A. Arbuckle, "Sponsorship's Biblical Roots and Tensions," *Health Progress* (September 2006): 13–16.

80. See John Paul II, Apostolic Constitution *Ex Corde Ecclesiae*, *Origins* 20, no. 17 (1990): 265–76.

constitution outlines four essential characteristics of Catholic universities and calls for them to make their Catholic identities known. The document examines theology's role in the university and vis-à-vis the teaching authorities in the church, the relationship with the local bishop, campus ministry, and the institution's dialogue with culture and the sciences. Also discussed are the roles of laity in the university, including those of non-Catholics, interdisciplinary education, the responsibility of civil governments, ecumenical dialogue, and evangelization. The four essential qualities of Catholic identities in universities, as stated in the document, are:

1. "A Christian inspiration not only of individuals but of the university community as such." It is not sufficient for individuals and individual faculties or individual courses to be animated by a Christian spirit; the whole university as an institution needs to mirror this inspiration.

2. "A continuing reflection in the light of the Catholic faith upon the growing treasury of human knowledge, to which it seeks to contribute by its own research." This quality refers to the rich Catholic intellectual tradition that has developed since the foundation of the church.

3. "Fidelity to the Christian message as it comes to us through the Church." This quality emphasizes the importance of adhering to the church's official teaching.

4. "An institutional commitment to the service of the people of God and of the human family in their pilgrimage to the transcendent goal which gives meaning to life."[81] This quality highlights the prophetic role of a university in the service of social justice, based on the principles of Catholic social teaching.

Evaluation

Though the emphasis in the document is on clarifying and maintaining Catholic identities in Catholic universities, there is much here that is applicable to all Catholic ministries, for example, research into Catholic identities and the importance of qualified people for ministry. The document is particularly relevant for the role of theology in relationship to tertiary secular research.

---

81. The list is found in ibid., 269.

Theology plays a particularly important role in the search for a synthesis of knowledge as well as in the dialogue between faith and reason. It serves all other disciplines in their search for meaning, not only by helping them to investigate how their discoveries will affect individuals and society, but also by bringing a perspective and an orientation not contained within their methodologies. . . . Catholic theology, taught in a manner faithful to Scripture, tradition and the Church's magisterium, provides an awareness of the Gospel principles which enrich the meaning of human life and give it a new dignity.[82]

The model, though it has significant positive qualities, requires a wide range of professional guides for its implementation, for example, canon lawyers and theologians. An inductive pedagogical method based on the Scriptures is needed to engage participants, who may or may not be Catholic, in order that they can meet the person of Jesus Christ, as explained in the following chapters.

Summary

• Since the 1970s the church can no longer define identity without constant reference to the cultural implications of postmodernity that affect all its ministries.

• The "secret of the [church's] educative power," as John Paul II wrote, "[is] not so much in doctrinal statements and pastoral approaches to vigilance as in constantly looking to the Lord Jesus Christ. Each day the church looks to Christ with unfailing love, fully aware that the true and final answer to the problem [of identity] lies in him alone."[83]

• Therefore, while normative definitions of Catholic identities are important, these cannot be imposed on people; they need first to meet the Jesus Christ of the Scriptures through an inductive pedagogical process he himself used; this method depends for its effectiveness on the evangelizer's creative imagination and persuasion, constantly nourished by love of Christ.

---

82. Ibid., 270.

83. John Paul II, *Veritatis Splendor* (Vatican City: Libreria Editrice Vaticana, 1993), 130.

Chapter Seven

Healthcare and Welfare: Refounding Catholic Identities

My design here is not to teach the Method which everyone should follow in order to promote the good conduct of his reason, but only to show how I have endeavoured to conduct my own.[1] *(René Descartes)*

[The parable is] a fiction capable of redescribing life.[2]
(Paul Ricoeur)

This chapter explains that:

- there are different models of healthcare and welfare: bio-medical, economic-rationalist, social, and foundational; the first model reduces the human person to a materialistic object and the second and third to a commodity
- the Good Samaritan parable "can be seen as one of the original building blocks out of which our modern universalist moral consciousness has been built"[3]; the parable

---

1. René Descartes (1596–1650), *Discourse on the Method and Meditations on First Philosophy*, ed. David Weissman, trans. Elizabeth Haldane and G. R. Ross (New Haven, CT: Yale University Press, 1996), 4.

2. Paul Ricoeur, "Biblical Hermeneutics," *Semeia* 4 (1975): 29–148, at 89.

3. Charles Taylor, *The Secular Age* (Cambridge: Cambridge University Press, 2007), 738.

contains values and truths that must form the foundation for holistic personal and social healing

• this parable is a springboard story, that is, the parable
can be used as the foundation for building our Catholic
identities through inductive learning in healthcare, welfare, and socioeconomic development ministries

In this chapter I take to heart René Descartes' approach and I endeavor to show how, after many negative experiences, I now conduct
identity workshops. I finally stumbled upon a method that provides
a safe environment in which people are able to craft Catholic identities for themselves personally and for their institutions. It is a method
that respects the dignity of the human person, follows the pedagogy of
Jesus Christ, and is fully in tune with the postmodern emphasis on the
importance of storytelling in achieving identities for individuals and
institutions. As I describe in this book's introduction, by adopting the
inductive method I cover far less material, but the learning that occurs
for participants of workshops significantly increases; people's lives are
being transformed through this experiential process. When working with
staffs of Catholic healthcare, welfare, and business institutions in the
early 1990s I followed the deductive or normative method for clarifying
the meaning of Catholic identity. That is, I would give a lecture that
neatly set out the normative definitions of Catholic identities (chap. 6).
I would then invite questions and discussion. The method failed to be
effective; participants in workshops were uninterested and unresponsive.

In desperation I adopted the inductive method; this meant first asking participants to highlight the issues that concerned them in their
work. Their experiences began to set the agenda and pace for the workshops, the dynamic of which rather dramatically changed. Participants
appreciated the chance to speak about their own struggles to achieve
personal and institutional identities as a consequence of the constant
changes impacting on their lives in the contemporary postmodern world.
This invariably led me to the next stage in the workshops, namely, the
need to explain from a cultural anthropologist's perspective, in an interactive manner and with ample examples, the mythological shift in
Western society from modernity to postmodernity that had become the
significant catalyst for their own identity confusions (see chap. 2). They
came to see for themselves the need to find mythological foundations

to give security in their lives and the value of storytelling in achieving identities.

Once participants had recognized the need for foundational stories in their lives, in the third stage of the workshops I would ask if they would like to hear and ponder the foundational story, the Good Samaritan parable, that has primarily shaped the development of all healthcare and welfare services in the Western world. The answer was always positive.[4] Having explained the characteristics of the Good Samaritan parable, I would then invite participants, in small groups, to identify values in the parable that they found important in their work. Invariably this would lead participants to connect their own experiences with the values of the parable. In the final stage of workshops on the parable I would concentrate in an interactive manner on drawing out the fundamental truths and values inherent in the story.

By allowing people to get in touch with, and re-own, the foundational stories of healthcare, welfare, and business institutions it is possible to begin the process of rearticulating their Christian, and therefore their Catholic, identities (see fig. 3.1). This is a process of refounding. In this chapter, therefore, I explain why the parable of the Good Samaritan is especially relevant to healthcare and welfare personnel, given the context in which they work. This will be followed by a cultural analysis of the parable.

Healthcare and Welfare Services

Context

Healthcare and welfare facilities exist to serve patients, yet this basic fact is too often forgotten because the values inherent in the Good Samaritan parable have ceased to have an impact on decision making. Therefore governments and others find it essential today to remind people that healthcare facilities exist for the service of patients. In Britain the government found it necessary in 2005 to recall the National Health Service (NHS) to its primary focus, namely, the welfare and safety of patients, not the well-being of clinicians and administrators![5] Donald

---

4. By the end of the 1990s I adopted the same approach, with modifications, when working with government-owned healthcare and welfare institutions.

5. See Department of Health, *Creating a Patient-Led NHS: Developing the NHS Improvement Plan* (London: Department of Health, 2005).

Berwick of Harvard Medical School, President Barack Obama's appointee as director of the Centers for Medicare and Medicaid Services, evoked widespread controversy in the United States when he reminded clinicians and others that patient-centered healthcare must be *the* priority in services. He wrote: "I . . . believe that we . . . would be far better off if we professionals recalibrated our work such that we behaved with patients and families, not as hosts in the care system, but as guests in their lives."[6] Why have healthcare and welfare services drifted from their primary purpose, namely, the need to respond to people's needs? The answer is to be found in the study of different models of healthcare and welfare that have evolved over the centuries. For the remainder of this chapter I will focus on healthcare, but the insights are applicable, with minor adjustments, to welfare services also.

The first type of healthcare is based on the *foundational model*, the Good Samaritan parable that is to be explained later.

The second type of healthcare is the *bio-medical model*, particularly favored by Western societies. Ill health is considered to an attribute of the physical body, or more particularly the inability of the body, for whatever reason, to function to its most desired level. In this model the body is equated with a machine and disease is a failure of this machine. The inner spiritual and/or psychological infirmity or *illness* quality of sickness is of no concern, that is, the state of the patient's mind is unimportant in medical assessment and treatment. Two dynamics alone are important: the physical *disease* and the *engineering* of the body back to health. Disease is a biological irregularity in a particular part of the body; the stress is less on the indicators given by the patient and more on signs that can theoretically be scientifically determined, often with the use of instruments. The medical expert's role is to return the body to good health again through medical expertise grounded in precise scientific laboratory techniques. Health, according to this model, is a commodity people possess, and if it is missing it can be restored by medical engineering. As with any commodity, investors are able to insure against loss or harm.

---

6. See Donald M. Berwick, "What 'Patient-Centered' Should Mean: Confessions of an Extremist," *Health Affairs* 28, no. 4 (2009): w555–w565, at 559. Accessible at http://content.healthaffairs.org/content/28/4/w555.full.html.

The third model, the *social model*, concentrates particularly on the prevention of sickness. It does not disagree that pathological or individual psychological factors cause sickness. It assumes, however, that health and sickness cannot be fully grasped or addressed unless the cultural and economic causes of poverty, unemployment, pollution, class, unacceptable personal and community lifestyles, and gender prejudice are positively confronted. If this model is to have constructive results, governments and other agencies must be prepared to direct suitable resources to empowering people to change.[7] Yet governments commonly want quick-fix solutions for the cultural causes of poor health and are not prepared to assign resources for the necessary long period.

The fourth type of healthcare is the *economic rationalist model*. The dramatic rise of for-profit hospitals in the United States, particularly in recent years, provides an excellent example of an unregulated economic rationalist model of healthcare. The primary purpose of healthcare administration is financial gain for shareholders, not the quality of service to patients or concern for the millions of people on the fringes of society. "The business," not the "the mission" becomes the motivating force in healthcare (fig. 7.1). Even the healthcare reform introduced by President Obama, although of significant assistance to millions of Americans, is still dominated by the economic rationalist model since administratively it remains under the control of for-profit insurance companies.[8] Two terms summarize the mythology behind economic rationalism as applied to healthcare: corporatization and privatization. Corporatization means that healthcare institutions must be managed according to strict business principles. What does not provide profit should be shut down. Competition between service providers is assumed to produce the best results for patients. The "twin concepts of choice and competition"[9] that are so popular with middle-class consumers are to be the guiding standards for decision making.

7. See Linda J. Jones, *The Social Context of Health and Health Work* (London: Macmillan, 1994), 32–38.

8. See Gerald A. Arbuckle, *Humanizing Healthcare Reforms* (London and Philadelphia: Jessica Kingsley Publishers, 2013), 94–95.

9. Rudolf Klein, *The New Politics of the NHS* (Oxford: Radcliffe, 2006), 257.

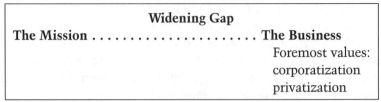

Figure 7.1: *Economic Rationalist Model of Healthcare and Welfare*

When the national health and welfare services of countries like Britain, New Zealand, Australia, and Canada were established, their founding mythology embraced the values inherent in the Good Samaritan story. It was taken for granted that healthcare is a fundamental human right. Healthcare should be provided by the state, paid for through taxation, and access guaranteed on the basis of need, not the capacity to pay. By the late 1970s and 1980s, however, these governments were increasingly threatened with serious questions about the financial sustainability of their healthcare systems, rising calls for choice especially from better-off middle classes, and aging populations. Governments wanted some quick solutions. The answer? Apply the principles of the market economy and management to healthcare, with its fundamental emphasis on profit. Discard local accountability and bring in a competitive quasi-market system. Lay managers with industrial and commercial expertise were to be in charge of the medical professionals, and market forces were to appreciably influence the distribution of services.[10] The false supposition behind these "solutions" is that healthcare can be easily transformed into a free, competitive market such as is found in any commercial business. Patients are to become consumers. Economic rationalist policies in these countries had to be modified in the 1990s. For example, in the European Union it was decided in 2006 that the core values should be universality; access to good quality health care for every person living in the European Union; equity; equal access to health care regardless of ethnicity, gender, age, social status, and ability to pay; and solidarity, people's primary right to healthcare and the duty of governments to ensure that this right is financially respected.[11] Assumed in the development of these healthcare systems are the other values at the heart of the Good Samaritan story such as compassion, respect, and dialogue.

10. See Allyson Pollock, *NHS plc* (London: Verso, 2005), 36–131.
11. See Scott L. Greer, *The Politics of European Union Health Policies* (Maidenhead: Open University Press, 2009), 7.

The Good Samaritan: Foundational Story[12]

> The Church . . . from century to century . . . has re-enacted the Gospel
> parable of the Good Samaritan, revealing and communicating her healing
> love and the consolation of Jesus Christ.[13]

The parable of the compassionate Samaritan is possibly the best
known of those from the master of storytelling, Jesus Christ. All of his
pedagogical skills are brilliantly evident in the parable. In the opening verses (Luke 10:25-28) the evangelist Luke tells us that one day a
certain lawyer confronted Jesus with a question structured to shame
him: "Teacher," he said, "what must I do to inherit eternal life?" (v.
25). Jesus, using his inductive pedagogical method, shrewdly responds
with a question of his own: "What is written in the law?" (v. 26). And
the lawyer correctly answers: "You shall love the Lord your God with all
your heart, and with all your soul . . . and your neighbor as yourself" (v.
27). The command to love God and neighbor are absolutely central to
Jesus' teachings, and in this parable "both commands have been fused
together."[14] In response, Jesus now takes the lawyer on a journey, the lawyer being blissfully unaware of the personally surprising and disturbing
ending. The lawyer is finally challenged to accept or reject the fact that
his boundaries of compassion, mercy, and justice thus far have been too
limited. His understanding of these virtues is turned upside down. Once
Jesus has finished his story he calls the lawyer to answer his original
question himself: "Which of these three, do you think, was a neighbor
to the man who fell into the hands of the robbers?" (v. 36). To save face
in the crowd, the lawyer must give the correct and startling reply that
goes directly against the culture of the time: "The one who showed him
mercy" (v. 37). His neighbor is not just a Jew, a member of his culture
only, but the one who relates even to his enemy with compassion and
mercy. Jesus has the last word: "Go and do likewise" (v. 37).

12. This section is more developed in my book *Humanizing Healthcare*, 75–84.

13. Pope John Paul II, *Contemplate the Face of Christ in the Sick*, Message for the
World Day of the Sick 2000 (Vatican City: Vatican Press, 2000), 13.

14. Klyne R. Snodgrass, *Stories with Intent: A Comprehensive Guide to the Parables of Jesus* (Grand Rapids, MI: Eerdmans, 2008), 349.

The philosopher Charles Taylor, when writing about the foundations of Western civilization, concludes that this story of the Good Samaritan "can be seen as one of the original building blocks out of which our modern universalist moral consciousness has been built."[15] Social ethicist Chris Marshall writes that the parable "carries tremendous rhetorical power, for it evokes one of the most seminal narratives in the Western cultural tradition." He further writes: "Indeed, it is hard to think of another story that has been more influential in moulding personal and political virtue. . . . It is a story that still serves, even in contemporary secular society, as a useful reference point for measuring policy options."[16] A sign of the story's remarkable legacy is simply the continuing widespread use in society of the phrase "good Samaritan" as an example of selfless concern to come to the aid of others in need.[17] Martin Luther King Jr. insisted that the parable's mandate is not just about charity, but charity accompanied by political, structural, and systemic conversion founded on justice.[18] In the early centuries of the Christian era the parable became the public and operative founding myth among Christians, and subsequently the monasteries in particular, obliging them to care for the sick in whom body and soul are united. Every stranger in need is a neighbor, the image of God and to whom the love of God ought to be expressed. Subsequently "permanent charitable institutions sprang up within a generation or two after the end of the persecution of the Christians"[19] in the fourth century. Christians formed "a miniature welfare state in an empire which for the most part lacked social services."[20] At the heart of this founding healthcare myth are the values of compassion, mercy, solidarity, equity, and social justice.

15. Charles Taylor, *The Secular Age* (Cambridge: Cambridge University Press, 2007), 738.

16. Chris Marshall, "'Go and Do Likewise': The Parable of the Good Samaritan and the Challenge of Public Ethics," 49–74, in Jonathan Boston, Andrew Bradstock, and David Eng, eds., *Ethics and Public Policy: Contemporary Issues* (Wellington: Victoria University Press, 2011), 53.

17. See Marshall, "'Go and Do Likewise'"; C. Daniel Batson, "Attribution as a Mediator of Bias in Helping," *Journal of Personality and Social Psychology* 32 (1975): 455–66; Hanokh Dagan, "In Defense of the Good Samaritan," *Michigan Law Review* 97 (1999): 1115–1200.

18. See Marshall, "'Go and Do Likewise,'" 53.

19. Gary B. Ferngren, *Medicine and Health Care in Early Christianity* (Baltimore: Johns Hopkins University Press, 2009), 145.

20. Paul Johnson, cited by ibid., 138.

The social democratic founders of the formation of the welfare state, therefore, in countries like Britain, New Zealand, Australia, and Canada[21] would have been deeply influenced, even unconsciously, by the residual myth of the Good Samaritan, which contains these values. Just as the suffering victim in the parable had a right to receive care from the Samaritan, so also everyone today has the right to healthcare. It is not a commodity to be bought only by those who can afford it. Aneurin Bevan, minister for health in Britain when he led the foundation of universal healthcare there in the late 1940s, often highlighted this fundamental right: "Society becomes more wholesome, more serene and spiritually healthier, if it knows that its citizens have at the back of their consciousness the knowledge that not only themselves, but all their fellows have access, when ill, to the best that medical skill can provide."[22] Therefore it was not surprising that Barbara Castle, when also minister for health in the 1970s and a close colleague of Bevan, stated that the British healthcare system "is the nearest thing to the embodiment of the Good Samaritan that we have in any aspect of our public policy."[23] In this statement Castle pointed to the Good Samaritan story as the primary founding myth of healthcare throughout the Western world, with its emphasis in modern times on good quality healthcare as a fundamental human right, rooted in human relationships and trust between health workers and patients. To ignore this human right is an act of violence, an affront to the dignity of the person. The Good Samaritan parable is so rich in meaning that I have been able to build an entire course for healthcare workers on its foundations, as I will later explain.

Pope John Paul II wrote that the parable of the Good Samaritan best articulates the heart of the ministry of Jesus Christ and the mission of healthcare; "those involved professionally or voluntarily in the world of health" are invited "to fix their gaze on the divine Samaritan, so that their service can become a prefiguration of definitive salvation and a

21. Tommy Douglas (1904–1986), architect of universal healthcare in Canada, was deeply influenced by the Social Gospel movement, which combined Christian principles with social reform.

22. Aneurin Bevan, quoted by Margaret Whitehead, "Is It Fair? Evaluating the Equity Implications of the NHS Reforms," 208–42, in Ray Robinson and Julian Le Grand, eds., *Evaluating the NHS Reforms* (London: King's Fund Institute, 1993), 210.

23. Barbara Castle, quoted by Rudolf Klein, *The New Politics of the NHS* (Harlow: Prentice Hall, 2009), 90.

proclamation of new heavens and a new earth 'in which righteousness dwells' (2 Pt 3:13)."[24] Then, in his first encyclical, *Deus Caritas Est* (God Is Love), Pope Benedict XVI pointed four times to the significance of the parable of the Good Samaritan as the model for holistic care in healthcare, welfare, and socioeconomic development ministries. The parable remains a standard that imposes universal love toward the needy, whoever they may be.[25] This masterpiece of literature sets out, he says, "the programme of Jesus . . . a heart which sees. This heart sees where love is needed and acts."[26] And Jesus calls all his followers to do the same. In brief, love of God and neighbor is at the very heart of Catholic identities: "This is my commandment: love one another as I have loved you" (John 15:12). The Good Samaritan parable depicts the primacy of this love. Love calls forth compassionate responses to the suffering of others, and the measure of these responses is the example of Christ himself, *the* Good Samaritan (John 15:13). Only decisions made in love can transcend the suffering within and around us. For this reason the ultimate way to Catholic identities is through the transforming process of identifying with, and acting on, the lessons contained within the Good Samaritan parable.

Biblical Insights

As explained in chapter 5, parables are stories that open up worlds of thought and experience for those who listen to them. They can evoke many meanings; in fact, to restrict them to one principle of interpretation destroys their rich pedagogical potential. As springboard narratives they can capture people's imagination and act as catalysts for listeners to grasp in an unthreatening manner key truths in their own lives.[27]

Health and Sickness: Illness and Disease

To grasp the relevance and the power of this parable, however, we first need to appreciate the Jewish understanding of health and sickness in the general cultural environment at the time in which the parable

---

24. Pope John Paul II, *Contemplate the Face*, 15.

25. See Pope Benedict XVI, *Deus Caritas Est* (Sydney: St Pauls Publications, 2006), 52.

26. Ibid., 54.

27. See Stephen Denning, *The Springboard: How Storytelling Ignites Action in Knowledge-Era Organizations* (Boston: Butterworth-Heinemann, 2001), xviii–xix.

was told. If we do not look closely at the culture of the time, the parable will remain so domesticated in the popular imagination that people will expect to see that there is nothing startlingly different and challengingly relevant for our modern world. Only by returning to the cultural background of the story is it possible to grasp its astonishing insights.

In the Bible, health is defined primarily in the holistic sense, that is, as a complete state of physical, mental, and social well-being.[28] It is used, especially in the Old Testament, to refer to the body corporate—Israel as a people—and only secondarily to the individual. We find the idea of healing applied in God's response to the pain of Israel's exile: "For I shall restore health to you, and your wounds I will heal, says the LORD" (Jer 30:17). When relationships based on justice are restored through God's initiative and the willing response of the people as a whole, there will be true peace (*shalom*). All are committed to work together for this peace. That is, the value of solidarity is fundamental to biblical thinking; we are responsible for our neighbor's well-being and they for ours. That millions of Americans remained without healthcare before the gradual introduction of the Affordable Care Act, initiated by President Obama, is totally foreign to this biblical thinking.

In ancient Jewish culture people identified two types of sickness: "disease" and "illness."[29] Certain diseases automatically marginalized the sufferers from all human contact. They became social non-persons, considered worthless, even dangerous to society. The Jewish concern about leprosy, for example, was not primarily that it was contagious but that it was ritually polluting. In the lament Psalm 88 the sufferer desperately appeals to God: "I cry out to you in your presence" (v. 1). He has a disease that has pushed him to the margins of society, and the anguish of heart is overwhelming: he feels his life is being drawn "near to Sheol" (v. 3), "like those forsaken among the dead, like the slain that lie in the grave" (v. 5). You can still feel the inner pain: "You have caused my companions to shun me; you have made me a thing of horror to them"

---

28. Today there is a growing emphasis on this holistic understanding of health, which is regarded as synonymous with well-being, that is, a state characterized by contentment, prosperity, and the fulfillment of fundamental human needs. According to the World Health Organization, health is "a state of complete physical, mental and social well-being and not merely the absence of disease or infirmity." World Health Organization, *Health Promotion Glossary* (Geneva: WHO, 1998), 1.

29. See Gerald A. Arbuckle, *Healthcare Ministry: Refounding the Mission in Tumultuous Times* (Collegeville, MN: Liturgical Press, 2000), 14–15.

(v. 8). He is not first asking for physical healing of his disease, but for God to hear and feel with him his feeling of abandonment, which is his illness. When God responds with his compassionate touch, the sufferer's heart will be healed. Contemporary medical anthropologists also make this distinction.[30] The disease is what you see, e.g., the cancer, the severe injury, the leprosy. The illness, however, is what you cannot see. It is the inner pain of the heart that accompanies significant disease, such as fear of the future, the grief that comes from the loss of good health. In today's language it is summed up in questions like: If I survive the cancer, will I have a job? If I die, who will look after my family?

Pope Benedict XVI explains in *Caritas Deus Est* how this distinction between disease and illness, and the priority to be given to the latter, is carried over into the New Testament. He writes that while professional competence for healing physical sickness is without doubt necessary, "it is not of itself sufficient. We are dealing with human beings . . . [who] . . . need heartfelt concern."[31] This is why he places such importance on the parable of the Good Samaritan, in which the theme of healing of the heart is of fundamental importance. In the parable the caregiver seeks to heal the body of the victim, but above all he seeks to respond to the sufferer's inner pain of rejection. The injured man has been made ritually impure by his bloody injuries. To touch him is to make oneself ritually impure. One can only imagine the depth of loneliness in the victim, for now he is socially a non-person. While still alive, he has ceased to exist. The late Cardinal Joseph Bernardin highlights this quality of Christian healthcare when he writes: "Our distinctive vocation in Christian healthcare is not so much to heal [the sickness] better or more efficiently than anyone else; it is to bring comfort to people by giving them an experience that will strengthen their confidence in life. The ultimate goal of our care is to give those who are ill . . . a reason to hope. . . . In this we find the Christian vocation that makes our healthcare truly distinctive."[32] Medical science does not have the solutions to all causes of suffering, not even all physical suffering, and certainly not the inner pains of the heart. Feelings of loneliness, fear

30. See Cecil G. Helman, *Culture, Health and Illness* (Oxford: Butterworth-Heinemann, 1994), 101–45.

31. Pope Benedict XVI, *Deus Caritas Est*, 52.

32. Joseph Cardinal Bernardin, *A Sign of Hope: A Pastoral Letter on Healthcare*, 18 October 1995 (Chicago: Archdiocese of Chicago Office of Communications, 1995), 5.

of the unknown, helplessness, hopelessness, and abandonment are all expressions of suffering that brilliant surgery and medical drugs cannot touch. It is particularly important to note that in the parable the story-teller does not say definitely that the victim lives. The primary focus is on the healing of the inner pain of marginalization. Such is the case also in incidents of actual healing by Jesus in the gospels.

Violence in the Parable

Significant violence occurs throughout the Good Samaritan story. Violence is not only physical; it also exists in whatever is insensitive to and oppressive of human persons. In the parable there are six types of brutality: verbal, physical, social, ritual, racial, and occupational. Since these types of violence are common in today's world, people can readily relate to what is happening as the story unfolds. The way Jesus tells the story provides profound lessons about how to relate to violence with compassion and justice. As already explained, the parable begins with a Torah scholar, or religious lawyer, who questions Jesus in a verbally aggressive, polemical manner: "And who is my neighbor?" (v. 29). In the culture of that time, questions in this form are public challenges to personal honor. The lawyer hopes that Jesus is unable to answer the question, for this would cause Jesus immense public shame. This is what is meant by the statement that the man "was wanting to justify himself" (v. 29).[33] The second act of violence is physical, namely, the assault by bandits on an innocent man (v. 30). At the time it was common for bands of ruffians to violently threaten affluent travelers, rob them, and often give the stolen goods to the poor.[34] The victim may have been a wealthy man. The third act of violence is ritual. Because there is blood on the victim he is automatically stigmatized as impure, untouchable, and therefore a social outcast. This stigma of defilement would have caused intense inner pain. People would be unwilling to help him because that would make them ritually impure, requiring lengthy rituals of purification. The priest and the Levite, religious ritual professionals, refuse to go to the aid of the victim for fear of contracting

---

33. This common negative interpretation of the scholar is questioned by Luise Schottroff, *The Parables of Jesus*, trans. Linda M. Maloney (Minneapolis: Fortress Press, 2006), 132.

34. See Bruce J. Malina and Richard L. Rohrbaugh, *Social-Science Commentary on the Synoptic Gospels* (Minneapolis: Fortress Press, 1992), 404.

ritual impurity. They should have known that their refusal to help goes against a fundamental law of the Torah, namely, to aid people in need. The fourth act of violence is the stripping of the victim (Luke 10:30). It was customary to strip prisoners naked before being scourged, and they suffered as much from the shame of involuntary nakedness as from the lash (see 4 Macc 6:2; Matt 27:28, 31),[35] but to strip a person naked, as Jesus was stripped before being crucified, is the final act of subjugation and social exclusion. The priest and Levite, two leaders of Jewish culture, illustrate a type of religious fundamentalism that had developed at that time. The Israelite tradition required that people must show compassion, especially to people who are poor and marginalized (Isa 58), but Jewish fundamentalists discarded this obligation, developing instead a religion that focused on external conformity to rituals of accidental importance. The priest going up to Jerusalem from his rural home refuses outright to help for two reasons: he fears being attacked by other roaming bandits if he pauses, but, more critically, he is not prepared to be defiled by touching the victim (v. 31). The Levite belongs to an order of cultic officials "for the service of the Lord" (Exod 32:28), inferior to the priests but nonetheless a privileged group in Jewish society, but he also declines to help for the same reasons (v. 32).

The traveler, as a Samaritan, focuses attention on a fifth form of violence. Samaritans were considered by Jewish people to be religiously and racially inferior. For this reason those who listened to Jesus telling the story would have been not only surprised but also shocked to hear that such a person—one marginalized by Jewish culture—becomes the caregiver. The story contains a sixth example of violence: work-related prejudice and discrimination. Traders in oil and wine, like the Samaritan, were marginalized because both Jews and Samaritans considered they had become rich through shady dealings. The Samaritan, like the victim, knows the pain of social ostracism and loneliness. Jews regarded the heretical Samaritans as religiously and racially inferior and the Samaritans had similar views of their Jewish neighbors. So, though there are two negative qualities stigmatizing him, it is this Samaritan—one considered religiously and racially inferior as well as occupationally dubious—who becomes the caregiver. In brief, the Samaritan is socially

35. See John J. Pilch and Bruce J. Malina, eds., *Biblical Social Values and Their Meaning* (Peabody, MA: Hendrickson, 1993), 121.

and racially a disadvantaged person, yet he is the one who freely and immediately acts to help the victim.[36]

Qualities of the Caregiver

The dramatic paradox in the story is that a Samaritan spontaneously aids the dying man. His compassion breaks through the many layers of violence after those who should act, the priest and the Levite, scorn the injured and marginalized victim. The story details the qualities of the Samaritan. He is courageous because he endangers his own life by getting off his mount, his only form of protection, becoming in consequence exposed to attack by thieves. Every moment he is off the mount the physical danger to himself intensifies. His courage is further tested when he walks and leads the mount to avoid exacerbating the sufferings of the victim, thus further risking an attack. The listeners to the story know that the road from Jerusalem to Jericho, with its tortuous bends and rocky sides, is ideal for bandits.

In addition to the physical risks there are the ritual and social consequences of touching the victim. We read that the caregiver "bandaged his wounds, having poured oil and wine on them" (v. 34). In order to bandage the victim the Samaritan must touch him, but since the Samaritans had similar laws about ritual impurity the caregiver himself becomes ritually contaminated. This readiness to venture to the very boundaries of society in service of healing expresses the depth of his love and compassion. The victim would have been profoundly comforted by this touch. At last there was someone who felt with him in his torment of ritual and social marginalization. Never in the story are we told that the victim survives physically, but through his touch we know with certainty that the victim's inner hurt is healed. That is the significant priority Jesus wanted to emphasize. The Samaritan heals the *illness* of the victim first and then, through the application of oil and wine to his wounds, he attempts to nurse the physical injury (that is, the *disease*).

The Samaritan practices the gift of hospitality. He contributes from his capital, the oil and wine he had intended to sell at the market. In biblical cultures hospitality is never confined to amusing one's friends or family members but refers primarily to receiving strangers and an

---

36. See John L. McKenzie, *Dictionary of the Bible* (London: Geoffrey Chapman, 1968), 766.

openness to share one's capital goods with them without anticipating any return. Outsiders are encouraged to stop being strangers and become honored guests instead.[37] The Jewish Law required this because, as the Israelites had been strangers in Egypt, so they should themselves show hospitality to outsiders (Exod 23:9; Lev 19:33-34). Jesus would develop this further, not just in this parable but through his example and his teachings. People who would receive the disciples of Jesus would in fact be receiving Jesus himself: "Truly I tell you, just as you did it to one of least of these . . . you did it to me" (Matt 25:40). To extend or refuse hospitality meant that the Gospel had been accepted or rejected.[38]

The inn in our Western society is traditionally a symbol of safety and hospitality, but the inn at the time of Christ was a hideout for thieves, and the innkeeper was the biggest scoundrel of all. There is a humorous touch to the Samaritan's relationships with the innkeeper because, despite the fact that the latter is a seedy character, the Samaritan deliberately aims to form a relationship with him. The caregiver is no romantic idealist, out of touch with the weaknesses of human nature; knowing from his own experience what to expect from the innkeeper, the Samaritan simply bribes him in order to ensure that the patient will be cared for and kept alive. He gives the innkeeper a certain amount of money but assures him of more when he returns (Luke 10: 35).[39]

Fundamental Truths and Values: Roots of Catholic Identities

In the last stage of workshops on the foundational story of healthcare and welfare services I would, in an interactive way, assist participants to recognize the fundamental values and truths inherent in the parable and how these form the roots of the Catholic identities of their ministries. Where appropriate I would introduce relevant deeper theological points for discussion. If the workshops covered several days it would often be possible to focus on critically important topics such as

37. See Pilch and Malina, *Biblical Social Values*, 104–7.

38. See Abraham J. Malherbe, "Hospitality," 292–93, in Bruce Metzger and Michael D. Coogan, eds., *The Oxford Companion to the Bible* (Oxford: Oxford University Press, 1993); Brendan Byrne, *The Hospitality of God: A Reading of Luke's Gospel* (Collegeville, MN: Liturgical Press, 2000), 100–102.

39. See Malina and Rohrbaugh, *Social-Science Commentary*, 346–48.

employer-employee relationships and the identification of and response to cultures of bullying. At all times it was possible to draw people back to the values and truths intrinsic to the parable.

Values

Values are action-oriented priorities of two types: *ultimate*, that is, values that must distinguish a sought-after end state, and those termed *directional*, that is, those values that assist or are essential for the achievement of the ultimate desired final state.[40] Ultimate values in the Good Samaritan story are: holistic health (the *illness* and *disease* are treated), equity (care is given with no reference to payment), and solidarity/social justice (peace and justice are restored as all peoples have fundamental rights to security and good health). Directional values are: compassion or empathy (the caregiver identifies with the feelings of the victim), respect for human dignity, hospitality (the caregiver shares his own capital wealth—oil, wine, and money—with the victim), courage, efficiency (the caregiver skillfully uses his talents and capital goods in the service of the victim), and dialogue (the caregiver's relationship with the innkeeper).

The primary binary opposition in the mythology of the Good Samaritan is that between what I call "the mission" and "the business."[41] The former, the mission, is to be the driving force behind the latter (fig. 7.2). The mission pole contains the values that are to guide all caregivers: compassion, empathy, communitarian solidarity, a preference for the marginalized, social justice. The Samaritan is sensitive to the distinction between disease and illness. While he does not neglect the disease or injury aspect, his primary concern is with the illness, the inner pain of the victim. Hence his emphasis on compassion, human solidarity, and social inclusion; by his actions the Samaritan overcomes the five forms of violence. By touching the victim the Samaritan caregiver expresses solidarity and compassion for the victim, since he is himself ritually marginalized by this action. His willingness to move to the margins of society as a caregiver demonstrates the depth of his love and compassion.

---

40. See Simon L. Dolan, Salvador Garcia, and Bonnie Richley, *Managing by Values* (Basingstoke: Palgrave Macmillan, 2006), 32–33.

41. See Brad H. Young, *The Parables: Jewish Tradition and Christian Interpretation* (Peabody, MA: Hendrickson, 1998), 101–88; John R. Donahue, *The Gospel in Parable: Metaphor, Narrative, and Theology in the Synoptic Gospels* (Philadelphia: Fortress Press, 1988), 128–34.

The victim is deeply comforted by this touch. At last there is someone who feels with him in his anguish and the marginalization imposed by the priest and the Levite. The Samaritan is also extremely brave, for he constantly risks his life on the brigand-ridden road in order to care for the victim.

The Mission Energizing . . . . **the Business**

Ultimate Values

   Holistic health
     Equity
     Solidarity/social justice

Directional Values
   Respect
   Compassion/empathy
   Hospitality
   Courage
   Dialogue
   Efficiency

Figure 7.2: The Good Samaritan: Foundational Values

But there are less recognizable "business" aspects to the parable. The Samaritan is a smart businessman. If he had not been an efficient wine and oil merchant he would have had no material goods of wine, oil, and money to assist the victim. His management skills are further evident in the way he relates to the innkeeper. To stop the innkeeper from robbing the victim once the Samaritan has gone, the alert Samaritan wisely bribes the innkeeper to be the caregiver. Surely this is an example of the values of efficiency and excellence!

The parable contains six interconnected truths (see fig. 7.3) that should form the foundation of Catholic healthcare and welfare ministries. Each truth contains values or action-oriented priorities. Because the truths are so interrelated, similar values will appear at times under different truths.

Good Samaritan Parable: Foundational Truths Catholic Healthcare/Welfare	1. Creation: gift of God Core Values: love of God and neighbor, hope, justice, hospitality 2. Commitment to stewardship Core Values: mercy, compassion, social justice, excellence, simplicity 3. Commitment to community building Core Values: mutuality, dialogue 4. Commitment to a preferential option for people who are marginalized Core Values: love, justice, compassion, humility 5. Call to holistic healing Core Values: justice, compassion, mercy 6. Call to prophetic leadership Core Values: memory, imagination, courage, trust in Divine Providence, hope

Figure 7.3: The Good Samaritan: Founding Truths and Values of Catholic Identities

1. All Creation Is to Be Considered a Gift of God[42]

The Samaritan, not the official religious representatives, well understood the fundamental fact: God created the world and God is our loving Parent, so well attested to in the Old Testament. Therefore the founding values are:

- Love of God and neighbor: Our love of God is to be expressed in concern for creation and the human dignity of all; human persons mirror God's power in the sense that they can think and act freely,

---

42. See wider explanation in Arbuckle, *Healthcare Ministry*, 155–79.

but this freedom must be exercised in ways that respect the purpose of the Creator.

- Justice: Every person should expect from society equitable access to what is necessary to live with dignity, in ways that respect the rights of others. This is the meaning of justice.

- Hope: The Samaritan offered the victim hope, an experience of "the new heavens and the new earth, where uprightness will be at home" (2 Pet 3:13), in a world of brokenness, despair, and violence.

- Hospitality: This value, in the sense already described, is a consequence of the fact that all creation is a gift of God. All goods ultimately belong to God, and when we receive a stranger we are but sharing what rightly belongs to all.

Hospitality in the Scriptures

The biblical understanding of hospitality helps to explain what is meant by a "preferential option for the poor." Hospitality is one of the most important virtues for Jewish and Christian living, more important than fasting (Isa 58:7). This is because hospitality is an application of the fundamental truth that all creation belongs to God and we all have the right to share equitably in its fruits. The Israelites, since they had been strangers in Egypt, were to show hospitality in turn to strangers in their midst (Exod 23:9). The book of Leviticus commands: "The alien who resides with you shall be to you as the citizen among you; you shall love the alien as yourself, for you were aliens in the land of Egypt: I am the Lord your God" (Lev 19:34). The prophets often speak of the duty of giving to the poor as an expression of hospitality, but their emphasis is primarily on its justice quality, not on what today we would call philanthropy, that is, giving from one's surplus. Philanthropy, however, is also encouraged (Prov 3:27-28; 28:27).

There is a strong emphasis on hospitality in the New Testament also; it is an integral part of Jesus' teaching and behavior (Luke 7:36-50).[43] Those who do not receive his disciples as guests are rejecting Christ himself (Matt 10:9-16).[44] Jesus insists in his conversation with the rich young man that to give *all* one's goods to the poor is a condition for becoming his follower (Matt 19:21; Mark 10:21).[45] The point he

---

43. See Byrne, *The Hospitality of God*, passim.
44. See Malherbe, "Hospitality," *Oxford Companion to the Bible*, 292–93.
45. See McKenzie, *Dictionary of the Bible*, 21.

is dramatically making is that all goods ultimately belong to God and one must therefore not be exclusively attached to them.[46] In the Good Samaritan story (Luke 10:29-37) we see an example of Jesus' emphasis on sharing even one's capital goods with strangers who lack necessities. The Samaritan, a trader in oil and wine, shares his capital with a person declared socially a non-person by both Jewish and Samaritan tradition.

In brief, hospitality requires that we give to those in need even out of our capital goods. While the Scriptures tell us that as good stewards we should use our resources wisely in view of future needs, they also direct us to take significant risks in drawing on our capital for the sake of people in need. Jesus tells several parables about the wisdom of careful and professional planning in business ventures. For example, the farmer who needs to build a tower to protect his crops and farm instruments must "first sit down and work out the cost to see if he had enough to complete it" (Luke 14:28). Then there is the wise builder who does not construct a house without first testing the solidity of the ground (Luke 6:47-49). But there are also key parables that insist that *all* economic decisions must be made through the lens of the imperative of an "option for the poor" (Luke 10:25-37; 12:16-21; 14:16-24; 16:19-31; Matt 22:1-14).[47] Careful discernment is required to find the right balance: planning for the future and at the same time risking giving from one's capital to fulfill the "option for the poor."

2. We Are to Use Creation as Stewards of God.

To be a steward is to hold something in trust for another person, that is, to use what has been entrusted to us in ways determined by that person. For us this means that we are called to cocreate with God, to continue God's creation in this world in ways that reflect the dignity of God. This truth contains the core values of justice, mercy, compassion, empathy, excellence, and simplicity. Because all creation comes from God we must use it as stewards of God.

- Mercy: As God has showed mercy toward us, so we are to do the same to those around us. Mercy is loving clemency or forgiveness of guilt (a theme that is more fully taken up in some other parables).

46. See Malina and Rohrbaugh, *Social-Science Commentary*, 244.
47. See Arland J. Hultgren, *The Parables of Jesus: A Commentary* (Grand Rapids, MI: Eerdmans, 2000), 130–79.

- Compassion: This has an interesting origin. The Samaritan traveler was moved with compassion (Luke 10:33). Compassion is a value originally founded on kinship obligations, whether natural or symbolic. The Hebrew word is derived from the word for womb, implying the need to feel for others because they are born of the same mother. God is that mother, and we are all children of that womb and must accordingly feel with, and care for, each other as brothers and sisters. Thus the Samaritan feels the inner pain of marginalization that the victim—his brother—is experiencing. Compassion asserts that there is nothing more urgent than the pain of another person "because that other person is profoundly, intimately, deeply connected to us through our common incarnation."[48] The more one feels the pain of the other person the more one is anxious to remove the injustices and oppressions that cause that pain. For this reason compassion is a powerfully subversive value, a value that can turn society upside down.

- Social justice: We must work for the good of all, especially people who are marginalized.

- Excellence: The value of excellence flows from the fact that our gifts come from God and are to be used in God's service. Excellence in this sense covers all human endeavor, including research, that is at the service of God and humankind. It allows for no selfishness, mediocrity, or laziness in the use of our talents. The Samaritan exercises this value when he uses his experience of human nature in relating to the innkeeper. Because one's talents come from God, excellence allows of no selfishness, mediocrity, or laziness in the use of such gifts.

- Simplicity: This value is not synonymous with ignorance that causes people to act imprudently. On the contrary, people with simplicity act with only the will of God in mind. Out of love, God gives creation to us to be used as God wishes; namely, with the single-minded commitment to justice and love in the service for others. There is to be no holding back, fuss, pretense, or double-dealing in our simple-hearted stewardship of God's gifts. Such is the example of the Samaritan.

---

48. David K. Urion, *Compassion as a Subversive Activity* (Cambridge, MA: Cowley Publications, 2006), 48.

3. Acting as Stewards, We Are Called to Collaborate in Building Communities of Healing

There is no support for individualism in the parable. In Jewish tradition people are expected to work together in imitation of God's desire to build community with the Israelites: "I will place my dwelling in your midst, and I shall not abhor you. And I will walk among you, and will be your God, and you will be my people" (Lev 26:11-12). Values of unity, collaboration, dialogue, and mutuality are marks of an authentic community as is evident in the way the Samaritan acts toward the victim and the innkeeper.

* Mutuality: This is an integral quality of any true community. The victim's pain of marginalization reminds the Samaritan of his own similar experience and his need for compassion. He gives from his own experience of vulnerability by first healing the victim's heart or illness caused by his marginalization from society.

* Dialogue: Dialogue is the interaction between people in which each one aims to give himself or herself as she or he is and seeks also to know the other as the other is. It is authentic if three conditions are met: people feel they understand the position of others, they also feel that others understand their points of view, and there is a readiness on the part of all to accept what is decided because the decision was reached openly and fairly.[49]

4. A Key Test of Our Authenticity Will Be Our Commitment to a Preferential Option for People Who Are Poor: This Can Be Achieved through Processes of Working with or for People Who Are Poor

This truth focuses on the core values of love, justice, compassion, and humility. Most commonly in the Scriptures the words "people who are poor," or "the little ones" refer to those who through no fault of their own are powerless in society. Structures of oppression condemn them to economic, social, and political poverty. In the parable Jesus identifies

---

49. See Gerald A. Arbuckle, *Refounding the Church: Dissent for Leadership* (Maryknoll, NY: Orbis Books, 1993), 111.

with the actions of the Samaritan, whose primary concern in this story is to be with one who is marginalized in society. By his actions and words Jesus frequently repeats this message: "I was hungry and you gave me food. . . . I was a stranger and you welcomed me" (Matt 25:35). Jesus becomes so identified with people who are poor that when we refuse them justice we are refusing him. The ultimate test of our concern for human dignity will be the priority we give to people who are especially socially or humanly disadvantaged, those people society considers worthless, having nothing to offer society, second-class citizens.

Humility, as a core value, is based on the fact that we are all brothers and sisters with a common God our Parent. No one can claim to be more exalted than others. This is evident in the Samaritan's behavior. As a successful trader he had much to be proud of. He could have regarded the victim as a social inferior. He did not do so. Flowing from this is the firm belief that other people can teach us truths from their own experience of life, if we are but open to hear. When the Samaritan is taken as a symbol of Christ we have here a powerful example of humility for caregivers. Matthew's gospel tells us that Jesus was no arrogant teacher, but "gentle and humble in heart" (Matt 11:29). He entered Jerusalem in an unpretentious way, seated not on a horse, a traditional war animal of power and status, but on a donkey, socially a lowly form of transportation (Matt 21:5).

5. We Are Called to Holistic Healing in Our Ministry, That Is, to Physical, Spiritual, and Social Healing

This truth emphasizes the core values of justice, compassion, and mercy. Pope John Paul II wrote that this parable "not only spurs one to help the sick, but also to do all one can to reintegrate them into society. For Christ, in fact, healing is also this reintegration: just as sickness excludes the human person from the community, so healing must bring them to rediscover their place in the family, in the Church and in society."[50] In addressing the two aspects of sickness—disease and illness—the Samaritan goes to the causes of marginalization, that is, he addresses the social stigma and poverty that entrap the victim.

---

50. Pope John Paul II, *Contemplate the Face of Christ*, 15.

6. In Fulfilling Our Ministry We Realize That Our Concern to Live the Values Inherent in Our Common Founding Story Will Require of Us at Times a Prophetic Leadership; This May Lead to Our Own Social and Political Marginalization

From this truth come the values of memory, courage, trust in Divine Providence, and hope. The biblical prophets of the Old Testament served Israel as its imaginative, creative, dynamic, and questioning memory.[51] As authentic leaders they could see the gap between God's call to justice and compassion and the absence of these qualities in their people's lives. As proficient storytellers they remember God's love for his people. They do not remain silent; they remind people in imaginative ways of God's commandments of love and justice and their failure to live accordingly. Despite their rejection by the people, they remain hopeful that God will still show compassion toward God's wayward people.

The Samaritan exemplifies these qualities of creative leadership. Not only does he risk his life for the victim on the bandit-infested road; he also suffers further ritual marginalization by Jewish people and those of his own culture because of his actions. Christ, the storyteller and the ultimate Good Samaritan, will of course give his life in the service of others. It is at this point that the symbolism of the cross in Catholic facilities can be explained.

Summary

- The parables are fictitious, imaginative stories Jesus used to explain his teachings and his mission. They challenged attitudes and invited people to transform their lives. The Good Samaritan parable, a fine example of Jesus' inductive method of teaching, is one of the most influential founding stories of our Western civilization; it continues to influence, at least in a residual manner, the way we are expected to relate to one another according to the values of love, compassion, and justice. The parable is not an academic discussion about these principles but a vivid reminder to see (vv. 31-33) and do (vv. 25, 28, 37–38).[52] Values are not truly values until they are actually being

51. See Gerald A. Arbuckle, "Maintaining Prophetic Cultures," *Health Progress* 86, no. 5 (September-October 2005): 19–24.
52. See Schottroff, *The Parables*, 132.

expressed in action; if values do not result in behavior they remain simply cognitive.

- In particular, the parable is the founding story of all Western health and welfare services; at times it is forgotten or deliberately overlooked, to the serious detriment of people's holistic health needs.

- It is startlingly evident from the Good Samaritan parable and Jesus' other parables that we must acknowledge the realities of personal and social sin; for holistic healing to take place we require not just changes in structures but also interior transformation of the heart.

- We desperately need refounding rebels in our health and welfare systems, leaders who are inspired by the memory of the founding story of healthcare, a story of equity, compassion, and social justice, but who also are able to create ways to embed these values in structures and strategies that are relevant to our contemporary conditions.

- In the following chapter we see that particular parables of Jesus Christ can be springboard or "trigger" stories to encourage business people to ethically critique the world in which they work; these parables, like the story of the Good Samaritan, can become for these people the foundations for their Catholic identities.

Chapter Eight

Crafting Catholic Identities in the Business World

[The] moral and political challenge we face today is . . . to rethink the role and reach of markets in our social practices, human relationships, and everyday lives.[1]
(Michael J. Sandel)

Today's international economic scene . . . requires a profoundly new way of understanding business enterprise. . . . [B]usiness management cannot concern itself only with the interests of the proprietors, but must also assume responsibility for all the other stakeholders *. . . the workers, the clients, the suppliers of various elements of production, the community of reference.*[2]
(Benedict XVI)

This chapter explains that:

- the major investment banking financial scandals and constant fear of more world recessions have increased public demand for more institutional and corporate ethical accountability

1. Michael J. Sandel, *What Money Can't Buy: The Moral Limits of Markets* (New York: Farrar, Straus and Giroux, 2012), 15.
2. Pope Benedict XVI, Encyclical Letter, On Integral Human Development in Charity and Truth (*Caritas in Veritate*) (London: Catholic Truth Society, 2009), 46–47.

- the biblical traditions in the Old and New Testaments that focus on the obligations the financially well-off have to people in need are relevant in today's world

- several parables of Jesus Christ insist that the profit motive must not dominate the way people relate to one another

- when businesspeople reflect on these parables *and* implement their values they are laying the foundations of Catholic identities in their lives

Michael Sandel, professor of government at Harvard University, argues that economic rationalism, the belief that unrestrained markets, not government, are "the key to prosperity and freedom," is now being seriously questioned in the aftermath of the world financial crisis. The world of business "has become detached from morals and . . . we need somehow to reconnect them."[3] Tony Judt, an internationally famous social critic and historian, writes that: "The Enlightenment vision . . . no longer convinces. What we lack is a moral narrative: an internally coherent account that ascribes purpose to our actions in a way that transcends them."[4] Capitalistic economic rationalism cannot provide the moral narrative to bring justice into the world of business. Massive scandals, such as occurred in Enron, WorldCom, Tyco, Parmalat, and others in the 1990s and early 2000s, and the world recession instigated by the collapse of the subprime mortgage market in the United States and elsewhere, demand that businesses be ethically critiqued. People are increasingly demanding that businesses become more accountable for their actions. Greed must be controlled. Hence "the real challenge in business education is to introduce business ethics into every area of the curriculum."[5]

This chapter, like the previous one, shows that relevant parables can be used by businesspeople as springboard narratives to ethically examine and guide their behavior. I have used these parables in workshops to

3. Sandel, *What Money Can't Buy*, 6.
4. Tony Judt, *Ill Fares the Land: A Treatise on Our Present Discontents* (London: Allen Lane, 2010), 183.
5. Jordi Canals, "Foreword," xiii–xiv, in Domènec Melé, *Business Ethics in Action: Putting People First* (Basingstoke: Palgrave, 2009), xiv.

stimulate discussion and action for businesspeople, but political, educational, and community leaders can also benefit from their lessons. When people's behavior conforms to the values inherent in these parables they are beginning to create transparently moral and ethical Catholic identities in whatever they do.

The chapter begins with a brief description of economic rationalism, followed by a summary of the biblical traditions that should guide all business and public relationships. This synopsis will form the background to the analysis of several parables that follow.

Context

It is rare these days to hear good news about the global economy. We still fear that another world recession will smother us. We are losing trust in the banking world and in the willingness and abilities of politicians to lead with transparency and integrity. We know that the rich are getting richer; the poor, poorer. On the global scene capitalism is ruling with fewer controls and less concern for the common good. Economic rationalism, or market capitalism, neoclassical capitalism, market liberalism, as it emerged in the 1980s, takes for granted that profit is the sole measure of value and the economics profession serves as its priesthood.[6] The assumptions are: sustained economic growth is the best way to distribute wealth; free markets, unrestrained by government interference, result in the most efficient use of resources; economic globalization, with the unrestricted flow of goods and finance, will benefit all; lower taxation and radically reduced government spending are desirable; governments must privatize services; the government's primary task is to support individual initiatives in commerce.[7]

Contained in the mythology of the economic rationalist culture, whose operational wing is called the "new managerialism," is the Social Darwinist assumption that the poor are poor through their own fault and therefore welfare services, which only make their poverty worse, must be reduced. Economic rationalists also aim to change public institutions

---

6. See David C. Korten, *When Corporations Rule the World* (London: Earthscan, 1996), 69; Gerald A. Arbuckle, *Violence, Society, and the Church: A Cultural Critique* (Collegeville, MN: Liturgical Press, 2004), 170–73.

7. See Arbuckle, *Violence, Society, and the Church,* 70.

into pseudo-businesses;[8] for example, healthcare is considered an economic commodity and must be subjected to the principles of supply and demand in the marketplace. Economic rationalists have adopted the postmodernist distrust of history. As John Saul commented in the 1995 Canadian Massey Lectures: "We have come to so forget our own history that we are compliantly acting in a suicidal manner, believing that economics can lead—whereas in the past it has always failed to do so. . . . We have fallen in love with an old ideology that has never paid off in the past."[9] However, the global economic meltdown of 2008 dramatically undermined confidence in economic rationalism, namely, the notion that people usually make rational decisions and that the market's invisible hand serves as a trustworthy corrective to any imbalance.[10] The cult of unrestrained individualism, or self-interest, the belief that greed is good, and the refusal to accept responsibility for the common good have proved to be economically and socially disastrous. Yet people refuse to learn this lesson. In the United States the poverty rate has risen to 14.3% in 2012, the highest increase in over thirty years; forty-three million of the population are listed as "poor."[11] Millions of Americans, encouraged by big business and the rise of the "tea party" movement, respond by demanding that the government cut back on taxes for the wealthy and further reduce welfare services. Tea party adherents love "to conjure up a mythic America of limited government, sing hymns to the constitution and denounce the federal bureaucracy in all its forms,"[12] but the human cost to millions of people on the margins of society is incalculable. A similar revitalization of economic rationalism is evident also in England, where the poverty gap continues to widen.

8. See Cris Shore and Susan Wright, "Coercive Accountability: The Rise of Audit Culture in Higher Education," 57–89, in Marilyn Strathern, ed., *Audit Cultures: Anthropological Studies in Accountability, Ethics, and the Academy* (London: Routledge, 2000), 63–65.

9. Paul R. Saul, *The Unconscious Civilization* (Toronto: Penguin, 1997), 123.

10. See Dan Ariely, "The End of Rational Economics," *Harvard Business Review* (July-August 2009): 78–84.

11. See *National Catholic Reporter* editorial, "Radical Individualism and the Poverty Rate" (1 October 2010): 28.

12. Lexington, "The Good, the Bad and the Tea Parties," *The Economist* (30 October 2010): 46; see Economist.com/blogs/lexington.

Obligations of the Rich: Scriptural Background to Parables

To appreciate the powerful and disturbing message of the parables that define the obligations of the rich to the poor, it will be helpful to summarize how the Old and the New Testaments viewed poverty and wealth.[13]

- The Scriptures are not against wealth but opposed to its misuse. Capital must be at the service of the common good; in aiding people on the margin believers are expected to give not only from surplus goods but also from their capital.

- People are just when they are in right relationship to God and to other people. The ultimate test of this right relationship is one's loving concern for people who are economically deprived in society and suffer the consequent social and political powerlessness.

- In both the Old and New Testaments there is a strong condemnation of well-to-do people for failing to use their wealth appropriately. People are entrapped in poverty and rendered politically powerless because of the greed of people who are wealthy.

These points will now be examined in detail.

Old Testament

Involuntary poverty, with its material and immaterial aspects, is contrary to fundamental truths of God's special relationship with the Israelite nation. All people are equal in dignity before God. All have the right to an equitable use of this world's resources and all are called to work collaboratively to ensure this right is respected. The test of the community's faithfulness to God is its concrete daily respect for these truths. "You shall love the Lord your God," says God, describing how the Israelites are to relate to him, "and keep his charge, his decrees, his ordinances, and his commandments always" (Deut 11:1). Thus "loving the Lord your God" is inseparably linked with "serving God" in building a community of justice and compassion (Deut 11:13). In return, God

13. See Gerald A. Arbuckle, *A 'Preferential Option for the Poor': Application to Catholic Health and Aged Care Ministries in Australia* (Canberra: Catholic Health Australia, 2007), 23–34.

promises that the Israelites "will eat [their] fill" (Deut 11:15). However, God warns about being "seduced into turning away, serving other gods and worshiping them" (Deut 11:16).[14] If they are seduced into politically and economically exploiting the poor, marginalizing vulnerable widows, orphans, and refugees, they are acting hypocritically. For this they are to be punished (Amos 8:4-6).[15]

The prophets in the Old Testament are Israel's creative and questioning memory. They repeatedly remind the Israelites of how God expects them to behave. Hence they unequivocally condemn the ruthless oppression of people who are poor by the rich and powerful: "Ah, you who make iniquitous decrees, who write oppressive statutes, to turn aside the needy from justice" (Isa 10:1). The prophet Amos scathingly decries the Israelites who "oppress the poor, who crush the needy" (Amos 4:1). Speaking through Amos, God condemns the Israelites' hypocrisy, performing their fine acts of worship while neglecting the rights of poor people: "I hate, I despise your festivals, and I take no delight in your solemn assemblies. . . . Take away from me the noise of your songs. . . . But let justice roll down like waters, and righteousness like an ever-flowing stream" (Amos 5:21, 23-24). By "justice" Amos means that people must meticulously avoid oppressing the poor and crushing the needy. Instead, they are to systematically pursue steadfast love in their regard for the poor and needy.

Ezekiel denounces the rich for their banditry against the poor (Ezek 22:29); Isaiah, their land grabbing (Isa 5:8); Jeremiah, their abuse of power (Jer 22:13-17). God will love the wealthy *only* when they are acting justly and using their power to help those on society's margins. They can enthusiastically pray with beautifully prepared rituals, even claiming to be utterly dependent in their hearts on God, but God will ignore them until such time as they act justly toward the defenseless: "Is such the fast that I choose, a day to humble oneself? Is it to bow down the head like a bulrush, and to lie in sackcloth and ashes? Will you call this a fast, a day acceptable to the Lord?" (Isa 58:5). The worship that pleases God is a search for justice and a special concern for those who are marginalized and oppressed (Isa 1:10-17; 58:6-7). The mission of

14. See Delbert R. Hillers, *Covenant: The History of a Biblical Idea* (Baltimore: Johns Hopkins University Press, 1969), 152.

15. See Mary Elsbernd and Reimund Bieringer, *When Love Is Not Enough: A Theo-Ethic of Justice* (Collegeville, MN: Liturgical Press, 2002), 41–46.

the future Messiah will be to defend the rights of the defenseless (Isa 11:4; Ps 72:2-4).

In the Old Testament three vulnerable groups of people are often singled out for special concern: widows, orphans, and refugees. In patriarchal cultures these people depend on male patrons for protection. In these times an independent woman did not exist; she had to rely for protection on her husband or father. When she became a widow she might be geographically distant from her father, making her particularly vulnerable to all kinds of oppression (Job 22:9; 24:21; Ezek 22:7). Her children could suffer the same fate. In the book of Exodus the Israelites are left in no doubt about what they must do: "You shall not abuse any widow or orphan. If you do abuse them . . . my wrath will burn, and I will kill you with the sword, and your wives shall become widows and your children orphans" (Exod 22:21-23).

In summary:

- The model of society in the Old Testament is not a competitive one but a neighborly network that supports people who cannot sustain themselves.[16]

- God does not denounce wealth or power as such but condemns their exploitation. However, the danger of being seduced by material goods is so great that their ownership is problematic. When people become selfishly attached to wealth and power, refusing to use them in the service of the community, then evil exists. They no longer have a right relationship with God (Ps 49:6).

- God has a preferential love for people who are economically poor, that is, for the powerless, because they have no one to trust but God: "But this is the one to whom I will look, to the humble and contrite in spirit, who trembles at my word. . . . Sing for joy . . . for the LORD has comforted his people, and will have compassion on his suffering ones" (Isa 66:2; 49:13) because the "poor soul cried, and was heard by the Lord and was saved from every trouble" (Ps 34:6). The poor are to become "a remnant of Israel" that the Messiah will draw together in a new relationship (Zeph 3:12-13).[17]

16. See Walter Brueggemann, *Reverberations of Faith: A Theological Handbook of Old Testament Themes* (Louisville: Westminster John Knox, 2002), 230.

17. See Xavier Leon-Dufour, *Dictionary of Biblical Theology* (London: Geoffrey Chapman, 1967), 386–87.

New Testament

In his teaching and lifestyle Jesus proclaims that people who are poor are to be the privileged "heirs of the kingdom" (Jas 2:5). He is to be the Messiah of the poor: "He has sent me to . . . let the oppressed go free" (Luke 4:18). After an ambiguous reaction from his listeners (Luke 4:22), Jesus reiterates by way of examples taken from the lives of the prophets Elijah (1 Kgs 17:17-24) and Elisha (2 Kgs 5:1-19) that his mission is preferentially directed toward those who are underprivileged and marginalized.

Jesus maintains this theme in all his preaching, although he is severely criticized, even threatened with death, for doing so. Jesus Christ is one of "the poor" from the time of his birth to his death on the cross. Having "emptied himself" (Phil 2:7) to share our humanity, he becomes a resident of a reviled village (John 1:46) in an isolated part of the extensive Roman Empire. He does not belong to a socially elite group but is known simply as a carpenter's son (Matt 13:55), living and acting in solidarity with ordinary people.[18] In the time of ancient Israel, God stands *beside* the oppressed, but with Christ there is to be total *identification* with the exploited. In Jesus' last speech before his passion he states unambiguously that the ultimate indication of social good health is whether or not the community is committed to justice, especially justice to the powerless, the hungry, the oppressed and deprived in society. Jesus so identifies with the defenseless that when people refuse them justice they are refusing *him*, even if they are unconscious of this fact: "For I was hungry and you gave me no food" (Matt 25:42).

We now examine several authors of the New Testament to see the emphasis they give to the Christian understanding of poverty and wealth.

Matthew's Gospel

In Matthew's listing of the Beatitudes, Jesus speaks of two groups of people especially loved by God. First, there are those whose attitudes and lifestyles are contrary to the unjust culture that surrounds them. For them wealth, power, and selfishness have nothing to do with one's happiness. True contentment is to be found only in being just, compassionate, and merciful. The second group of people are advocates who stand up to protect the rights of the powerless and, suppressing self-love

18. See Donal Dorr, *Mission in Today's World* (Dublin: Columba Press, 2000), 151–52.

and ambition, show mercy. They struggle to develop peace in an unjust society and are prepared to suffer for the defense of justice: "for these is the kingdom of heaven" (Matt 5:3). They are people with wealth and power who are detached from undue love of material goods and power. They offer themselves and their gifts for the service of God in their sisters and brothers. They seek to build solidarity with the economically poor and powerless and may even identify with them, sometimes in radical ways, just as Jesus does.[19]

Luke's Gospel

Luke, the author of the third gospel and the Acts of the Apostles, speaks even more forcefully than does Matthew about riches, poverty, and the use of resources. He is writing for Christian communities throughout the Graeco-Roman empire, which is strikingly similar to our contemporary world. It is a society in which a working person's wage never allows her or him to live far above the hunger line. One day without employment would result in hunger.[20] In contrast to Matthew's version, in which people who are poor are generally referred to metaphorically, in Luke's text Jesus speaks of the materially or sociologically poor: "Blessed are you who are poor" (Luke 6:20) but "woe to you who are rich" (Luke 6:24).[21] The rich must use their resources to build a just community. These verses do not praise the lack of money or condemn people possessing it, but what the Beatitudes address, as in the Old Testament, is the gap between the two that makes people defenseless. The rich are challenged to renounce a significant amount of their wealth and also to undertake unpalatable deeds, such as offering risky loans (Luke 6:35) and canceling debts (6:37).[22] Zacchaeus, the chief tax collector of Jericho, is praised by Jesus for giving up half his possessions to the poor, but Zacchaeus still remains a wealthy man (Luke 19:1-10).[23]

---

19. See Leonardo Boff and Clodovis Boff, *Introducing Liberation Theology* (Maryknoll, NY: Orbis Books, 1987), 48–49.

20. See Hermann Hendrickx, *Social Justice in the Bible* (Quezon City: Claretian Publications, 1985), 85.

21. See Elsbernd and Bieringer, *When Love Is Not Enough*, 49.

22. See David J. Bosch, *Transforming Mission: Paradigm Shifts in Theology of Mission* (Maryknoll, NY: Orbis Books, 1991), 103.

23. See Roger Charles, *The Social Teaching of Vatican II* (Oxford: Platter Publications, 1982), 302.

In Luke's gospel, Jesus is conveying more bluntly than in Matthew's text that the chasm between rich and poor cannot be justified, and in the reign of God there will be an economic reversal.[24] Thus those who are poor are called blessed not because their poverty is something good in itself, but because when the reign of God takes shape they will be the preferential beneficiaries of the changes that occur. In brief, Jesus describes a key sign of the reign of God: those who are powerless take the first place. Riches are evil whenever people become so preoccupied with them that they entirely control people's lives.

There are seven parables in Luke's gospel that are stories of social, economic, and political reversal, that is, the marginalized are given preferential status: the Samaritan is good, not the status-proud priests and Levites (Luke 10:33-37); the last seated at the banquet are good, not the rich invited ones (Luke 14:15-24); Lazarus is good, not the wealthy rich man (Luke 16:19-31); the tax collector is good, not the Pharisee (Luke 18:10-14); and the prodigal son is good, not his envious and self-righteous brother (Luke 15:11-32). In all these parables Jesus teaches the stupidity of becoming overly committed to material things.

The Letters of John and Paul

John, writing toward the end of the first Christian century, summarizes his understanding of what Jesus Christ expects of a true follower: "How does God's love abide in anyone who has the world's goods and sees a brother or sister in need and yet refuses help? Little children, let us love, not in word or speech, but in truth and action" (1 John 3:17-18).

Paul goes to a great deal of trouble to organize a collection for people in poverty in Jerusalem and tells the Corinthians that their generosity is a sign of their genuine love of God (2 Cor 8:8). He develops the theme of communal solidarity for justice when he uses the analogy of the human body: "For just as the body is one and has many members, and all the members of the body, though many, are one body, so it is with Christ. . . . Now you are the body of Christ and individually members of it. . . . If one member suffers, all suffer together with it" (1 Cor 12:12, 27, 26). He then speaks of the different tasks and obligations of each member of the body (v. 28). A body has many diversified members—foot, eye, ear—so has the church many members with different functions. This means that

---

24. See John L. McKenzie, *Dictionary of the Bible* (London: Geoffrey Chapman, 1965), 684.

an official leader of a local church or group will have more responsibility to implement strategies for justice than one who has no leadership role. But because of the unity and solidarity of the one body of Christ, whatever one person does in the name of justice, all share in that action: "Now there are varieties of gifts, but the same Spirit; and there are varieties of services, but the same Lord. . . . To each is given the manifestation of the Spirit for the common good" (1 Cor 12:4, 5, 7). For Paul, as for Jesus Christ, covetousness is a form of idolatry, the worship of fake gods (Col 3:5). In his letter to the Galatians he ends with this instruction on corporate responsibility: "Bear one another's burdens, and in this way you will fulfill the law of Christ" (Gal 6:2). The ultimate test of our sincerity as Christians is, for Paul, our concern for other people in need, especially those on the margins of society (see Rom 14:9; 1 Cor 8:11-13).

To summarize, in the New Testament, as in the Old Testament:

- God is the creator and owner of all material things.

- We, therefore, are but stewards of these goods, called to continue God's creation in a spirit of love and justice.

- Special concern is owed to the plight of people on the margins of society.

- At the same time, since material goods can become ends in themselves, we must avoid all forms of greed or covetous behavior.[25]

Parable 1: Solidarity: Obligations of the Rich (Luke 16:1-31)

Relevance

Today the term "executive compensation" means the entire remuneration given by business firms to top-level executives in a corporation. There is growing worldwide anger over the often staggering payouts to executives of large firms, especially in times of economic turbulence. In sizable American corporations this reward can reach many millions of dollars annually. There is a massive disparity between the amounts received by top executives and those provided to shop-floor workers. It is estimated that the pay of the average worker in the United States

---

25. See Ben Witherington, *Jesus and Money* (London: SPCK, 2010), 141–52.

rose from $14,000 in 1980 to $15,900 in 2004 (a total increase of 7%, or 0.3% per year), while the payment given to CEOs increased from $625,000 in 1980 to $4,500,000 in 2004 (an increase of 614%, or 8.5% annually).[26] Little wonder that people complain that greed, not concern for the equitable distribution of wealth, is outrageously out of control in the senior levels of the business world. Moreover, since the global financial crisis hundreds of thousands of low-paid workers have been thrown into unemployment and poverty through no fault of their own, while senior executives, often those whose greed caused the financial upheaval, have kept their positions of obscene wealth and privilege.

The Parable Explained

The social drama of the rich man and Lazarus (Luke 16:1-31) has two parts. Part 1 (vv. 19-26) sets the scene. Predictable order has been turned upside down. As Mary in her earlier hymn of praise and thanksgiving prophesied: "He has brought down the powerful from their thrones, and lifted up the lowly" (Luke 1:52). The fortunes of Lazarus, a beggar, and of the rich man have been dramatically reversed. The rich man is in "Hades, where he is being tormented . . . [and] in agony in [its] flames" (vv. 23-24). Lazarus, by contrast, is at peace beside Abraham (v. 23). The second part is the liminal stage of the drama (vv. 27-31) in which the rich man struggles to get back to his past position of wealth and power by bullying Abraham into helping him, his father, and his five brothers. He fails because he chooses not to be transformed by the opportunity given him. The result is that the rich man must now suffer God's judgment. His covetousness is sinful, but even worse is his apathy about the plight of people who are poor, as symbolized by the sufferings of Lazarus.[27]

This brief summary does not do justice to the powerful symbolic language adopted by the storyteller.[28] The rich man is extravagantly clothed

26. See Melé, *Business Ethics in Action*, 188.

27. See Brad H. Young, *The Parables: Jewish Tradition and Christian Interpretation* (Peabody, MA: Hendrickson, 1998), 280.

28. I am particularly indebted to the analysis provided by William R. Herzog, *Parables as Subversive Speech: Jesus as Pedagogue of the Oppressed* (Louisville, MI: Westminster John Knox, 1994), 117–30; Stephen I. Wright, "Parables on Poverty and Riches," 217–39, in *The Challenge of Jesus' Parables*, Richard N. Longenecker, ed. (Grand Rapids, MI: Eerdmans, 2000), 230–33; Klyne R. Snodgrass, *Stories with Intent: A Comprehensive Guide to the Parables of Jesus* (Grand Rapids, MI: Eerdmans,

in purple and linen garments, and daily eats excessively of the very best foods. The purple dye of his clothes is reserved for those who are especially wealthy and powerful within the urban elite, a social class distinguished by oppression of the poor and belief that wealth is the sign of God's special favor toward them. Lazarus, however, is not only an impoverished beggar; he is also covered in weeping sores. It was assumed that his poverty was the result of his own sinfulness, a punishment by God. Socially this was bad enough, but at least a beggar had the right to plead for food. However, Lazarus's sores place him well below even the status of a beggar. Not only does his poor health make it increasingly impossible to find work; it also further removes him from social contact with people because sores render him ritually impure, someone to be shunned even by other beggars. Lazarus is socially a non-person. Exhausted and starving, Lazarus has no energy to defend himself against the equally ravenous street dogs. They await his death in the hope of relieving their hunger. The storyteller notes that Lazarus lay at the gate of the rich man (v. 19). He is so exhausted he has no energy to sit upright, which would have given him some chance to chase the dogs away. Lazarus's exclusion from society is further reinforced by the fact that he lies at the gate, an extravagantly designed entrance to the rich man's house. The gate symbolizes the enormity of the divide between the rich and the poor. The latter can never hope to rise to the social heights of power and prestige of the rich elite.

In the middle of the story the focus shifts to the verbal interaction between the now-suffering rich man and Abraham. As someone used to commanding social inferiors, the rich man addresses Abraham in a lordly manner. Lazarus must become a messenger, "an errand boy to do Abraham's bidding."[29] Abraham refuses. The rich man fails to see that Abraham is the mythical father of Lazarus and all socially rejected people, not just of himself. He and Lazarus are kinsfolk because Abraham is their common father. The rich man must change his entire life and become committed to justice and solidarity with the oppressed. But he does not listen to Abraham's politely delivered message; he tries now to plead and bargain rather than command: "I beg you to send him to my father's house—for I have five brothers—that he may warn them" (vv. 27-28). Abraham responds with a sharp reminder that he should know better. He, his father, and his brothers should be well aware of

---

2008), 419–35; Bruce J. Malina and Richard L. Rohrbaugh, *Social-Science Commentary on the Synoptic Gospels* (Minneapolis: Fortress Press, 1992), 377–78.

29. Herzog, *Parables as Subversive Speech*, 123.

the fundamental teachings of Moses and the prophets; they do not need to be reminded of what is at the heart of Israel's traditions (v. 29). His family members, no doubt rich business partners, are leading selfish and unloving lives, living as though death will end everything, so they will not be punished for their injustices toward the poor.

But the rich man still does not get the message. He is so accustomed to having his commands obeyed because of his wealth and power that he tries once more to manipulate Abraham into doing what he wants. Wealth has blinded him to the realities of poverty and his own role in the oppression of the poor. So he goes on pleading for special treatment for his family: "if someone goes to them from the dead, they will repent" (v. 30). Abraham sharply refuses by again reminding the petitioner of the principle of solidarity, that is, all people are equal before God. Nothing in the teachings of Moses and the prophets could be clearer than this. So many signs have been given his family in these teachings that no new sign will bring them to their senses. They are spiritually blinded by their own pride and self-importance.

Parable 2: Battles over Inheritance (Luke 12:13-21)

Relevance

A Google search discloses more than a million references to conflicts over inheritance. Disputes over inheritance are commonly bitter in the extreme, especially between family members, no matter how rich they might already be; the acrimony generated is apt to pass from generation to generation. This is why I find the parable of inheritance and a foolish businessman as relevant today as it was at the time Jesus told it. In the Scriptures, particularly in the Old Testament, there are quite detailed rules regarding inheritance and disinheritance.[30]

The Parable Explained

The catalyst for Jesus' parable is particularly significant. Jesus is asked to settle a dispute about inheritance of property: "Teacher, tell my brother to divide the family inheritance with me" (Luke 12:13).

---

30. See Jonathan Burnside, *God, Justice, and Society: Aspects of Law and Legality in the Bible* (Oxford: Oxford University Press, 2011), 183, 190–92. The parable of the prodigal son, to be discussed later in this chapter, is an example of a domestic quarrel about inheritance.

But Jesus refuses to become directly involved. Instead, he recounts the parable to remind all involved in inheritance disputes to examine their motives. If greed is the motivating force there can no lasting resolution to a dispute: "Take care! Be on your guard against all kinds of greed; for one's life does not consist in the abundance of possessions" (v. 15).[31] The question to the hearers is: are they genuinely seeking justice inspired by love? If not, then anger between the disputants will only intensify, with no possible lasting reconciliation between family members. This aspect of the parable is as relevant today as it was at the time the story was first told.

The wealthy farmer's properties have produced so much that his barns cannot contain the abundance. He plans to construct more spacious buildings in order to cope with the incoming harvest. At first sight the rich man seems to be acting responsibly in preparing for his future. But enough is never enough. He wants more for himself without considering the needs of others. He is more interested in his long-range security than in the immediate needs of people who are poor. He says to himself: " 'I will pull down my barns and build larger ones, and there I will store all my grain and my goods. And I will say to my soul: 'Soul, you have ample goods laid up for many years; relax, eat, drink, and be merry' " (Luke 12:18-19). God then visits him: " 'You fool! This very night your very life is being demanded of you. And the things you have prepared, whose will they be?' So it is with those who store up treasures for themselves but are not rich toward God" (Luke 12:20-21).

There is a humorous touch to the story. This caricature of a rich, though inept, farmer raises a very serious question about the meaning of life. He is so greedy that he is prepared to pull down his existing barns while the crops are still in the fields waiting to be harvested. He will end up without storage space while his crops rot on the ground; he should have anticipated the good harvest coming and done his rebuilding program in time for the new grain. The listeners to this story would have seen the stupidity of the farmer and mocked him.[32] Of course, the deep meaning of the story is that economic prosperity in itself does not give a lasting sense of personal satisfaction. If the farmer had been

31. See Wright, "Parables on Poverty," 221.

32. See Charles W. Hedrick, *Parables as Poetic Fictions: The Creative Voice of Jesus* (Peabody, MA: Hendrickson, 1994), 158–62.

more concerned with the welfare of others he would have distributed the abundantly good harvest to people in need.[33]

This parable concentrates on human mortality and the divine command to use money to alleviate the burdens of people who are marginalized.[34] Wealth as such is not the issue, but Jesus is dramatically condemning greed and the refusal to use material things for the common good, especially for the relief of poverty. Greed is a form of idolatry, the adoration of material goods instead of God. The stupidity of the farmer is his belief that his obligations in life finish when he narcissistically secures his own economic welfare. Rather, he should be focusing his efforts on following the will of God in the use of material goods. The foolish man had no sense of his obligations to the community; he was concerned for nothing but his own aggrandizement. He would have died all alone, "in social isolation, for greed cuts us off from the neighborhood."[35]

Parable 3: Affirmative Action Approved (Matt 20:1-16)

Relevance

"Affirmative action" is frequently used to mean "positive discrimination," that is, the controversial social policy that aims to reverse historical trends that have forced minority groups into positions of disadvantage, especially in education and employment. Fundamentally the policy aims to encourage educational institutions and different types of industry to provide access and promotion to members of groups that have experienced manifold hardships.[36] It can be an effective instrument for confronting inequalities, especially if it is the only way "to overcome discriminatory effects that could not be eliminated in some other way."[37] The policy can, however, arouse envy and jealousy among those who belong to the power groups in society. The following parable, I find, helps to raise discussion about affirmative action to a more objective level.

33. See Charles W. Hedrick, *Many Things in Parables* (Louisville: Westminster John Knox, 2004), 96–99.

34. See Snodgrass, *Stories with Intent*, 389–401; Wright, "Parables on Poverty," 221–24.

35. Walter Brueggemann, "The Bible, the Recession and Our Neighbor," *Health Progress* 91, no. 1 (January–February 2010): 48–52, at 50.

36. See E. Ellis Cashmore, *Dictionary of Race and Ethnic Relations* (London: Routledge & Kegan Paul, 1984), 1.

37. See Melé, *Business Ethics*, 262.

The Parable Explained

The parable of the hiring of the day laborers by the landowner is initially a puzzling one. Why should those who worked only for a short time be paid the same as those who toiled the entire day in dreadful heat? What message is Jesus wanting to convey? I argue that the parable has a twofold aim: first, to illustrate that God is overwhelmingly generous: "God's treatment of people, his judgement, is not based on human reckoning and human standards of justice."[38] The second aim is to emphasize that solidarity commits followers of Christ to ensure that all people have the necessities of life. In contemporary terms this means that governments must make sure all citizens have the right to a basic wage and health services and that the rights of refugees be respected.

The social drama, as always, has three stages: the description of the scene in which a rich landowner hires laborers at different times of the day (Matt 20:1-7), then the liminal phase in which conflict over values erupts between the landowner and several of his former employees (20:9-10), followed by the reactions of various people in the drama (20:11-16).

In the opening scene the landowner is desperate for additional laborers to work in his vineyard, so early in the morning he goes to the marketplace to hire them. He agrees to pay them "the usual wage" (v. 2). But he miscalculates the number needed, so he returns "about nine o'clock" (v. 3) for more, then noon (v. 5), then three o'clock (v. 5), finally again at five o'clock (vv. 4-8). Each time he agrees to pay them "what is right" (v. 4).

There is a touch of dry humor in the way the landowner speaks to the eleventh-hour unemployed: "Why are you standing here idle all day?" (v. 6). It is clear to all why they have remained inactive. They make the obvious response: "Because no one has hired us" (v. 7). The tone of their reply would have conveyed the intense sadness they experienced for not having been selected earlier in the day. The generosity of the landowner in hiring them is particularly clear to any observer of the scene, for they would have been already exhausted by the heat and their inability to find nourishing food. They would not have made energetic workers.

The landowner belongs to the rich urban elite class and is desperately concerned to harvest his grape crop before the intense heat destroys it. The day laborers, by contrast, are at the lowest level of the economic and social scale. Unless they can get some employment they and their families risk

---

38. Snodgrass, *Stories with Intent*, 376.

starvation and eventually death. But the competition for work is intense; the marketplace is filled with unemployed laborers with no bargaining power. Slaves are even better off than these men because the landowner has a vested interested in maintaining their health and well-being.[39]

The key phase of the story's drama begins when the landowner sends his estate manager at the end of the day to pay the laborers (v. 8). Jesus is at pains to describe the intensity of the heat. Those who were hired at earlier times while the sun was at its height obviously expect to be paid more than those who were hired at five o'clock, as the sun was setting. Great is their consternation when they discover that all are to be paid exactly the same (v. 9): "they grumbled against the landowner, saying, 'These last worked only one hour, and you have made them equal to us who have borne the burden of the day and the scorching heat'" (v.11-12). The owner refuses to accept their argument. He has paid them exactly according to the original work contract: "did you not agree with me for the usual daily wage? Take what belongs to you and go" (vv. 13-14). They have no grounds to complain; they have received exactly what they had agreed to. However, their claim that he is unjust comes only because they are not paid more than the latecomers. The owner then sharply reprimands them, accusing them of envy and a lack of generosity toward those employed late in the day: "Or are you envious because I am generous?" (v. 15). In this stage of the parable it is the landowner who is transformed by the experience, not the grumbling laborers. The landowner takes pity on the latecomers because he is aware that they urgently need to pay for food for themselves and their families. If they go another day without employment they risk starvation, and the less they eat the less energy they have to work or to be employed by managers who demand healthy workers. The envious laborers are self-centered and view life solely in economic terms, with the result that they refuse to recognize the needs of their neighbors whose very lives are in danger.

Parable 4: In Praise of Whistleblowing in Corporate Organizations (Luke 19:11-27)

Relevance

Whistleblowing in business ethics means the reporting by an existing or former employee of unethical practices or an institution's unprincipled

---

39. See Herzog, *Parables as Subversive Speech*, 88.

behaviors (see chap. 4). If the reporting is done within the institution it is termed "internal whistleblowing"; if it is done publicly it is referred to as "external whistleblowing."[40] Sociologist Robert Jackall writes that the "fundamental rule of corporate life is to protect oneself and, if possible, one's own."[41] Hence, given that loyalty is the preeminent virtue in corporate and other institutions, the pressure to maintain silence is considerable. People daring to break the code of secrecy and silence in order to reveal unethical behavior are in danger of automatic expulsion or, in mafia-like organizations, even death. It is indeed rare for a whistleblower to survive without significant personal cost to him- or herself.[42]

The responsibility for exposing ethical coverups increases as one moves higher in the hierarchical structures of an organization; for example, directors have a more serious duty to call the group to be openly accountable than does the financial officer. All ordinary avenues for dealing with unethical practices need to be followed before a person reveals them to outsiders. However, whistleblowers may have no option but to go public, especially when they reasonably judge they will not be listened to by the appropriate internal authorities and they risk being socially and economically scapegoated.[43] This is especially a challenge when the whistleblower encounters a culture of corruption so deep that no one in the organization can be trusted. Sometimes the whistleblowers fear that even external authorities will not listen to them, but, motivated by their concerns for the wider common good, they proceed to expose the injustices. They may suffer severe consequences for their integrity.

40. See Marcia P. Miceli and Janet P. Near, *Blowing the Whistle: The Organizational and Legal Implications for Companies and Employees* (New York: Lexington, 1992), passim; Melé, *Business Ethics*, 140–41; Arbuckle, *Violence, Society, and the Church*, 95–99.

41. Robert Jackall, *Moral Mazes: The World of Corporate Managers* (New York: Oxford University Press, 2010), 95.

42. Michael Woodford provides a vivid personal case study of the perils of whistleblowing. In 2011 he became the first foreign president of the Japanese camera-maker Olympus. Six months later he was dismissed for correctly questioning $1.7 billion in suspicious transactions. See his *Exposure: Inside the Olympus Scandal; How I Went from CEO to Whistleblower* (London: Bloomsbury Academic Press, 2012).

43. See Melé, *Business Ethics*, 141; Arbuckle, *Violence, Society, and the Church*, 136–50.

The Parable Explained

The parable begins simply with a nobleman about to leave for a distant country in order to be crowned king, despite the fact that his citizens hate him so much that they do not want him back as their ruler (Luke 19:14). He calls ten of his slaves and gives them each one pound (i.e., a *mina*), which in the currency of the day is a considerable amount, equal to one hundred days' wages for a common laborer.[44] They are commanded to invest this money: "Do business with these until I come back" (19:13). The central phase of the social drama begins when the king returns. How will the slaves react when summoned to give an account of their investments? And how will the king question them? Two of them have been very active and are extravagantly rewarded: the first has made ten pounds, so is given charge over ten cities; the second made five pounds and is to govern five cities (19:16-19). But the third comes to the king and responds in vivid contrast to the previous slaves. He has buried the pound, which evokes an incredibly harsh punishment from the angry king: "[Y]ou wicked slave! You knew . . . that I was a harsh man, taking what I did not deposit and reaping what I did not sow? Why then did you not put my money into the bank? Then when I returned, I could have collected it with interest" (19:22-23). The pound is immediately taken from him and given to the one who has ten. He will probably have suffered the same fate as the enemies of the tyrant: "as for these enemies of mine who did not want me to be king over them—bring them here and slaughter them in my presence" (19:27).

The traditional understanding of this parable stresses the duty everyone has to use to the fullest the gifts given us by God.[45] However, this reading has been seriously questioned in light of social science research.[46] I agree with Luise Schottroff when she writes that to see the "third slave as the embodiment of people who reject God's righteousness and God's Torah is simply unbearable."[47] Schottroff points out that in Matthew's text (Matt 25:14-30) the parable is immediately followed

---

44. See Snodgrass, *Stories with Intent*, 528.

45. See ibid., 519–43; Bernard Brandon Scott, *Hear Then the Parable: A Commentary on the Parables of Jesus* (Minneapolis: Fortress Press, 1989), 217–35.

46. See Barbara E. Reid, *Parables for Preachers: The Gospel of Matthew* (Collegeville, MN: Liturgical Press, 2001), 202–10; Herzog, *Parables as Subversive Speech*, 150–68; Malina and Rohrbaugh, *Social-Science Commentary*, 149–50.

47. Luise Schottroff, *The Parables of Jesus*, trans. Linda M. Maloney (Minneapolis: Fortress Press, 2006), 223.

by "the great mythic vision of the eschatological judgment of the Son of Man over all the nations."[48] The ultimate test before the judgment seat of God will be whether or not we have fed the hungry and clothed the naked (Matt: 25:31-46). The investments of the first two slaves result in exorbitant monetary returns. To have achieved this, they would have had to exploit peasants by demanding increases in such things as rents on property, or the peasants would have had to take out loans from banks at ridiculously excessive interest rates to save their crops or properties, with the consequence of further enslaving them.[49] It was normal to torture and imprison defaulting debtors (Luke 12:58; Matt 18:28-34). But it is the third slave who refuses to collude in the financially corrupt behavior of the king and the other two slaves. In other words, the third slave is a whistleblower and suffers the fate of one who refuses to participate in the economic oppression of the poor. The parable, therefore, is a scathing condemnation of contemporary free market economies in which investment bankers' unrestrained greed for profits is esteemed as a virtue.

Parable 5: The Profit Motive Must Not Dominate Education (Luke 15:11-32)

Relevance

Martha Nussbaum begins her recent book with the startling statement: "We are in the midst of a crisis of massive proportions and grave global significance."[50] She is referring directly not to economic or environmental crises, but to "a world-wide crisis in education."[51] She continues: "Thirsty for national profit, nations, and their systems of education, are heedlessly discarding skills that are needed to keep democracies alive."[52] She passionately decries the increasing marginalization of the liberal arts at all levels of education. Historically, the humanities have been pivotal to education because they have been correctly considered essential for creating proficient democratic citizens. Instead,

48. Ibid.
49. Herzog notes that interest rates for peasants could range between 60 and 200 percent; *Parables as Subversive Speech*, 161.
50. Martha Nussbaum, *Not for Profit: Why Democracy Needs the Humanities* (Princeton, NJ: Princeton University Press, 2010), 1.
51. Ibid., 2.
52. Ibid.

governments, with the collusion of educators, increasingly focus on national economic growth as the primary purpose of education rather than exhorting students to think critically and become knowledgeable and empathetic citizens. This overemphasis on financial growth and profit, accompanied by a cult of individualism and material achievement, has weakened our capacity to think critically and to question the values and actions of those in authority. It has lessened our ability to be sympathetic toward members of different cultures and those on the margins of society, as well as reducing our skills for understanding and solving multifaceted global issues.

Nussbaum cogently argues that in order to counter this overemphasis in education on economic growth we must again make the humanities the foundation of education. Literature, such as the great novels, can engage people in what she terms "the narrative imagination."[53] This means the facility "to think what it can be like to be in the shoes of a person different from oneself, to be an intelligent reader of that person's story, and to understand the emotions and wishes and desires that someone so placed might have."[54] She writes of the value of the soul, which she uses in a secular sense to indicate "the faculties of thought and imagination that make us human and make our relationships rich."[55] She encourages the Socratic ideal of the "examined life" and its meticulous commitment to questioning, in particular questioning tradition and authority. She does not demonize concern for economic growth. It is rather a question of providing foundational values, such as empathy and solidarity, so that politics and economics can be used wisely for human and community growth.

Case Study: Commercialization of Sport and Catholic Identities

The disturbing fact is that economic and corporate factors have come to dominate professional sport as never before,

---

53. Ibid., 95.
54. Ibid., 96.
55. Ibid., 6.

even at times invading sporting activities in schools and colleges.[56] When capitalistic values take over sports, the bottom line becomes a substitute for the goal line.[57] It is a win-lose philosophy, encouraged by capitalistic values of envy and jealousy, so that a sporting event is judged in terms of the amount of money it produces for sponsors of a winning team. The markers of success are the numbers of spectators, media contracts, and merchandise sales a game attracts. Even stadiums are named after corporate sponsors. Players are judged not only in terms of their physical skills but also by their ability to entertain their admirers by behavior on and off the field. Invariably this increases the financial return to investors. Never before in history have economic realities so dramatically controlled decisions about sport, "and never before have economic organizations and corporate interests had so much power and control over the meaning, purpose and organization of sport."[58] In Australia television and broadcasting rights for sport are the media companies' biggest source of revenue. In the United States, the NFL initiated an eight-year, $17.6 billion contract with television companies in 1998. By the year 2000 world football had a yearly turnover of over $403 billion, equivalent to the gross national income of Holland.[59] The profit motive has become the emphasis. As one observer noted: "Sports is not simply another big business. It is one of the fastest-growing industries . . . and is intertwined with virtually every aspect of the economy. . . . [Sports are] everywhere, accompanied by the sound of a cash register ringing incessantly."[60] Even amateur sports are now heavily financed by corporate groups whose primary interest is profit.

56. See Jay Coakley, Chris Hallinan, Steve Jackson, and Peter Mewett, *Sports in Society* (North Ryde: McGraw-Hill, 2009), 150.

57. Ibid., 342.

58. Ibid., 341.

59. See Richard Giulianotti, *Sport: A Critical Sociology* (Cambridge: Polity, 2005), 28.

60. Michael K. Ozanian, "Following the Money: FW's First Annual Report on the Economics of Sports," *Financial World* 164, no. 4 (14 February 1995), quoted by Coakley et al., *Sports in Society*, 342.

A distressing quality of much contemporary sport is its overemphasis on male power supremacy; the mass media repeatedly proclaim the message of gender domination through their extensive coverage of male sporting events. In addition, encouraged by capitalistic values, sports, especially for men, become forms of ritualized violence.[61] And praise of ritualized violence is taken for granted in commercial sports journalism: there is admiration for the victors when they have been able to wound the "enemy" in such sports as boxing and wrestling. Participation by boys in sport is often a kind of initiation ritual into manhood. Players who are physically superior marginalize the less gifted who do not survive the initiation rituals. They are pushed to the sidelines. Nor is it uncommon in the business world, dominated by male values, for female executives wishing to advance in business to have to acquire the cultural language of male sport. If they do not appear at the latest big game of male players accompanied by their clients they are in danger of being ostracized by their corporate colleagues as irrelevant.

This culture of commercialized sport is invading school systems; corporate sponsors use school sports primarily for their own advantage.[62] The question is: how can the mission of the Catholic school be maintained when the business side of sport, even in schools, begins to dominate? Sport has no place in Catholic schools unless it is organized to attain educational outcomes for competitors, in particular, and all students, even the least talented, in general. School programs undermine the achievement of educational goals when they are based primarily on financial outcomes for corporate sponsors and others. Not to stand up to commercial pressures in sport is to collude in them. In view of these conclusions it is urgent that educators in Catholic schools resist the invasion of capitalistic sporting values that are contrary to the Gospel message. Hence the importance of the following parable, which downplays the profit motive in education.

61. See Arbuckle, *Violence, Society, and the Church*, 113–14.
62. See Coakley et al., *Sports in Society*, 128–55.

The Parable Explained[63]

This parable, which is normally called "the prodigal son," appears at first sight to focus on the conversion experience of one son, but in fact the description of his elder brother is equally instructive because, unlike his younger brother, he refuses the opportunity for transformation.[64] Jesus wants to show in this wonderful parable that God's love is unconditional and that God is constantly calling us to be open to this love. We respond positively only if that we acknowledge before God our own failings and pride; if we fulfill this requirement we will be successfully initiated through God's overwhelming compassion and love into union with Christ. To give us a model, Jesus first describes in detail the journey of the first son, who carries on in a rather spectacular way. The journey of his jealous and envious elder brother, who is solely motivated by the financial profit motive, is less startling, but its lessons are equally important. At the same time, the father in the parable is deeply saddened to discover that his education of his elder son has been a failure, but he rejoices when he discovers that the traumatic experiences of his formerly wayward son have led the young man to reflect on the stupidity of his ways. This is a parable that wonderfully illustrates the importance of reflective or inductive learning.

The first stage of the prodigal son's transformative journey is brief (Luke 15:11-12): the brash, self-centered adolescent, acting within his rights according to the custom of the time, asks for his share of his father's property and then leaves for a distant country where he squanders his wealth on "dissolute living" (Luke 15:13). He views his father purely in economic terms, that is, as a source of money. Then follows the central stage of the story. Utterly destitute and alone, the son is forced to accept what is culturally one of the lowest and most shaming employments for a Jew: working with pigs. Thus the pigpen is a powerful anti-symbol of the chaos in this adolescent's journey into mature adulthood. In this liminal stage he begins a process of conversion by acknowledging that his troubles are his own fault. He recalls the love and compassion of his father, which in his self-centredness he has long ignored and even considered unmanly. This energizes him to return to seek forgiveness

---

63. For a fuller background to this parable see Gerald A. Arbuckle, *Laughing with God: Humor, Culture, and Transformation* (Collegeville, MN: Liturgical Press, 2008), 70–90.

64. See Young, *The Parables*, 130–57.

and reconciliation, but he does not expect his father will openly receive him. Hence he will offer himself to his father as just another hired laborer. But the father, seeing his son in the distance, runs to him and embraces him in a gesture of profound compassion and forgiveness. The actual running is itself a culturally antistructural symbol because no man of his social standing would do such a thing.

The last stage of the young man's transformation is marked by the feast of celebration called for by his father. It is a celebratory graduation ritual. The son has graduated with honors! The lesson to Jesus' listeners is this: the mythological heart of Christ's message is that God's love is unconditional and God is constantly inviting us to let go of our attachments to worldly things. We must abandon our secular myth of the narcissistic desire for power and material things and embrace God's message of Christ's unconditional love and concern for those who are marginalized. If we do so, we also will rejoice with an inner peace that cannot be measured in merely human terms.

The elder son's failed journey of initiation into maturity is in stunning contrast to that of his brother. Something of his selfishness is indirectly depicted at the beginning of the parable; avarice hides behind a façade of filial piety. By custom the elder son must act as the mediator in disputes between younger brothers and the father, but he fails to do so. People listening to Jesus would have known this and developed a negative view of his behavior. But worse is to come. Hearing of his sibling's return, he is overwhelmed by destructive jealousy and envy. Jealousy is the sadness that arises when a person either fears losing or has already lost a meaningful status or relationship to a rival. On the other hand, envy is the sadness a person experiences because of what someone else has and the desire or wish that the other did not possess it. Jealousy and envy can lead to violence. The elder son is jealous because he fears he will lose the capital goods he thinks belong to him (Luke 15:29). He is envious because his brother now possesses what he lacks: a mature adult relationship with their father. Despite his protestations of maturity, he has not grown up to be a responsible person. He wants his brother punished for his earlier adolescent selfishness, so he attempts to belittle his brother and thus destroy the father's joy; the father will not, however, be seduced into destroying the mature relationship he and his younger son have established. The elder son, by refusing to even begin an initiation ritual of conversion, remains consumed by the anger and sadness of his envious and jealous feelings. In addition, by custom the elder son should be the host of the party, but he refuses even to enter the house, thus publicly insulting the dignity of his father and his reconciliation with his brother. Yet the father still encourages him to begin the journey of conversion; his words to him about his failure to accept his brother are not harsh, but a kindly invitation to acknowledge his own need of conversion (Luke 11:31-32). As we are not told if the elder son accepts his father's invitation, the story ultimately ends on a sad note.

Summary

- In the formation of Catholics it is important but insufficient that they *know* the ethical values and norms expected of them. As Aristotle writes,[65] a sound ethical evaluation can only come from a *virtuous* person; values belong to the cognitive sphere, whereas virtues are gained by the repetition of good actions.

- The parables of Jesus Christ aim to foster not just a knowledge of values, but above all virtuous behavior in listeners; the parables motivate people to implement in action values that are integral to Catholic identities in the world of business, politics, the workplace, and recreational activities.

- Secularism, as Charles Taylor explains, does not deny the existence of God, but it relegates God to the transcendent level, which is considered supernatural, beyond the human world, and consequently "unbelievable." God has nothing to say to us in the "beyond world." However, in the parables God enters our world, calling us to reflect and act morally in our everyday life according to values of justice and love. Through reflective contemplation on the parables we are motivated to break through the culturally supported narratives of greed and the desire to dominate others.[66]

65. See Aristotle, *Nicomachean Ethics* II, 6.
66. See Charles Taylor, *A Secular Age* (Cambridge, MA: Harvard University Press, 2007), 534.

Chapter Nine

Adult Rural Education: Refounding Catholic Identities

[Rural development needs educators with] a great deal of devotion. But how to teach devotion. . . .[1] *(René Dumont)*

With one heart all these joined constantly in prayer . . . including Mary the mother of Jesus. (Acts 1:14)

This chapter explains that:

- cultural obstacles are among the major barriers to rural village development in developing countries

- the movement from subsistence farming to a money economy demands a profound shift in people's identities and behaviors

- adult non-formal rural education requires educators to be skilled technologically, but above all they need the gift of devotion

- devotion of staff ministry, illustrated in the case study of rural non-formal education, comes from a deep commitment to the Gospel story of Mary, mother of God

---

1. René Dumont, "Green Revolution: Priorities in Melanesian Development," *Catalyst* 2, no. 2 (1972): 3–33, at 26.

In the language of this book, my theme is that the founding and refounding of the identities of Catholic institutions and their members, the way they survive, grow, and know who they are, are conveyed through a ministry of storytelling. Certainly, dogmas and creeds are important; they normatively define academically what *should* be the uniqueness of our institutions. However, unless institutions and their members are able to recount how their own stories intersect with or diverge from the truths of the gospel narratives these normative proclamations have little or no impact. But the process of storytelling energizes, gives direction to what people do, and it is especially needed in these turbulent times. Faith comes alive.

This chapter is a case study of the founding and ongoing refounding of a unique rural, adult agricultural training center in Fiji, South Pacific. The Catholic identities of this faith-based, non-profit institution continue to be clarified in the context of the ever-changing social and economic realities in Fiji and elsewhere in the South Pacific. René Dumont (1904–2001), the French ecologist and agricultural economist, when reflecting on the obstacles to rural development in emerging economies, went to the heart of the problem. Rural development, he wrote, desperately needs educators gifted with "a great deal of devotion. But how to teach devotion, commitment. . . ."[2] This case study illustrates how devotion can be "taught" and "caught" through non-formal education, if led by devoted teachers skilled in the art of gospel storytelling. The non-formal educational approach encourages participants to think critically and innovatively.[3] After explaining the cultural and economic context of the institution, the chapter describes the process of the founding and refounding of the center in the light of a changing environment.

Context of the Project

Fiji, with a population of approximately 900,000, is a developing South Pacific country with a largely subsistence-based economy. Over half the population lives in rural areas where unemployment, especially among youth, continues to rise. As a recent report notes: "Youth unemployment together with the creation of worthwhile rural livelihoods has

2. Ibid.

3. See Thomas H. Groome, *Will There Be Faith?* (New York: HarperOne, 2011), 13.

emerged for decades as major intractable problems."[4] The problem of unemployment is associated with the widespread failure to commercialize agriculture on traditional land. There are the usual obvious obstacles to economic progress in developing countries, for example, poor transportation facilities for marketing goods and limited financing. But the two major factors inhibiting commercial agricultural development are cultural barriers and the lack of appropriate rural agricultural training programs for young people.

Cultural Barriers

The "inherent weakness of most Fijian societies continues to lie in the apparent inability to dissociate their economic activities from the traditional social background of Fijian life."[5] A Fijian anthropologist summarized his frustration nearly fifty years ago: "The major problem for economic development is to extricate the economic process from social relationships and establish it on new foundations."[6] This problem endures well into the twenty-first century. The indigenous Fijian village culture is premodern, that is, its founding mythology emphasizes group harmony, cohesiveness, togetherness, stability, patriarchalism, hierarchical authority and power structures, and the sacredness of tradition. So powerful is the pressure to conform to group norms that individuals find it difficult to develop their own sense of personal autonomy and initiative. The fear of being mocked, gossiped about, shamed, and punished by spirits if one goes against tradition can informally enforce conformity to the group's norms.

These premodern cultural values discourage individuals who wish to break away from tradition in order to initiate and sustain a much-needed productive, market-oriented method of farming. Villagers, it was said in 1960, "have indeed become conditioned to authoritarian leadership, so that for the most part they tend to do little but what they are told to do."[7] Not much has changed since this was written. The

4. Andrew McGregor, Livai Tora, with assistance of Geoff Bamford and Kalara McGregor, *The Tutu Rural Training Centre: Lessons in Non-Formal Adult Education for Self Employment in Agriculture* (Suva: FAO, 2011), ix.

5. *Fijian Council Paper* 20 (1951): 8.

6. Rusiate Nayacakalou, *Traditional and Modern Types of Leadership and Economic Development among Fijians* (Suva: Institute of Pacific Studies, 1964), 24.

7. O. H. K. Spate, "Under Two Laws: The Fijian Dilemma," *Meanjin* 19, no. 2 (1960): 166–81.

conclusion of a Fijian government report in the same year still remains true in 2012: "An energetic and progressive man [*sic*] can be completely ruined by his predatory relatives."[8] The demands of hospitality are frequently and oppressively excessive, because to give evidence of thrift or apparent miserliness is to sin against tradition.[9] This emphasis on generosity, when abused, inevitably discourages many individuals from saving and investing in agricultural development.[10] Moreover, the village cultural system was "designed in such a way that the older generation effectively exploited [younger people] who have little alternative than to be submissive."[11]

The customary system of communal land tenure further inhibits the better development of local land resources. Land ownership in villages is communal, but under the authority of the chief; tradition decrees that rules governing the use of land have been set by the ancestors and cannot be significantly changed.[12] Hence, an individual is loath to invest time and limited resources in improving the land unless he or she is certain that its use and produce will remain under his or her own control. Little wonder that many individuals who want to change farming methods feel a sense of hopelessness and fatalism when confronted with these cultural obstacles.

Many young Fijian people, particularly the most innovative and educated, try to escape from the constraints of village life and seek employment in urban areas, but then, of course, the traditional conservatism in rural areas is only reinforced. This drift to urban areas is encouraged by parents, because paid employment there is considered a sign of success in the contemporary world. Moreover, the problem is not helped by the fact that too frequently educational programs are unrelated to the needs of rural life. Some 18,000 students graduate from school annually, but only 8,000 are able to find places in the urban professions or as short-

---

8. *The Burns Commission Report*, Fiji Council Paper 1 (1960): § 66.

9. See Gerald A. Arbuckle, *Violence, Society, and the Church: A Cultural Approach* (Collegeville, MN: Liturgical Press, 2004), 33–54.

10. See comments by Marshall D. Sahlins, *Moala-Culture and Nature on a Fijian Island* (Ann Arbor: University of Michigan Press, 1962), 203–14.

11. Mary Low, Michael McVerry, and Ron Crocombe, *Education for Rural Development: The Tutu Experiment and Its Relevance for the Pacific* (Suva: Institute for Pacific Studies, 1984), 2.

12. See Cyril S. Belshaw, *Under the Ivi Tree: Society and Economic Growth in Rural Fiji* (London: Routledge and Kegan Paul, 1964), 181.

term casual workers in, for example, the tourist industry. This means that about 10,000 annually must return to the villages and are classed as failures in their own estimation and that of their parents. The impact of sustained unemployment on young people in the villages is humanly devastating because a chronic youth subculture of poverty develops: an experience of powerlessness, shame, stigma, diminished citizenship, a loss of self-worth, a weary, apathetic fatalism.[13] What self-esteem they retain further disintegrates as the years go by. With nothing personally rewarding to do, many village youth cope by sinking into an "invisible cycle of daily life": afternoon football followed by drinking sessions with kava (*yaqona*), the locally popular non-alcoholic and relaxing beverage, late into the night, then rising late in the morning, "with little interest in allocating significant labour inputs in agricultural production."[14] It is a very depressing and dehumanizing scene!

Rural Training Programs

It was recognized in the late 1950s that Fijian farming methods and levels of efficiency could improve only under the guidance of adequate and sympathetic rural extension services.[15] Experts have, however, become increasingly frustrated as attempts to find practical solutions have repeatedly failed. In an effort to break the cycle of poverty for rural youth, three broad types of training programs have been promoted over the last fifty years in Fiji and elsewhere:[16]

- Institutional: that is, agricultural education of youth that is not experiential; it is of a deductive type in institutions situated away from village life.

- "On-farm": educational programs that are village-based and inductive; however, it is impossible to supply expert educators simultaneously in all villages, and, moreover, student farmers need periods away from their villages to develop a sense of objectivity and to bond with, and learn from, fellow students in other villages.

13. See Gerald A. Arbuckle, *Culture, Inculturation, and Theologians: A Postmodern Critique* (Collegeville, MN: Liturgical Press, 2010), 50–51.

14. McGregor et al., *The Tutu Rural Training Centre*, 10.

15. See Cyril S. Belshaw, *Small-Scale Industry for the South Pacific* (Noumea: South Pacific Commission Technical Paper 1959), no. 89, 1.

16. See ibid. and Geoff Bamford, *Report on Training Rural Youth for Farming in the Asia and Far East Regions* (Bangkok: FAO, 1972), 6.

- Comprehensive: that is, educational programs that are institutional *and* "on-farm."

Programs in the first and second categories have rarely succeeded. This is fundamentally due to their inability to relate to the needs and aspirations of rural youth who want to be farmers.[17]

The Tutu Rural Training Centre (TRTC), Fiji

The Tutu Rural Training Centre (TRTC), a ministry conducted by the Fathers and Brothers of the Society of Mary (Marists), fits within the third category. Since its foundation thirty years ago it has repeatedly been praised by international consultants for its unique successes. It offers a range of programs that respond to the needs of villagers at all levels, such as young farmers, married couples, young single women, and parents.[18] The Mission of TRTC "is to provide a place/presence in which [principally] the people of Cakaudrove [an administrative province of Fiji] are empowered to become more autonomous, and take charge of their lives, in a rapidly changing world; it involves a transforming and reciprocal outreach to the peoples of the Pacific." The TRTC is a "non-formal adult education training centre for a specific geographical area, for rural self-employment using the participants' own resources, locally focused but with an international character."[19] And the TRTC achieves its transforming non-formal educational aim for its participants primarily through the processes of storytelling.

Non-formal Education

Non-formal adult education is an educational process that focuses on the needs of learners who themselves are involved in its organization and curriculum. As opposed to traditional formal education, which is planned and directed by teachers, non-formal education is "bottom-up," that is, it involves trainees at all stages of the planning and implementation of the process. Non-formal educators assume "that people feel a commitment to a decision in proportion to the extent that they feel they have participated in making it."[20]

17. See McGregor et al., *The Tutu Rural Training Centre*, 14.
18. Ibid., xiii.
19. Ibid., xiv.
20. Malcolm Knowles, Edwood F. Holton, and Richard Swanson, *The Adult Learner* (Oxford: Butterworth-Heinemann, 2011), 264.

Non-formal education aims to be transformative; trainees are encouraged through non-formal education to critically evaluate their cultural environment and assume their own authority in decision making, to become self-directing or autonomous persons.

Non-formal educators, unlike educators in "top-down" institutions, must be creative and flexible, willing to adapt to meet the changing needs of their trainees. The educational process is two-way, as teachers are themselves learners. They are constantly open to learn from the experience of the trainees.

TRTC: Reasons for Success Explained

The laudatory report on the TRTC in 2010, initiated and sponsored by the Food and Agriculture Organization of the United Nations (FAO), listed several reasons for its success. The following is a summary of and commentary on their findings.

Inductive Learning through Storytelling

People learn through articulating and sharing their experiences in a trusting atmosphere. As Father Michael McVerry, the TRTC principal, notes: "The truths we live by are the ones we discover for ourselves, not what others tell us; the learner is in charge of the process, sets the agenda, begins with felt needs and must discover for themselves the real needs."[21] The definition he has adopted for adult education is: "A process whereby a person in and through community assumes responsibility for their growth. It is a process of liberation by which, under skilled guides, they reflectively grow in freeing themselves from the constraints of personal, social and cultural orders."[22] The TRTC emphasizes the fundamental importance of participants' developing responsibility for self-growth—physical, emotional, community, and spiritual—that is, as McVerry frequently says, the TRTC stresses the need for participants to develop their own autonomy in decision making, a challenging task in view of the cultural obstacles explained above.

21. Michael McVerry, TRTC archives, n.d.
22. Gerald A. Arbuckle, *From Chaos to Mission: Refounding Religious Life Formation* (London: Geoffrey Chapman, 1995), 102.

Reality-Based

"The starting point for all our participants is to recognize their communal, cultural background."[23] The challenges of oppressive village life must be acknowledged and ways found by participants to rise above them while remaining in and contributing to village life. "Any rural transformation programme has to be rooted in the realities of agriculture and village life and not in the pleasure that salaried people take in exhorting the poor to work harder."[24] Because the TRTC is reality-based, its staff has the ability to help people discover for themselves what really worries them. This is far more difficult than may at first appear. It demands that educators be willing to spend considerable time listening to people's stories. [25]

Begin Small

Projects that begin and remain small are flexible, easily altered in response to the changing needs of participants' lives. Moreover, if a project is too big people are unable to see the reasons for their mistakes and thus learn from them.

Community Focused

An integral quality of authentic self-growth is concern for community needs. An external assessment of the TRTC in 1977 made this comment: "The government-run institutions seem . . . to give inadequate attention to ethical concern and community responsibility and thus to produce an elite which is disproportionately concerned with advancing its own interest vis-à-vis those of the less privileged elite."[26] Also, as participants will be working in their villages it is essential that TRTC educators and participants themselves involve their parents and elders in the learning process. Without their permission and encouragement it would be impossible for participants to obtain the use of land and control over their produce. McVerry writes: "Attitudinal change is slow particularly in rural areas, and the same staff who must relate to young people must also be able to [win] the trust of the old people whose

---

23. Michael McVerry, TRTC archives, n.d.

24. Fiji Government Paper, *Education for Modern Fiji* (1969): 9.

25. See Gerald A. Arbuckle, *Earthing the Gospel: An Inculturation Handbook for Pastoral Workers* (Maryknoll, NY: Orbis Books, 1990), 196–203.

26. Institute of Pacific Studies, *Education for Rural Development: The Tutu Experiment and Its Relevance for the Pacific* (Suva: University of South Pacific, 1977), 30.

support is essential if participants are to use communally owned land without interference."[27]

Oscillation Principle

The TRTC has adopted the "oscillation principle," that is, training programs that are a mixture of institutional and on-site village praxis. Staff members are able to supervise the practical implementation in villages of theory already acquired in the institutional setting. The four-year course for young farmers, for example, requires that they follow the repeating cycle of residing for five weeks at the TRTC and five weeks on their home farm. This "allows trainees to put into practice and to test the principles they learn at the training centre on an ongoing basis. . . . As a result . . . during the course, young farmers are able to make a relatively seamless transition from life as trainees to self employed village based farmers."[28] McVerry comments that when participants are on their home farms "they are in charge of the process and the staff [when visiting them] are the uncertain ones. They are guests, as it were, of their trainees."[29] In these times the trainees become the educators of the staff, fostering an interesting role reversal requiring openness and humility on the part of the staff.

No Dependency

There are no admission fees, but participants are expected to make a significant contribution in kind or in voluntary work; there must be no handouts or loans.

Participatory Management

The participatory management style of the principal, Michael McVerry, has "contributed to Tutu's flexibility and responsiveness to the changing needs of its constituents."[30]

Devoted Leadership

The FAO report frequently refers to the dedication of staff members (the vast majority are laypersons). The TRTC would not be successful without devoted staff members gifted with empathetic listening skills;

27. Communication of Michael McVerry to Gerald A. Arbuckle, 4 April 2011.
28. McGregor et al., *The Tutu Rural Training Centre*, 63.
29. Michael McVerry to Gerald A. Arbuckle, 4 April 2011.
30. McGregor et al., *The Tutu Training Centre*, 65.

they regularly visit the villages to assess on-site the progress of trainees and help educate their communities in the aims and principles of the TRTC. The FAO report notes the staff "are required to be frequently away from their own families and spend long working hours in village based consultations. Most civil servants and college graduates are likely to be reluctant to take on such work."[31] Again, the report notes that the "success of [the TRTC] can in no small measure be attributed to the high calibre of the staff and the exceptional leadership of [people like] Brother Kevin Foote and Father Michael McVerry."[32]

The Source of Devotion

The FAO report does not, and cannot, explain the ultimate driving force behind the devotion of staff and principal. The TRTC is like a two-sided coin. The report analyzes it from a socioeconomic perspective, but the other side of the Centre is that it is a *faith-based* institution. Agricultural economist René Dumont concluded that to stimulate and sustain agricultural rural growth in emerging economies it is essential to have "low-key development extension workers" equipped with a very practical education and gifted with "a great deal of devotion." Yet Dumont, as noted in the introduction to this chapter, could find no solution to the challenge, namely, *"how to teach devotion."*[33] Yet a solution does exist. Economists in developing countries have too often neglected the role of religion in people's lives. It is thought to be irrelevant, if not an obstacle to development. The TRTC, however, recognizes that Fijians are very religious people; religion permeates every area of their lives. The TRTC acknowledges this and builds its entire training program on this reality. Although the TRTC is a Catholic and non-government organization it is open to people of all traditions and proselytizing is forbidden. Still, it unashamedly draws on the gospels as its source of devotion. "The Gospel stories are the handbook of Tutu," declares McVerry. Ultimately this is the reason for the TRTC's accomplishments. Through the gospels and the inductive teaching method of Jesus Christ the TRTC's leaders have learned *how to inspire devotion*.

In summary, a social and economic analysis alone is inadequate to unlock the causes of the TRTC's radical effectiveness. The TRTC is a faith-based institution possessing a unique faith story that is the ulti-

---

31. Ibid., 64.
32. Ibid.
33. Dumont, "Green Revolution," 26. Italics supplied.

mate source of the devotion of educators and participants. This story has motivated people in the founding and refounding of the Centre. We now identify and explain the founding and refounding of the TRTC through the art of gospel storytelling, the ultimate source of its Catholic identities.

The Tutu Rural Training Centre: Founding/Refounding Identities

There are two stages in the historical development of the TRTC.

Stage 1: Founding: 1969–1972

The training of Pacific Islanders as Brothers of the Society of Mary had been a failure for many years. Their formation from 1953 onward, such as it was, took place at an institution in an elegant middle-class suburb of Sydney, Australia, but most professed brothers eventually left the community on return to the Pacific, as they found the adjustment from city life back to isolated islands too demanding.[34] In 1969, under the initiative of an energetic Marist priest, Father Michael Bransfield, the training program was transferred to rural Fiji on a property of 1,200 acres owned by the congregation. His assistant was the saintly Brother Kevin Foote, who had been a highly successful farmer in New Zealand. Foote could see the plight of rural youth in Fiji and yearned to do something about it. Both founding figures eventually felt the need to provide not just updated training for brothers in religious life but also their formation as "low-key rural multi-skilled extension workers" equipped with the gift of devotion to serve the needs of the rural Fijians. The two aims were interdependent. Then both men realized that the rural formation side of the training program should be opened to young people in the local villages. Brothers could not be trained in isolation. The programs they intended to offer were multifaceted, that is, they would be concerned not only with agricultural issues but also with whatever was considered necessary to help village people grow as persons: for example, through family life enrichment programs. Bransfield would later define his approach in this way:

34. Between 1961 and 1969, 39 Brothers were professed and 29 left. Eventually most of those who initially survived also left the congregation.

> If the value of a training facility is to be secure, its members, though aware of the advantages for themselves, must be absolutely sincere in their desire to help the local people. As an apostolic community, Marists (must) attempt to empathize with the people in their own environment, and beyond. . . . They need to be open to them, meet them with mutual respect and trust and genuinely desire integral development for them.[35]

Unfortunately, despite the inspiring quality of this vision Bransfield was unable to provide detailed analysis of how the project was to be practically implemented. By 1971 the TRTC was in deep trouble, short of funds and increasingly lacking competent staff to continue the programs. I was asked by the Marist provincial and encouraged by Bransfield to assess the entire project and presented my report in October 1971.[36] I concluded that if the project continued to focus on forming agricultural extension workers in local villages, as originally intended in the founding of the TRTC, much more capital and qualified staff had to be made available. Above all, the congregation had to be prepared to appoint a competent successor to Bransfield. That person had to be not only technically equipped but also gifted with "the vital human virtues essential for development of peoples."[37] I stated that the congregation "has a serious obligation in this matter for the sake of the people to be trained and the funding organizations who contribute."[38] I concluded that if the congregation was not prepared "to provide the core qualified personnel, then, out of justice to the people and the government, the congregation must withdraw totally from all sections of the scheme. Development of peoples through grass-roots agricultural/technical training is not the work of amateurs in human relations."[39] The congregation accepted the report and acted immediately to appoint Father Michael McVerry, a Marist missionary working in the Solomon Islands. I knew from working with him that he had exceptional skills for communicating

---

35. Michael Bransfield, *Tutu: Its Purpose and Function*, Marist Archives, Suva (16 October 1972), 1.

36. See Gerald A. Arbuckle, *The Agricultural Training Centre: Tutu—Taveuni Island, Fiji* (29 October, 1971), Marist Archives, Suva.

37. Ibid., 25.

38. Ibid.

39. Ibid., 27.

through storytelling, as well as a remarkable ability to involve people in decision making and planning.[40]

Stage 2: Refounding the Ministry of the TRTC: 1972–Present

With the arrival in 1972 of Michael McVerry as the new principal the TRTC began to move slowly forward from being a well-intentioned amateur-run project for rural development to a professionally organized training center for non-formal adult education in rural living. This required quantum-leap thinking and strategizing by McVerry at two levels: first, the founding story needed to be further deepened and communicated in ways that related to the local people's faith beliefs; second, educational programs had to devised according to these principles and in close cooperation with villagers. The results were immediate. Visiting experts praised what was happening; for example, one educationalist wrote in 1973 that "Tutu is exciting. . . . There is no place like it in the Pacific."[41] A South Pacific economist, Ron Crocombe, concluded a year later: "Perhaps the most important aspect of Tutu . . . is the effective integration of work with study."[42] In 1976 a group of eight academics reported their findings. They observed that the project had not "developed a highly sophisticated organizational framework with large-scale financial resources." If it had, "it could not have been as effective or identified closely with local people who have little finance and uncertain resources. One of its greatest strengths has been that it has evolved out of very close contact with the people it aims to serve. There was freedom to experiment and grow from the ground up."[43] They felt that "the real worth of the spiritual training at Tutu is deep, and personal."[44]

Certainly McVerry radically upgraded the professional and organizational aspects of the TRTC. His most significant gift from the 1970s onward, however, has been his role as its refounder through rediscovering and revitalizing the TRTC's transformative founding mythology so that it ultimately underpins and permeates the activities of staff and trainees

---

40. In a later publication I describe Michael McVerry as an example of one who has above-average skills of communicating with premodern cultures. See Gerald A. Arbuckle, *Earthing the Gospel*, 201.

41. *Report: Youth Education Officer* (South Pacific Commission, 1973), Marist Archives, Suva, 3.

42. Ron Crocombe, *Report on TRTC* (3 August 1974), Marist Archives, Suva, 4.

43. *Education for Rural Development* (1977), 3.

44. Evaluation Team Report, *Education for Rural Development*, 15.

to this day. McVerry's predecessors, Michael Bransfield and Kevin Foote, had never fully and formally articulated the founding story, although it had implicitly influenced their efforts. However, given the turmoil that the Centre was going through in the 1970s it was imperative that the founding story be reidentified and communicated in order to be the driving force behind relationships between staff and participants. This storytelling process at the TRTC is what theologians call inculturation, that is, "a dialectical interaction between Christian faith and cultures in which these cultures are challenged, affirmed, and transformed toward the reign of God, and in which Christian faith is likewise challenged, affirmed, and enhanced by this experience."[45] The dialectical interaction that is occurring at the TRTC is between the gospel story of Mary, mother of God, and the local Fijian culture; in Mary's story people are challenged to change cultural values that hinder their authentic development, as well as affirming and enhancing those values that are in accordance with Gospel imperatives.

McVerry describes how the mythology unfolded:

> To our surprise we found that the land on which the TRTC was built had originally been dedicated to Our Lady of Lourdes (in the Fijian language this is translated as *Marama ni Lura*) on 1st July 1914. A large statue of Marama ni Lura given by a companion Sister of St. Bernadette, to whom Our Lady had first appeared on 11th February 1858, had been erected at the entrance of the property in 1908. We re-dedicated the land and the TRTC with much ceremony to Marama ni Lura on 1st July 1974. Each year, on 1st July we meet as a community around the statue to celebrate Mass, listen again to the story, and sign a re-consecration to be Mary and to carry out her work in her place of Lura. The TRTC is truly "Mary's Place." Mary and her story are at the very heart of the founding story of the TRTC. Our staff and participants are invited to "be Mary," to re-live her courageous spirit. And people energetically respond to this vision because Mary means so much to them.[46]

In light of the intimate role Mary has in the founding story, McVerry chooses his key staff carefully and trains them according to the Marian story. As Mary was called to the ministry of bearing and nurturing Jesus, so staff members, in imitation of Mary, are invited to minister to one another and to the people they are to serve. They must have given evi-

---

45. Arbuckle, *Culture, Inculturation, and Theologians*, 152.
46. Communication of Michael McVerry to Gerald A. Arbuckle, 4 April 2011.

dence of their ability to work beside participants at courses in a listening and empathetic way. As he says: "Rural people are in general suspicious of experts who come with theoretical answers and proposals without listening to people's stories, but they are more accepting of other farmers who listen and talk with integrity from experience."[47] For McVerry, staff members are not primarily to be teachers, but "formators" whose task is to help people transform their attitudes and lives. But to undertake this critical role, he argues, staff members must first live the qualities of Mary, the model of formators. In advising TRTC's staff members, McVerry leads them into the lessons of the Annunciation. On hearing the lessons his students learn to apply the message to their ministry. McVerry tells them:

> First, there is fright at the angel's message. She is left speechless, but she did not block the dialogue with the angel. So we also when we enter the uncertainties of what may be ahead of us in the villages, we are frightened, but we trust in God. We question, but we are open to God. God will give us an answer when we allow Him to break through the narrowness of our human capacities.[48]

Speaking to the staff of the TRTC about the biblical story of Mary in the upper room waiting for Pentecost and what this means for their work, he has said:

> Mary graciously chooses us to do her work. As at Cana she is saying to us personally "This is what I want!" As she was hidden at Nazareth, so too she is hidden in the upper room. She occupies no position like Peter and the apostles, but rather is behind them supporting them. She is like a mother hidden behind the curtain prompting her child on stage to move forward confidently. We are to be like Mary in being present to the people we work with and for. Like her we do not push ourselves onto people. No, we are to empower people to discover for themselves their own dignity. We do this by listening, caring, encouraging, being concerned for people in what they judge to be their "felt needs." Then we work beside them to go deeper to discover what the "real needs" are. We, like Mary, must listen with our hearts—patiently, not judging.[49]

47. Ibid.
48. Ibid.
49. Ibid.

Rituals that mirror the founding story are to be commemorative and transformative. A second statue of Mary was ritually erected on July 1, 2000, and the plaque beneath it further explains Mary's central role in the TRTC's founding story. As the 180th meridian line runs through the property, it was decided to commemorate the Millennium Year by an appropriate text:

> This statue was . . . placed here . . . to enable us to remember that Mary was the first human being to pass from the Old to the New Covenant. With Mary, here in Tutu, her Place, we are always being called to move from the old to the new, from yesterday to today, and from today to tomorrow.

A staff member, Marist Father Donato Kivi, described for me one key ritual that reminds participants in courses what it means to call the TRTC *"Mary's Place"*; the ritual further enriches the conventional Fijian understanding of land. As explained earlier, in the traditions of the Fijian people land is never to be reduced to an economic unit. It is a gift from the ancestors, a source of life and of relationships between people down through the ages. "Now," he said, "this land is Mary's land. She is our mother, our ancestor ever present to us. Through her land Mary nourishes us as a mother, gives us water, protects us. When participants are allotted a piece of land at the TRTC to cultivate, they are invited to rub soil respectfully in their hands, to smell it. Then each day before beginning work on their garden they pick up a handful of soil and thank Marama ni Lura for being able to use her soil. It is a soil packed with symbolic meaning, for it is Mary's land. We hold her land in trust, for she is our ultimate ancestor, and so we must use it with respect."[50]

Mary: Theological Clarification

As the role of Mary, mother of Jesus, is pivotal in Tutu's founding story, McVerry's application of contemporary Marian theology needs to be put in the context of the local culture and people's needs.

> Contemporary theological reflection has revealed a deeper understanding of Mary's role in the church. For example, her Magnificat is seen as the bridge between the Old and New Testaments; she states without ambiguity that Jesus has come especially for the healing of *anawim*. Her

---

50. Donato Kivi, personal communication to Gerald A. Arbuckle, 12 October 2011.

hymn is one of the most forthright *subversive* statements in all world literature. This is contrary to some images of Mary in popular religiosity as a submissive, passive, retiring woman in a patriarchal culture. For the faithful trapped in oppression her song expresses a deep and dangerous hope of a better world.[51] The hymn proclaims three revolutions: a *moral* revolution ("He has shown strength with his arm/ he has scattered the proud in the thoughts of their hearts" [Luke 1:51]); a *social* revolution ("He has brought down the powerful from their thrones/and lifted up the lowly" [Luke 1:52]); and an *economic* revolution (He has filled the hungry with good things/sent the rich away empty" [Luke 1:53]).[52] Jesus explains the radical nature of this hymn when he defines his mission of justice (Luke 4:16-21), in the proclamation of the Beatitudes (Luke 6:20-26), and in his Judgement Discourse (Matt 25:31-46).[53]

McVerry is conscious that Catholic Fijians have had a deep personal devotion to Mary since the early missionary days of the nineteenth century. He builds the refounding mythology and its rituals on their traditional popular religiosity but further develops these in view of contemporary Mariology. One of the significant criticisms of Latin American liberation theology in its early stages of development was its condemnation of popular religiosity with its colorful devotions to Mary and to various saints and their healing rituals.[54] This disapproval of popular religiosity was a serious mistake because this religiosity in premodern cultures is in fact a rich expression of people's faith; McVerry is deeply aware of this. He concentrates on Mary as a listening follower of Jesus, his first disciple. This is not a passive Mary, but a Mary who intercedes with her Son in matters that worry people in their daily lives; hence the emphasis on Mary at the Annunciation as one who fears the unknown but trusts God, or at the Visitation where she fulfills her first duty, as a listener to her Son, of sharing the Good News with others. The speed and enthusiasm of her response, and the physical dangers she is prepared to undergo on the four days' journey to visit her cousin are confirmation that she is radically converted to her role. It will take courage for people

51. See Walter Brueggemann, *First and Second Samuel* (Atlanta: John Knox, 1990), 21.

52. See Hermann Hendrickx, *Bible on Justice* (Quezon City: JMC Press, 1978), 50; William F. Maestri, *Mary: Model of Justice* (New York: Alba House, 1987).

53. See Gerald A. Arbuckle, *Healthcare Ministry: Refounding the Mission in Tumultuous Times* (Collegeville, MN: Liturgical Press, 2000), 169.

54. See Gerald A. Arbuckle, *Culture, Inculturation, and Theologians*, 135.

in Fijian villages to confront cultural obstacles, courage like that of Mary traveling through uncertain territory to visit Elizabeth. It takes daring to empower villagers to discover for themselves their ability to stand on their own feet and make decisions for themselves. The local culture is an authoritarian one; people are instructed from above about what they are to do. Mary's role of empowering models a contrary view. One further incident in Mary's life that is important in the refounding story of the TRTC is her presence in the Upper Room, supporting and uniting the disciples (Acts 1:14). On this point McVerry says: "We are not a commune . . . a group of people who lose their individual identity. We are rather called to be one in mind and heart while acknowledging our individual differences and need to maintain our individual autonomy."[55]

Michael McVerry has the qualities of a refounding person in faith-based projects, for example, a willingness to live and work in the darkness of faith, the ability to articulate a vision inspiringly and in an empowering way through the art of storytelling, a collaborative style of management, a non-judgmental respect for people even if they reject his ideas and vision, a tremendous commitment to hard work. Like other refounders he has the gift of being able to go to the roots of problems and create imaginative ways to overcome them. A contemplative who does, he deeply thinks through issues before acting. This does not mean he is not prepared to take risks; quite the contrary, but they are risks founded in faith. Yet, like all refounders, McVerry has had to face significant opposition, mainly from members of his congregation. For example, between 1972 and 1974 his provincial was repeatedly pressured to close the TRTC. In 1975 McVerry was transferred to another part of the South Pacific, but he was reappointed as principal in 1982. As explained earlier in this book (see chaps. 4 and 5), it is a depressing fact that most founding and refounding projects eventually meet disapproval, if not outright resistance, from people not involved. Resistance to the project has lessened over the years, but it has not entirely disappeared.

The Tutu Rural Training Centre must now face a further crucial stage of refounding, namely, the establishment of structures, including the formation of an effective management board, that will guarantee that the founding story remains alive and vibrant. McVerry has already set the process in motion. It is recognized that a management board must above all be a guardian of the TRTC's values. It must ensure that the

---

55. Communication of Michael McVerry to Gerald A. Arbuckle, 4 April 2011.

founding story continues and never drifts from its original vision. Expert decisions about socioeconomic development projects can never be a "substitute for deliberations and explicit pronouncements on values."[56] Peter Drucker is right: "[Nonprofit institutions] exist for the sake of their mission, and this must never be forgotten."[57]

Summary

- Cultural factors are among the most intractable barriers to rural agricultural development in developing countries; the change from subsistence farming to a money economy requires a profound alteration in people's identities and behavior.

- One major reason for cultural resistance to change is the inability of many agricultural experts to mold rural educational programs that intimately involve villagers themselves in the planning and execution of these programs. Requisite are skilled and devoted educators who are prepared to lead their trainees through a lengthy process of story-telling in and through which they are able to see that transformative change is possible. But *the* problem is to find educators who are gifted with the devotion and the willingness to listen. Frequently Western educators in developing countries have neglected the role of religion as the source of devotion.

- The case study of the Tutu Rural Training Centre illustrates that a rural village development project owes its success ultimately to the fact that the educators are able to engage the gospel story of Mary as the inspirational source of cultural change. Mary is at the heart of the founding and refounding story of the Catholic identities of the TRTC, its staff, and its trainees.

- This case study also testifies to the key lesson of this book: the gospel stories are at the very foundation of Catholic identities and we desperately need in the church today people gifted with the art of lovingly relating these stories to contemporary issues. When this happens our ministerial identities are truly being refounded.

---

56. John Carver, *Boards That Make a Difference* (San Francisco: Jossey-Bass, 1997), 17.

57. Peter Drucker, *Managing the Nonprofit Organization: Practices and Principles* (New York: HarperCollins, 1990), 45.

Index